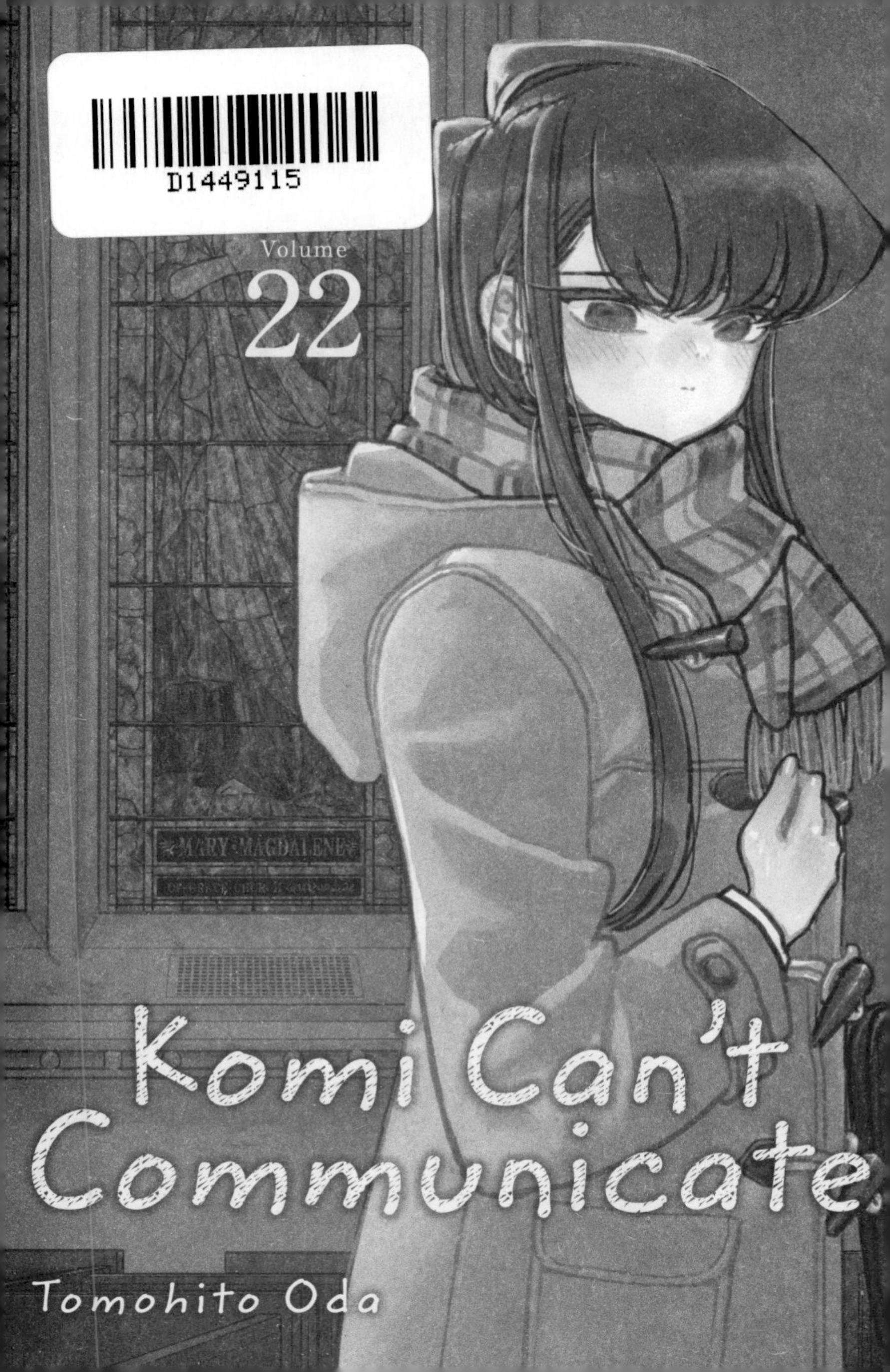
MARY MAGDALENE

Volume 22

Komi Can't Communicate

Tomohito Oda

Contents

22

Komi Can't Communicate

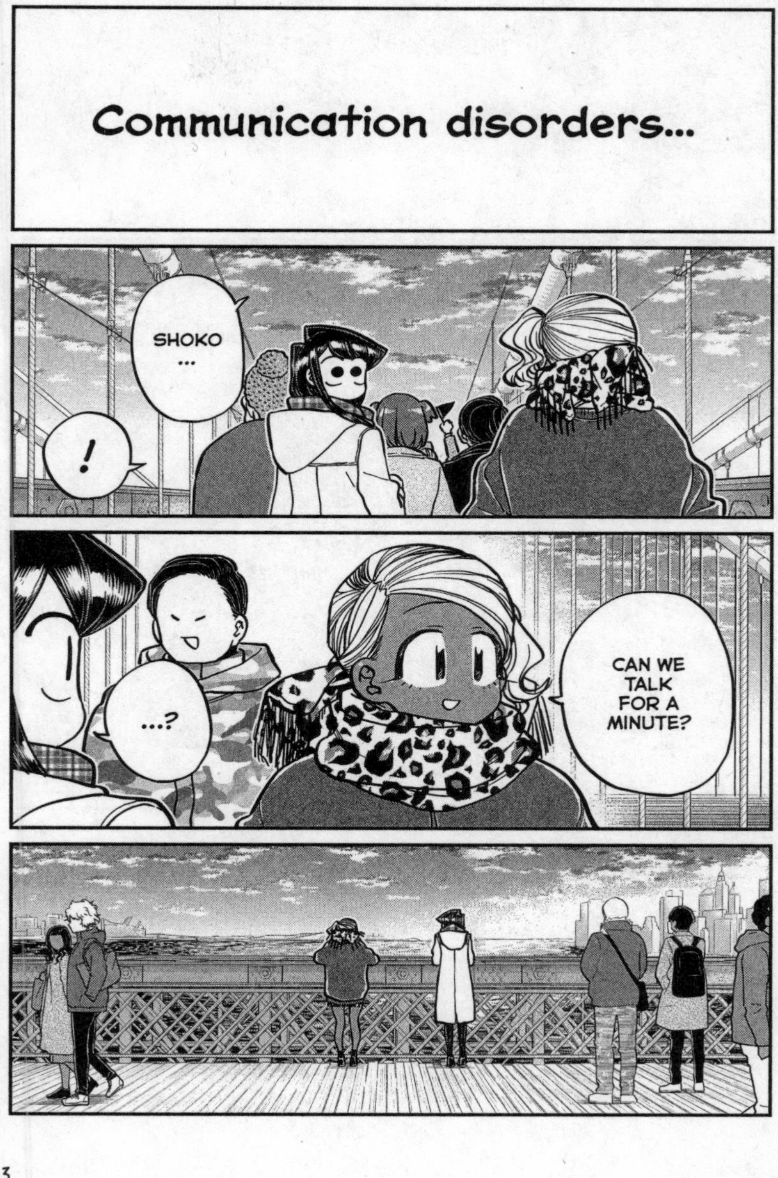
Communication disorders...
SHOKO ...
!
CAN WE TALK FOR A MINUTE?
...?

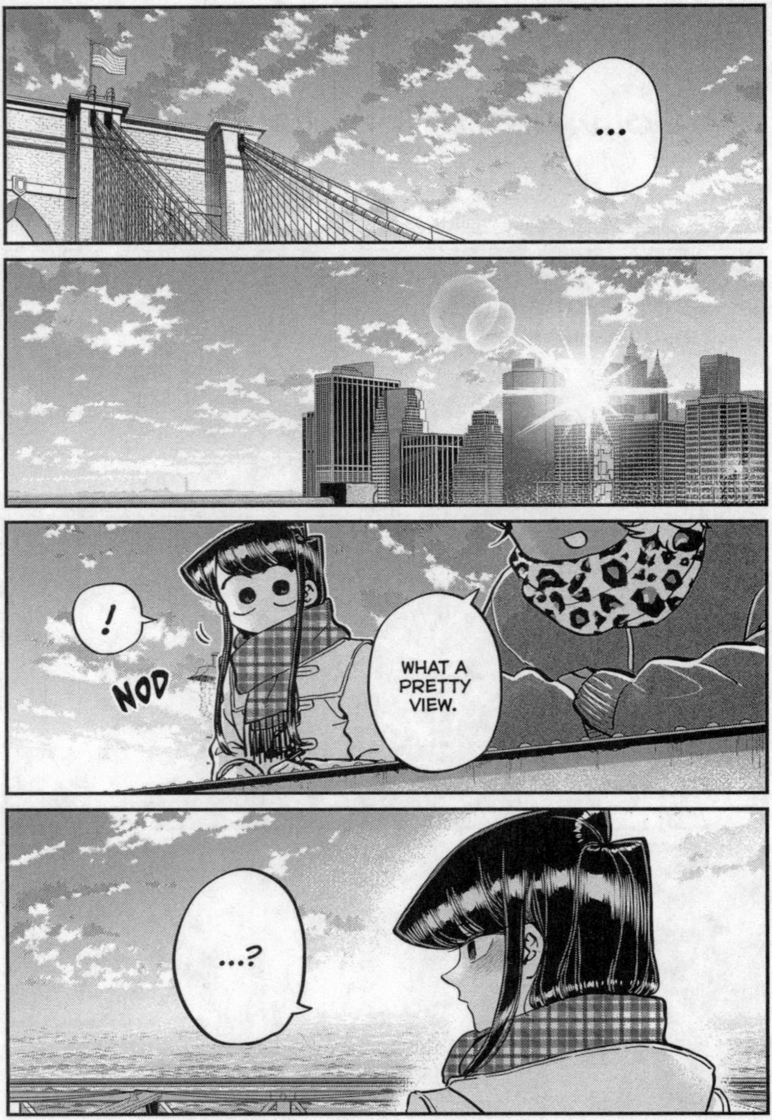
...
WHAT A PRETTY VIEW.
!
NOD
...?

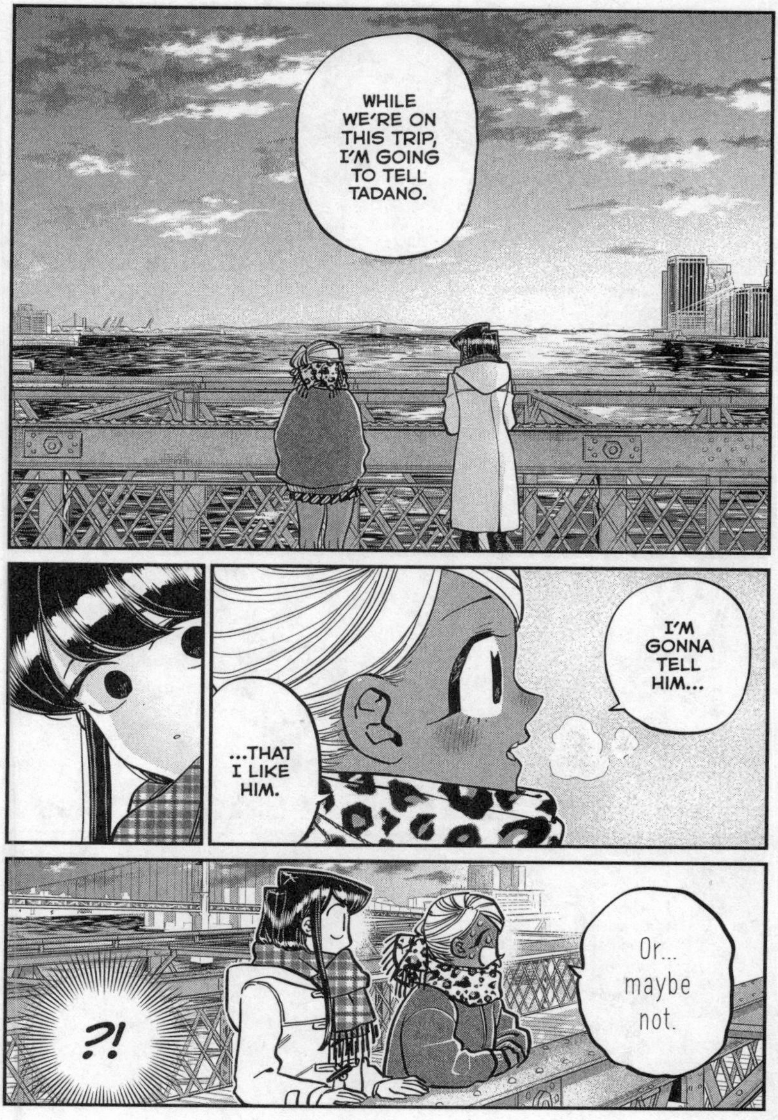
WHILE WE'RE ON THIS TRIP, I'M GOING TO TELL TADANO.
I'M GONNA TELL HIM...
...THAT I LIKE HIM.
Or... maybe not.
?!

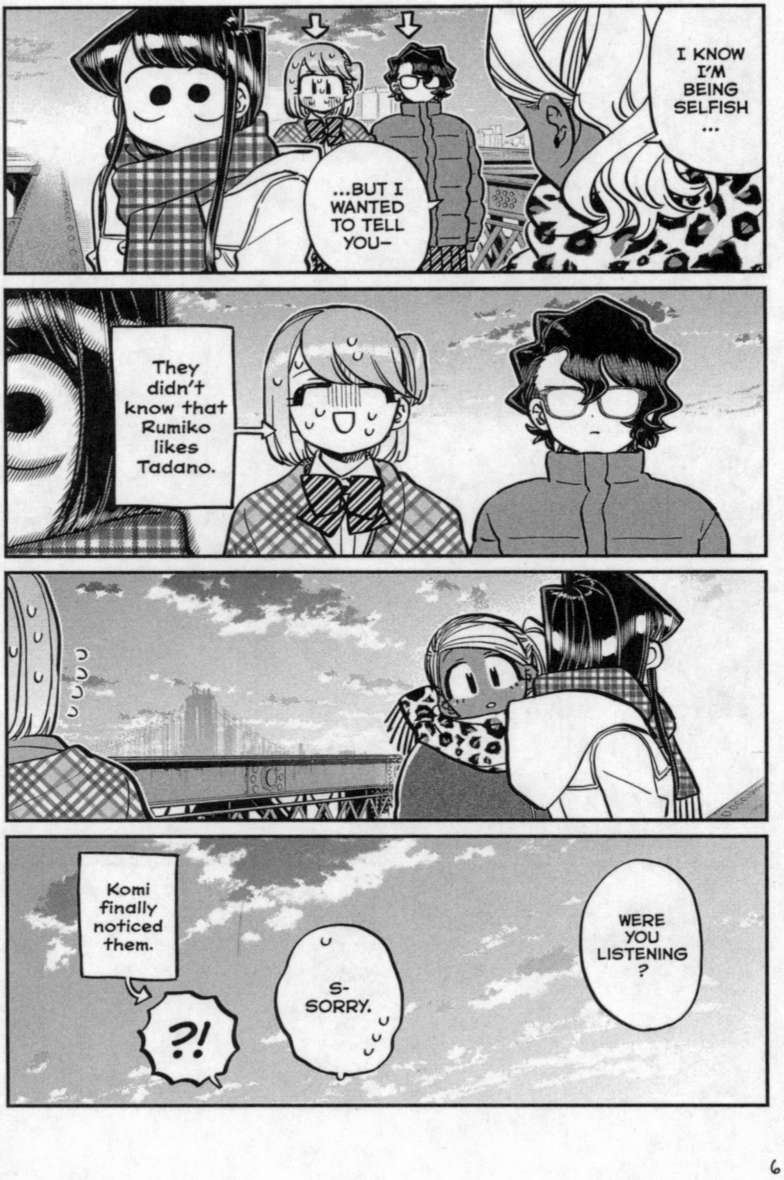
I KNOW I'M BEING SELFISH ...
...BUT I WANTED TO TELL YOU–
They didn't know that Rumiko likes Tadano.
WERE YOU LISTENING ?
S- SORRY.
Komi finally noticed them.
?!

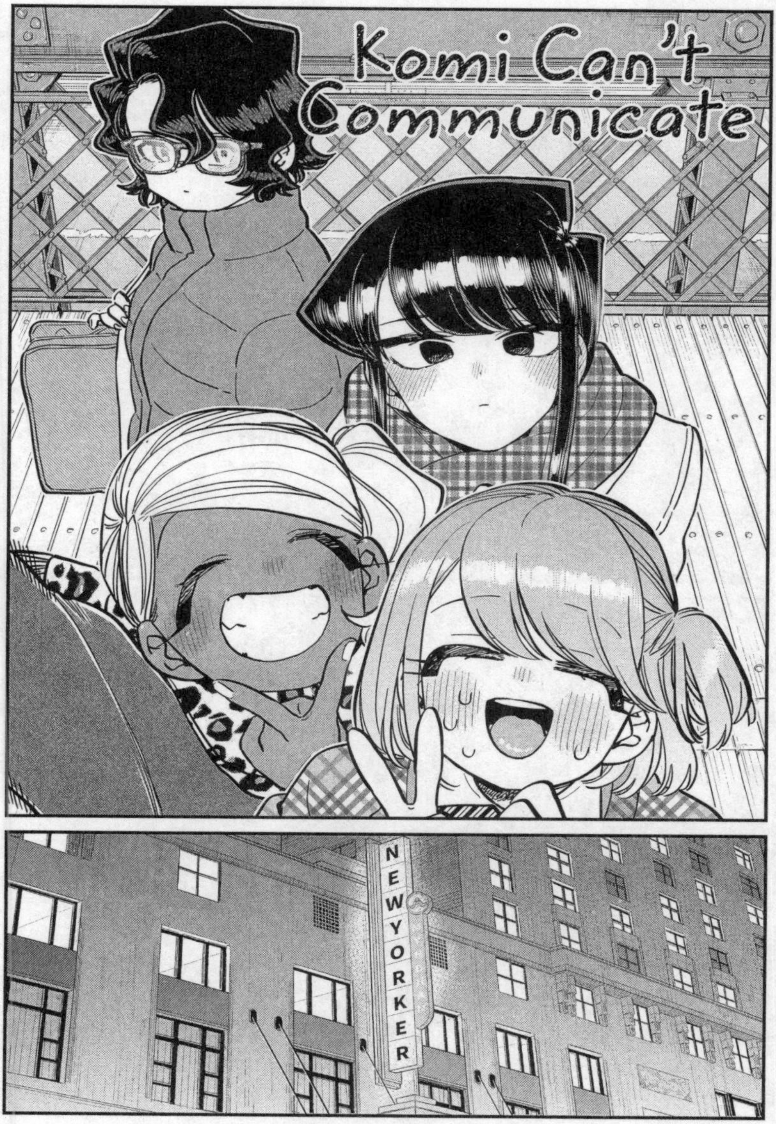
Komi Can't Communicate
NEWYORKER

Communication 285: Against It but Not Against It

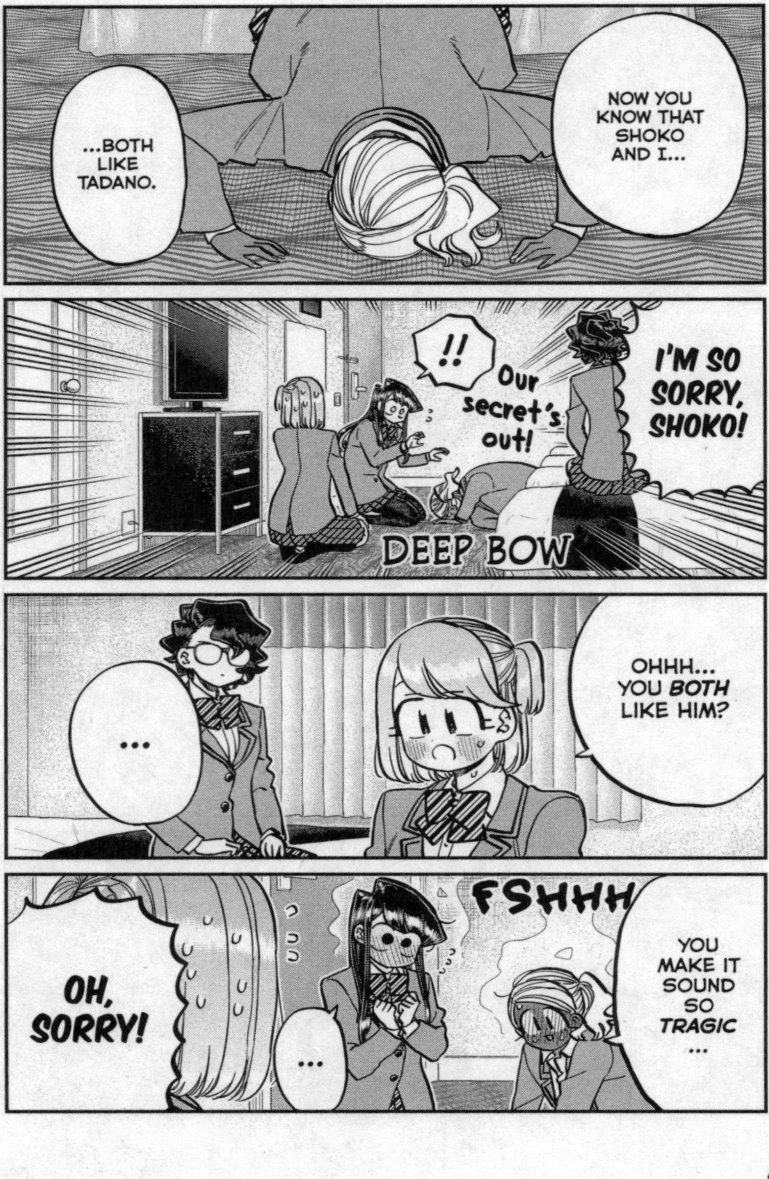
NOW YOU KNOW THAT SHOKO AND I...
...BOTH LIKE TADANO.
I'M SO SORRY, SHOKO!
!!
Our secret's out!
DEEP BOW
OHHH... YOU *BOTH* LIKE HIM?
...
YOU MAKE IT SOUND SO *TRAGIC* ...
FSHHH
...
OH, SORRY!

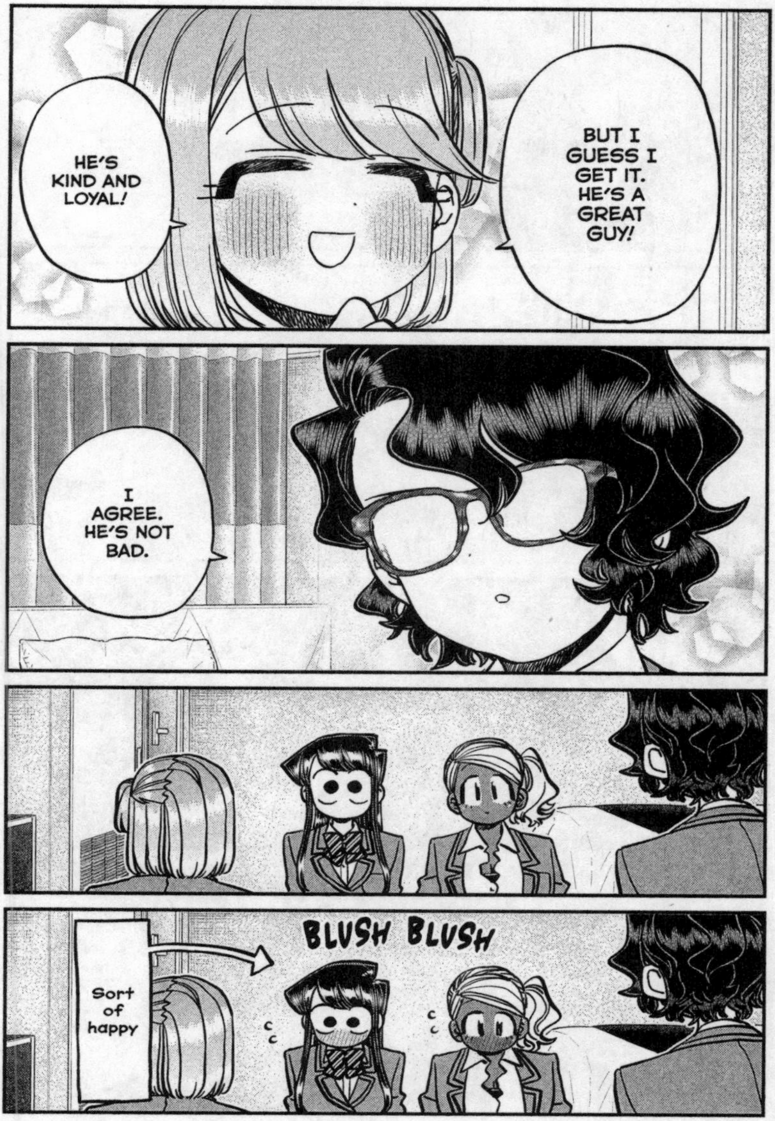
BUT I GUESS I GET IT. HE'S A GREAT GUY!
HE'S KIND AND LOYAL!
I AGREE. HE'S NOT BAD.
BLUSH BLUSH
Sort of happy

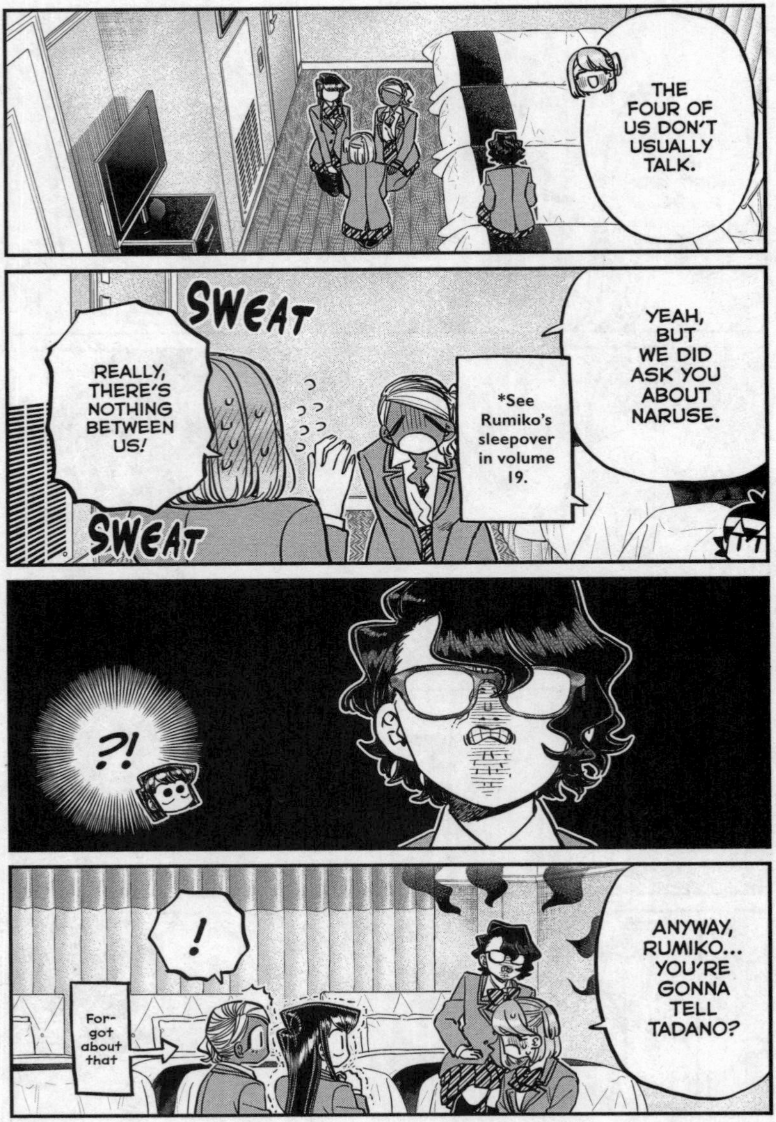
THE FOUR OF US DON'T USUALLY TALK.
YEAH, BUT WE DID ASK YOU ABOUT NARUSE.
*See Rumiko's sleepover in volume 19.
SWEAT
REALLY, THERE'S NOTHING BETWEEN US!
SWEAT
?!
ANYWAY, RUMIKO... YOU'RE GONNA TELL TADANO?
!
For-got about that

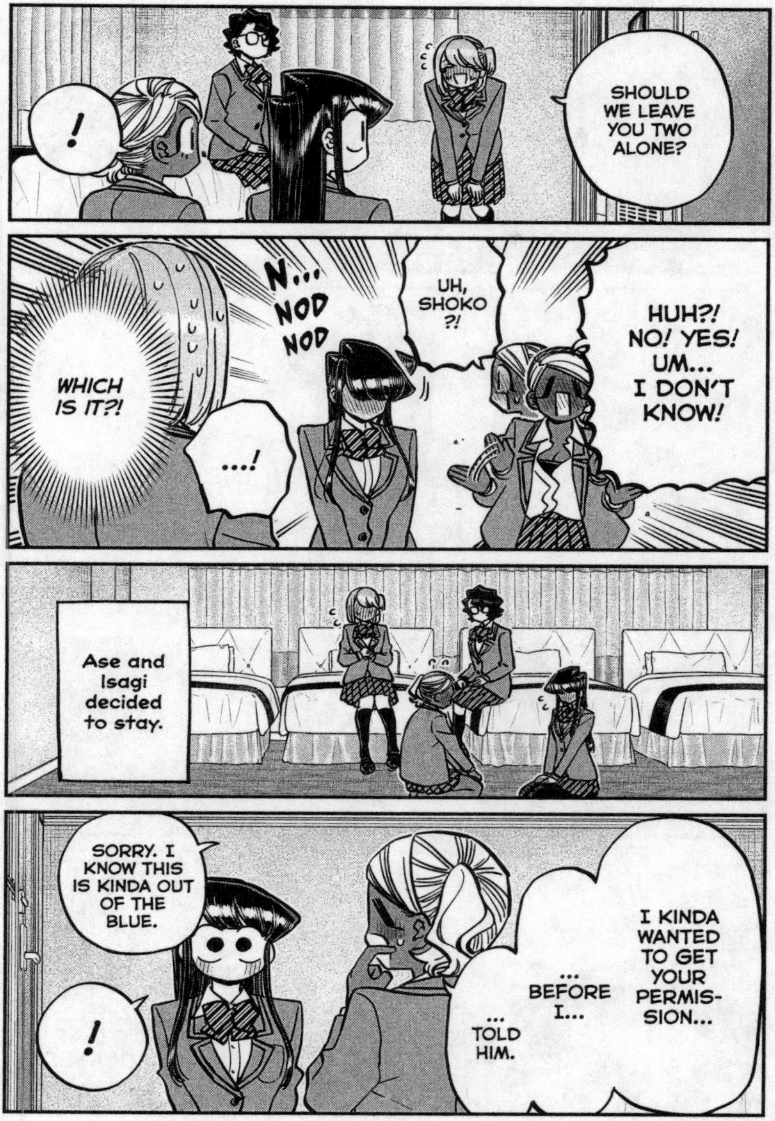
SHOULD WE LEAVE YOU TWO ALONE?
!
HUH?! NO! YES! UM... I DON'T KNOW!
UH, SHOKO?!
N... NOD NOD
...!
WHICH IS IT?!
Ase and Isagi decided to stay.
I KINDA WANTED TO GET YOUR PERMIS-SION...
... BEFORE I...
... TOLD HIM.
SORRY. I KNOW THIS IS KINDA OUT OF THE BLUE.
!

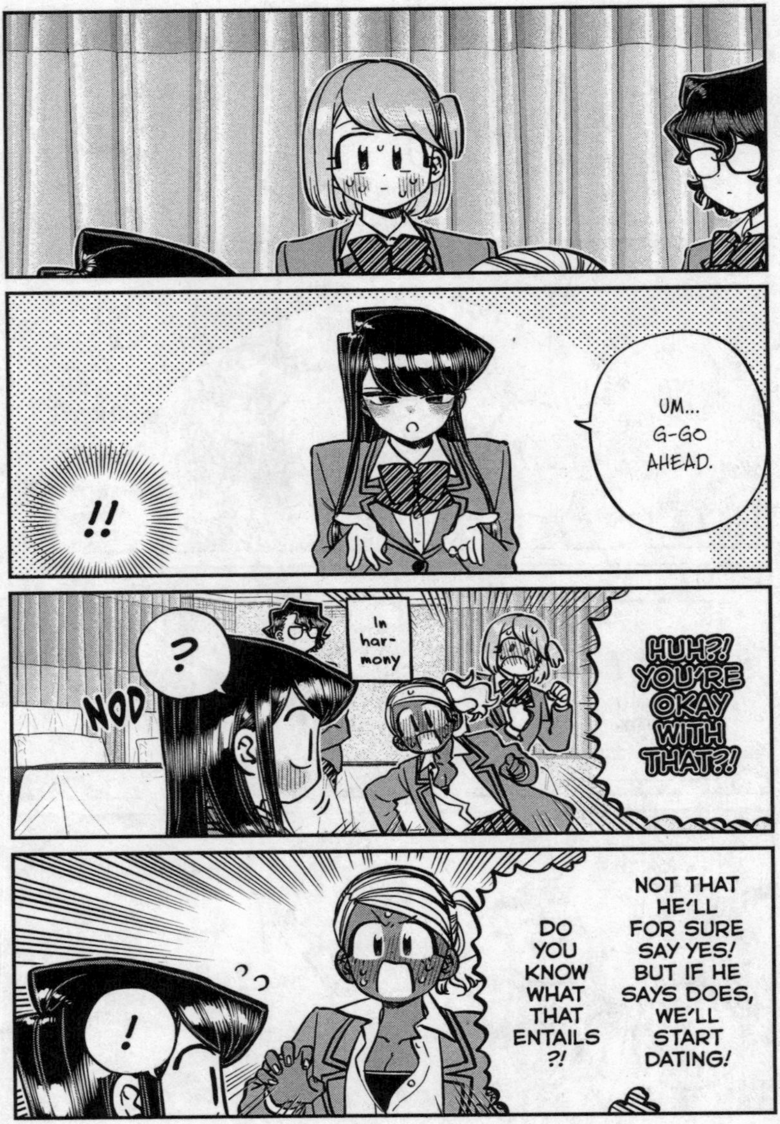
UM... G-GO AHEAD.
!!
HUH?! YOU'RE OKAY WITH THAT?!
In har-mony
?
NOD
NOT THAT HE'LL FOR SURE SAY YES! BUT IF HE SAYS DOES, WE'LL START DATING!
DO YOU KNOW WHAT THAT ENTAILS ?!
!

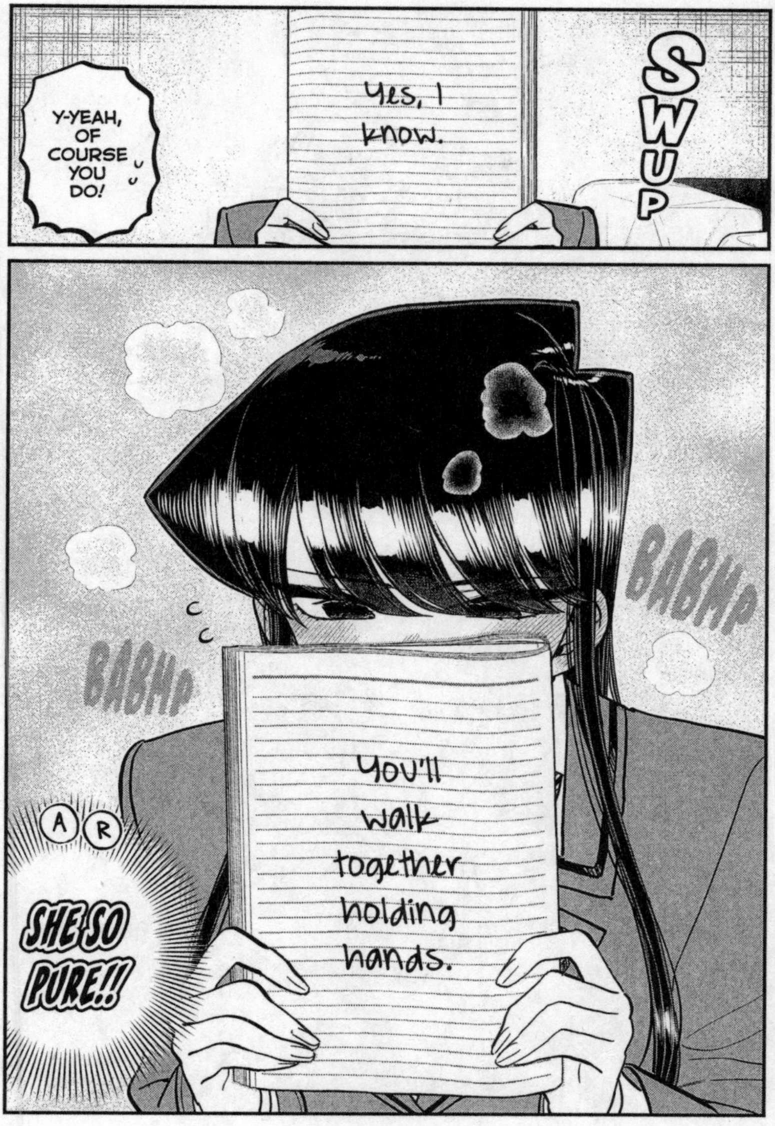
SWUP
Yes, I know.
Y-YEAH, OF COURSE YOU DO!
BABMP
BABMP
You'll walk together holding hands.
SHE SO PURE!!

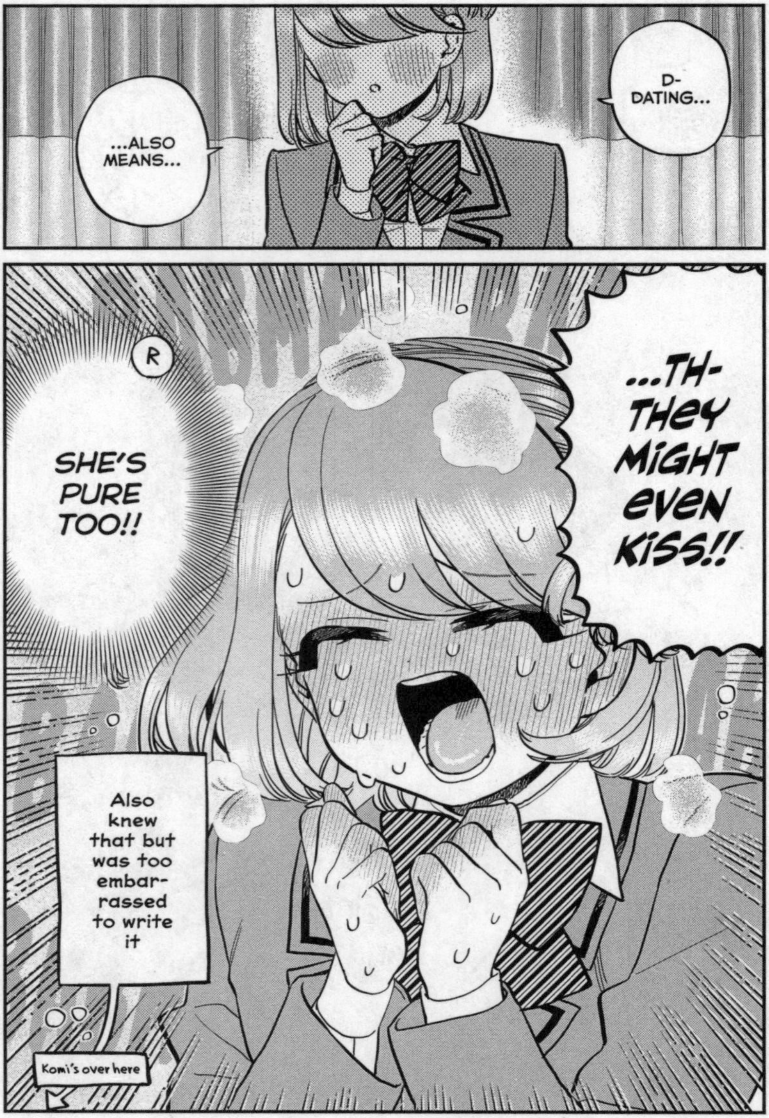
D-DATING...
...ALSO MEANS...
...TH-THEY MIGHT EVEN KISS!!
R
SHE'S PURE TOO!!
Also knew that but was too embarrassed to write it
Komi's over here

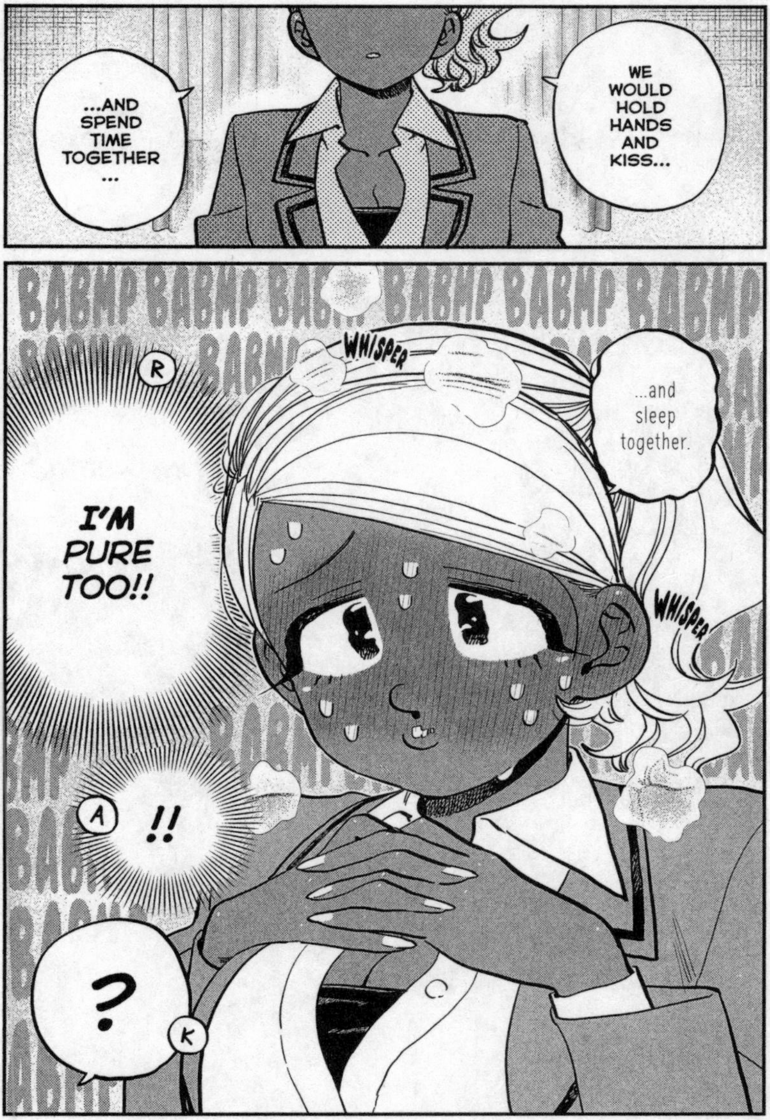
WE WOULD HOLD HANDS AND KISS...
...AND SPEND TIME TOGETHER ...
BABMP BABMP BABMP BABMP BABMP BABMP
WHISPER
...and sleep together.
WHISPER
R
I'M PURE TOO!!
A
!!
?
K

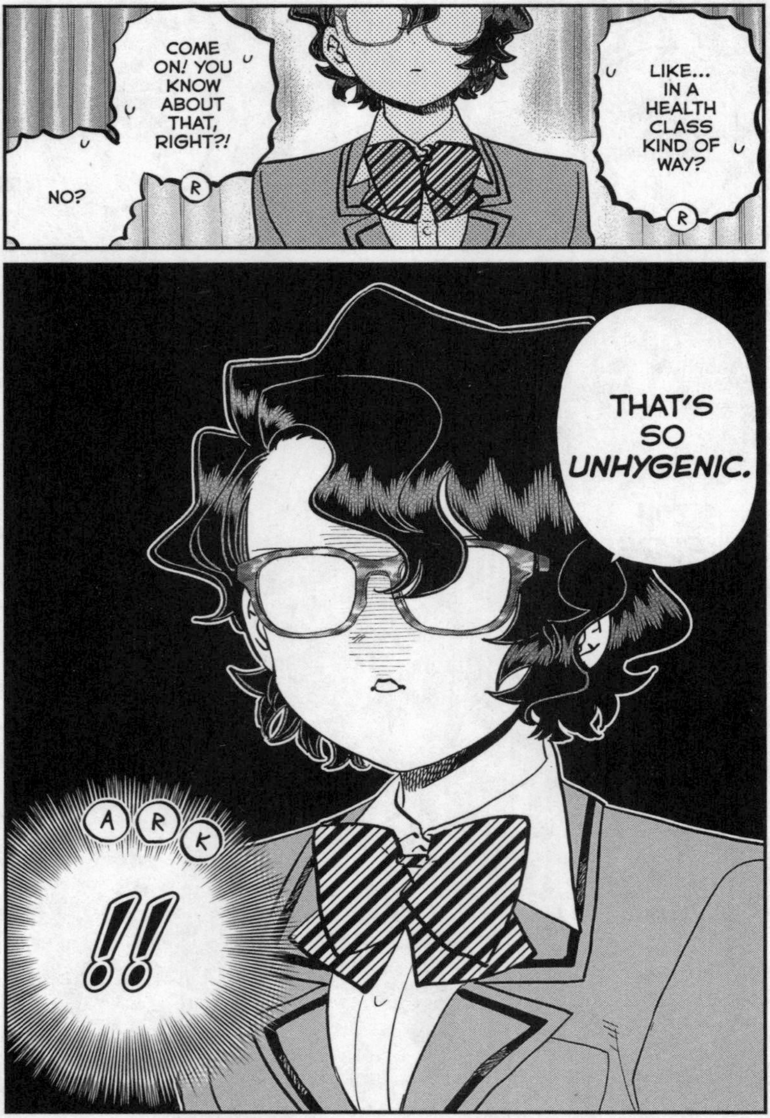
LIKE... IN A HEALTH CLASS KIND OF WAY?
R
COME ON! YOU KNOW ABOUT THAT, RIGHT?!
R
NO?
THAT'S SO *UNHYGENIC.*
ARK
!!

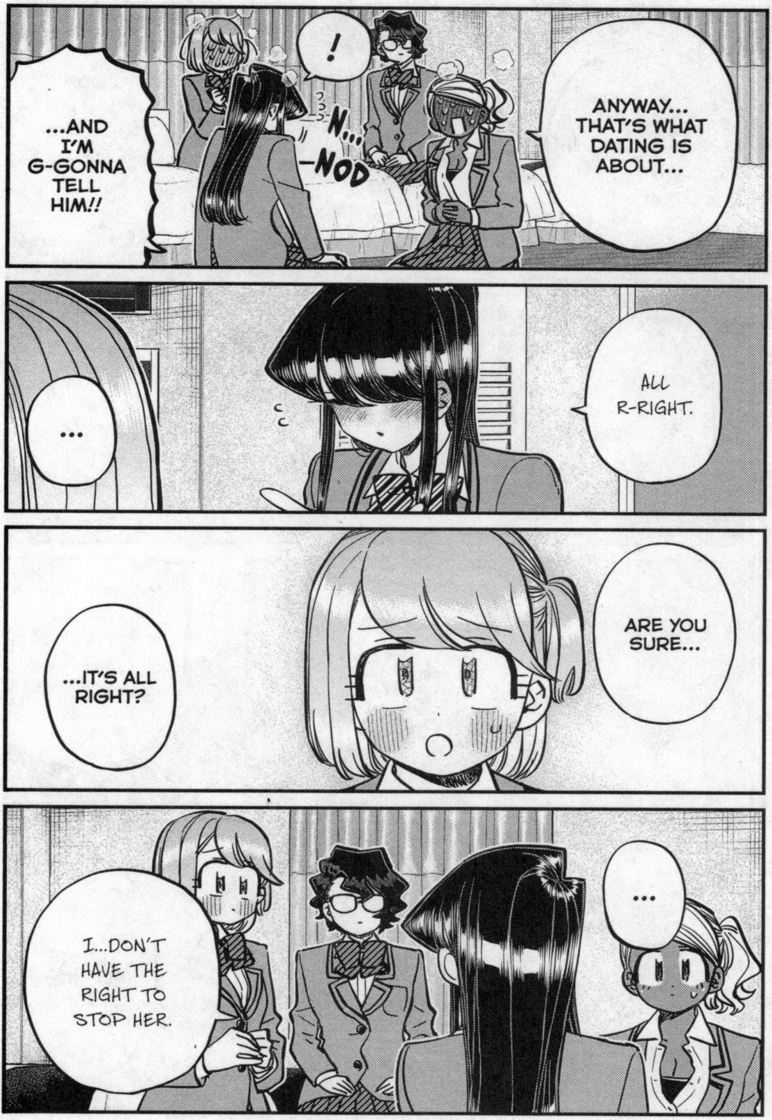
ANYWAY... THAT'S WHAT DATING IS ABOUT...
!
N... —NOD
...AND I'M G-GONNA TELL HIM!!
ALL R-RIGHT.
...
ARE YOU SURE...
...IT'S ALL RIGHT?
...
I...DON'T HAVE THE RIGHT TO STOP HER.

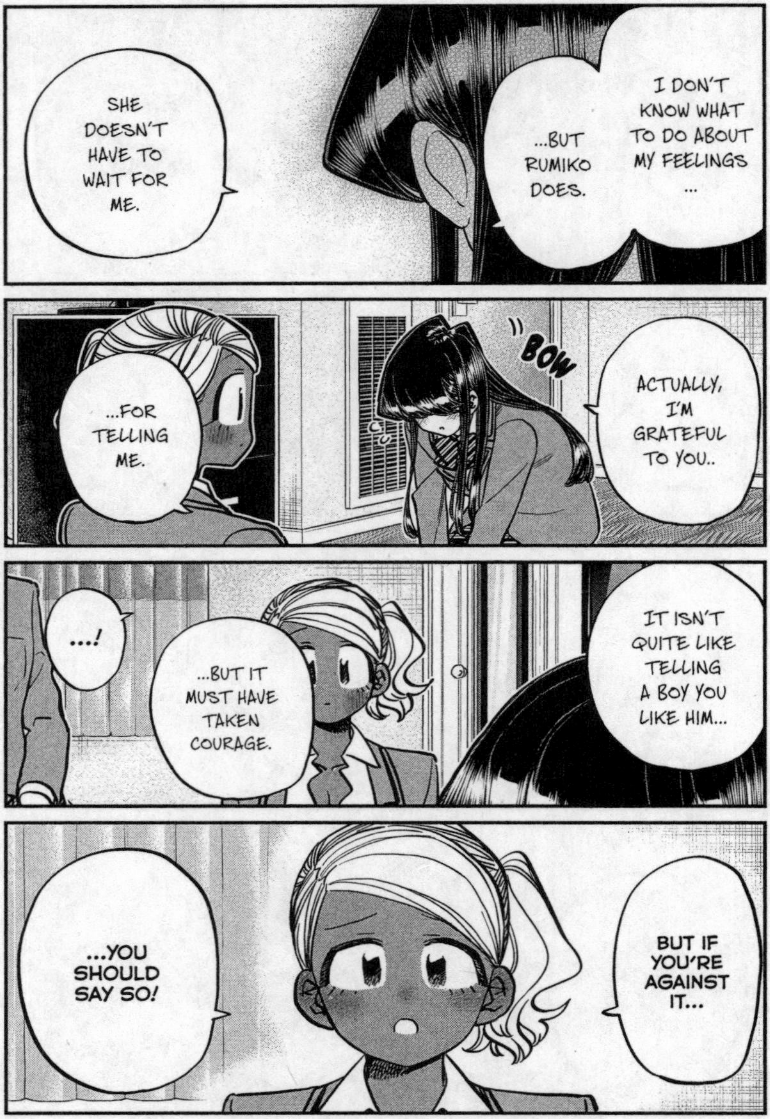
I DON'T KNOW WHAT TO DO ABOUT MY FEELINGS ...
...BUT RUMIKO DOES.
SHE DOESN'T HAVE TO WAIT FOR ME.
ACTUALLY, I'M GRATEFUL TO YOU..
BOW
...FOR TELLING ME.
IT ISN'T QUITE LIKE TELLING A BOY YOU LIKE HIM...
...BUT IT MUST HAVE TAKEN COURAGE.
...!
BUT IF YOU'RE AGAINST IT...
...YOU SHOULD SAY SO!

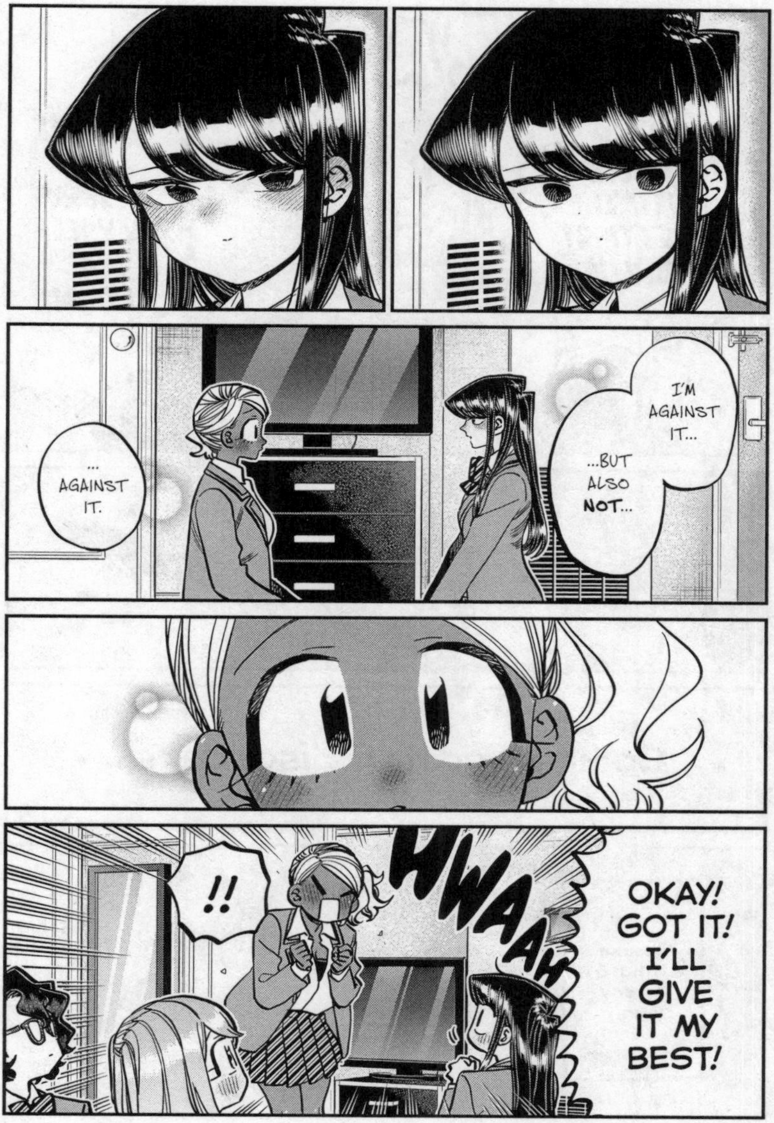
I'M AGAINST IT...
...BUT ALSO NOT...
... AGAINST IT.
OKAY! GOT IT! I'LL GIVE IT MY BEST!
HWAAAH
!!

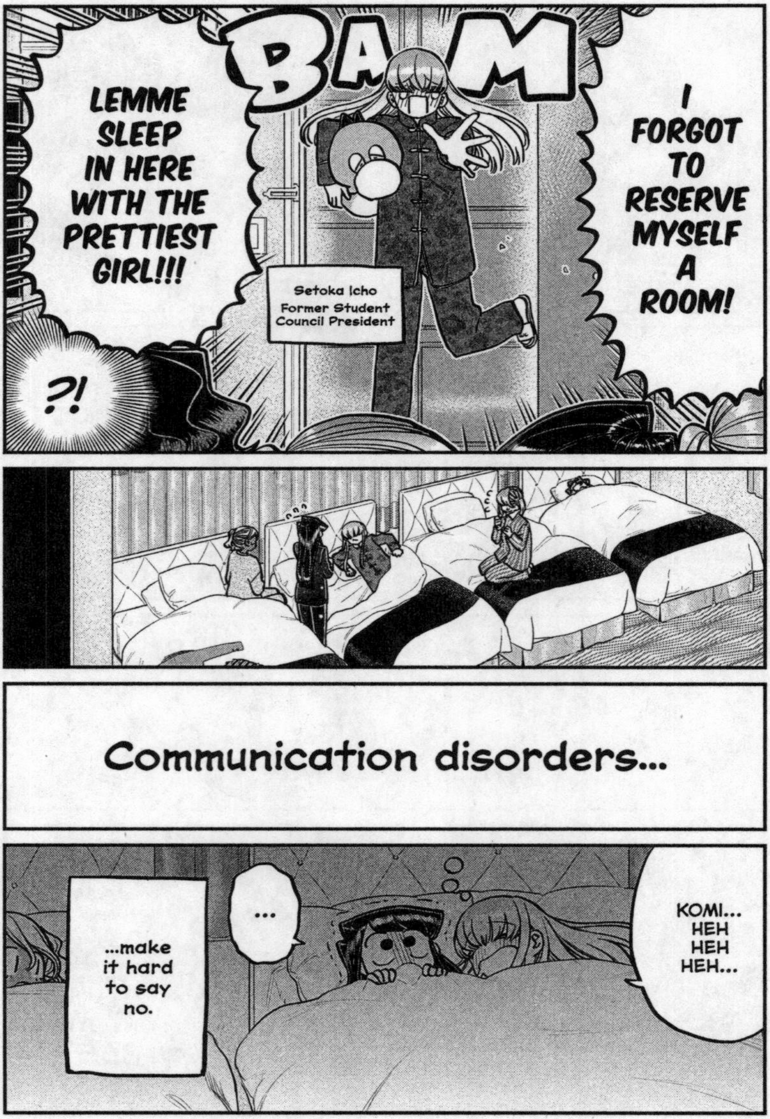
I FORGOT TO RESERVE MYSELF A ROOM!
BAM
LEMME SLEEP IN HERE WITH THE PRETTIEST GIRL!!!
Setoka Icho Former Student Council President
?!
Communication disorders...
KOMI... HEH HEH HEH...
...
...make it hard to say no.

Communication 285 — The End

Komi Can't Communicate

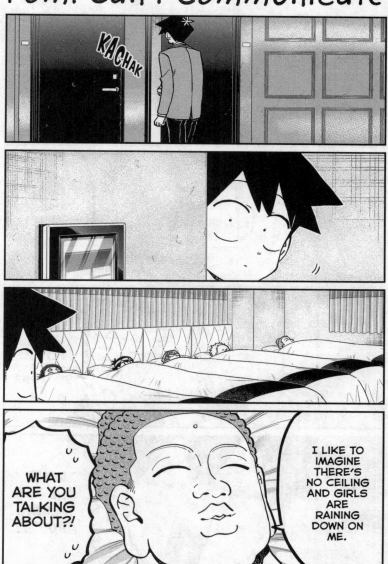

KACHAK
I LIKE TO IMAGINE THERE'S NO CEILING AND GIRLS ARE RAINING DOWN ON ME.
WHAT ARE YOU TALKING ABOUT?!

Communication 286: The Boys' Room

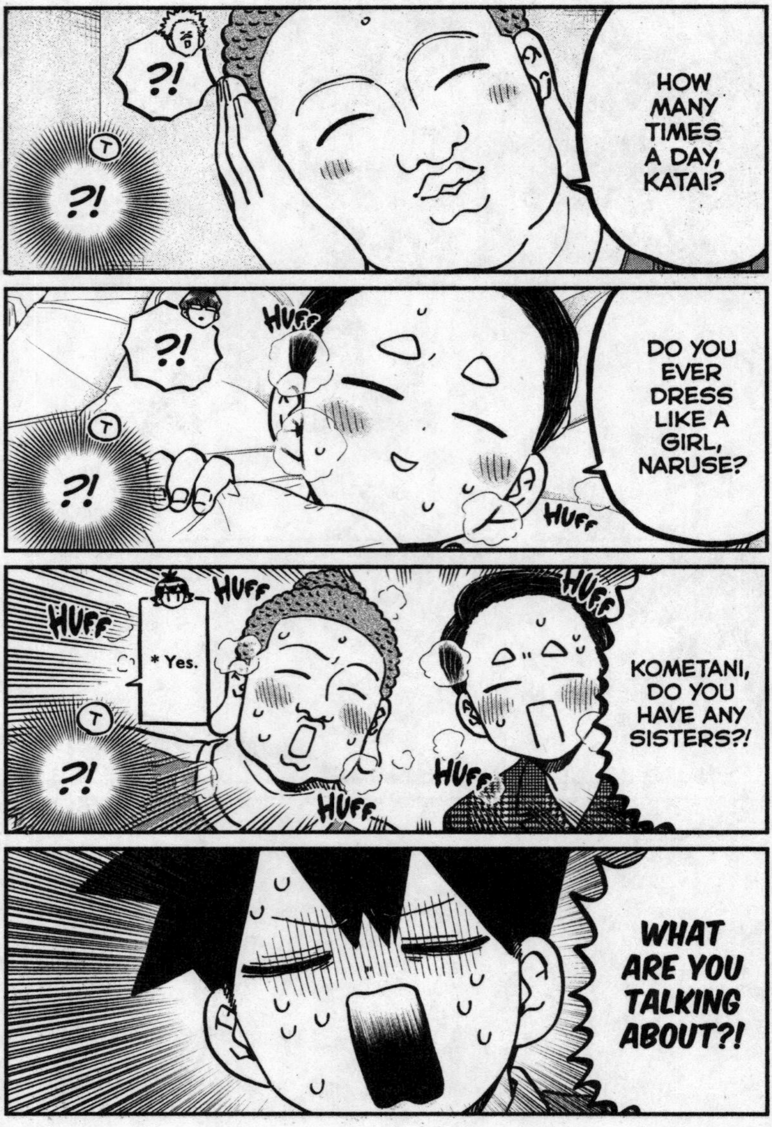
HOW MANY TIMES A DAY, KATAI?
?!
T
?!
DO YOU EVER DRESS LIKE A GIRL, NARUSE?
HUFF
HUFF
?!
T
?!
KOMETANI, DO YOU HAVE ANY SISTERS?!
HUFF
HUFF
HUFF
HUFF
* Yes.
HUFF
T
?!
WHAT ARE YOU TALKING ABOUT?!

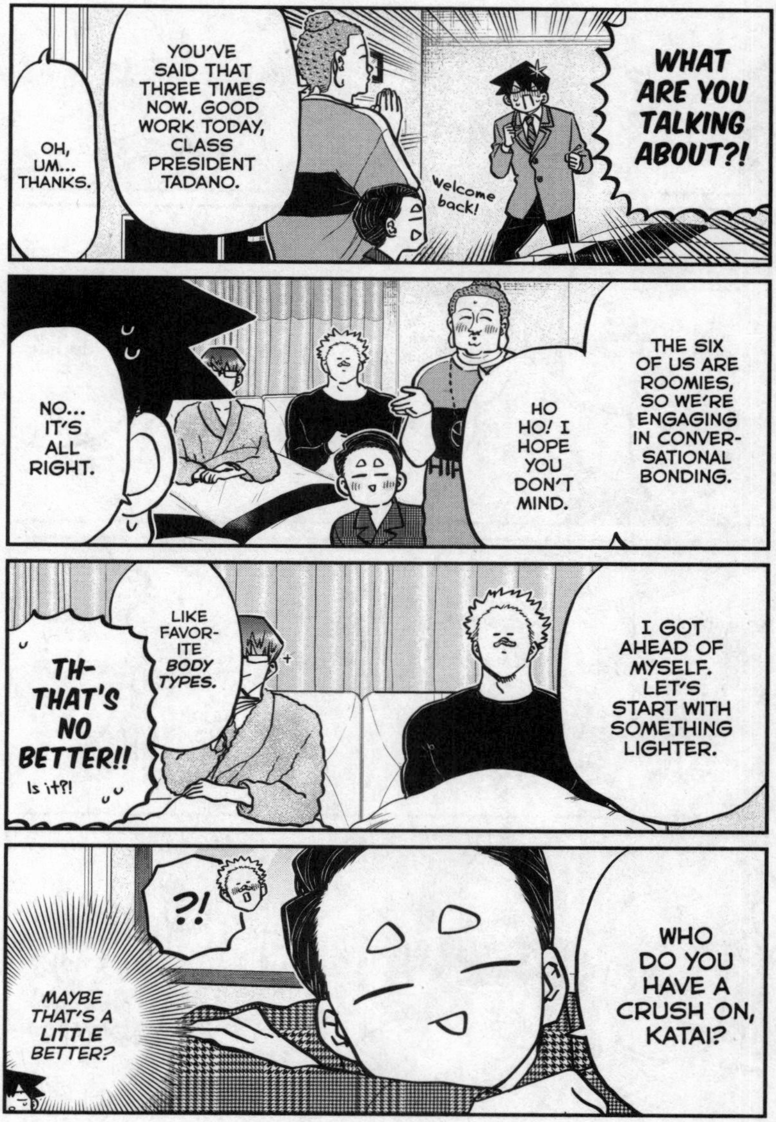
WHAT ARE YOU TALKING ABOUT?!
Welcome back!
YOU'VE SAID THAT THREE TIMES NOW. GOOD WORK TODAY, CLASS PRESIDENT TADANO.
OH, UM... THANKS.
THE SIX OF US ARE ROOMIES, SO WE'RE ENGAGING IN CONVERSATIONAL BONDING.
HO HO! I HOPE YOU DON'T MIND.
NO... IT'S ALL RIGHT.
I GOT AHEAD OF MYSELF. LET'S START WITH SOMETHING LIGHTER.
LIKE FAVORITE BODY TYPES.
TH- THAT'S NO BETTER!!
Is it?!
WHO DO YOU HAVE A CRUSH ON, KATAI?
?!
MAYBE THAT'S A LITTLE BETTER?

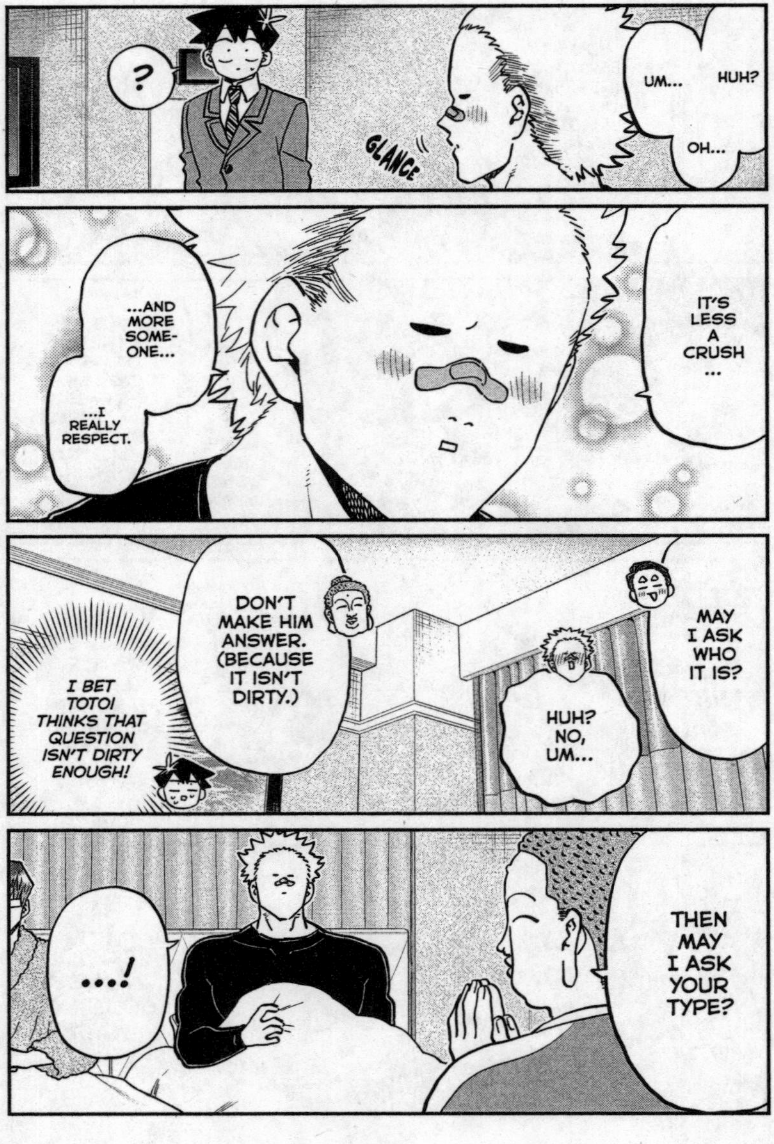
UM... HUH? OH...
GLANCE
?
IT'S LESS A CRUSH...
...AND MORE SOMEONE... ...I REALLY RESPECT.
MAY I ASK WHO IT IS?
HUH? NO, UM...
DON'T MAKE HIM ANSWER. (BECAUSE IT ISN'T DIRTY.)
I BET TOTOI THINKS THAT QUESTION ISN'T DIRTY ENOUGH!
THEN MAY I ASK YOUR TYPE?
...!

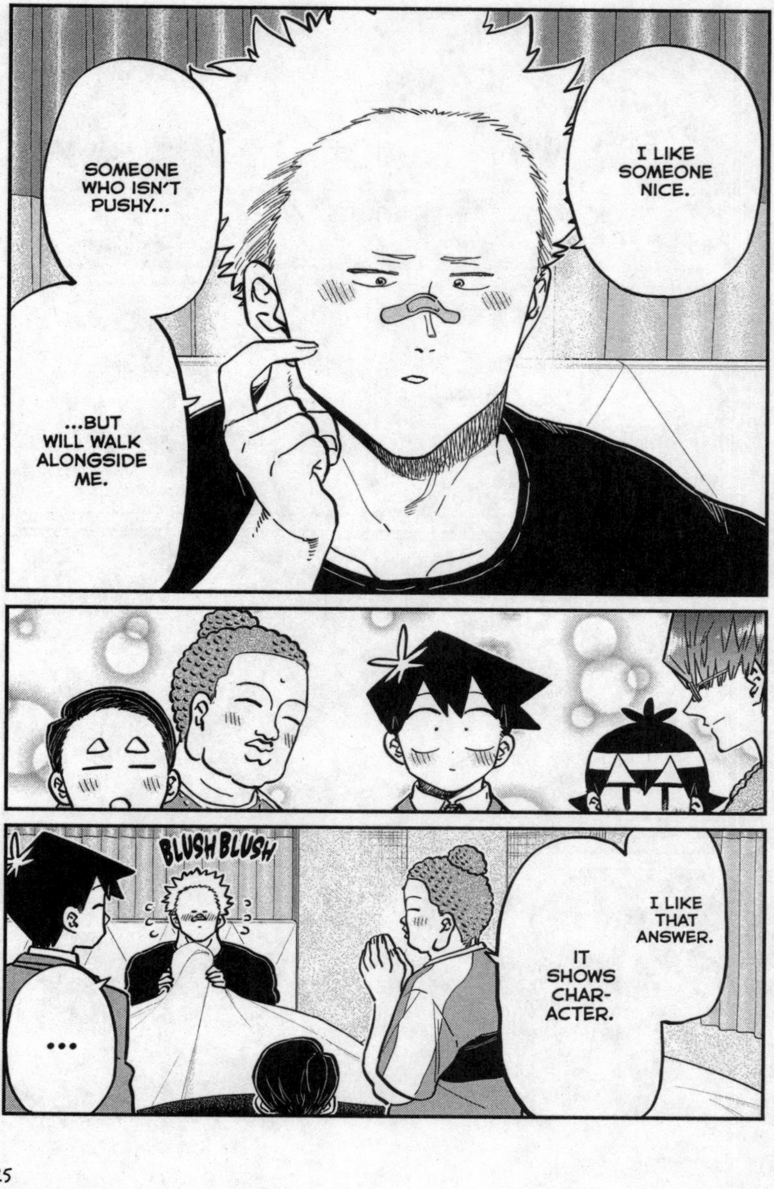
I LIKE SOMEONE NICE.
SOMEONE WHO ISN'T PUSHY...
...BUT WILL WALK ALONGSIDE ME.
I LIKE THAT ANSWER.
IT SHOWS CHAR-ACTER.
BLUSH BLUSH
...

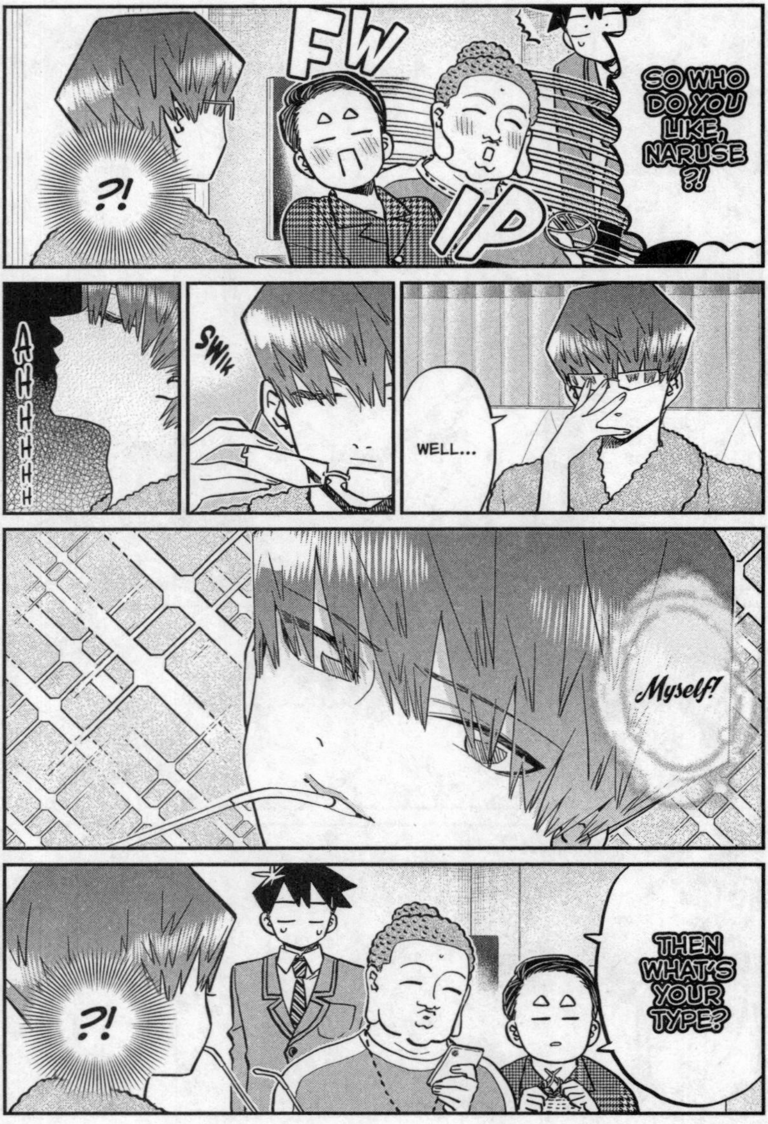
SO WHO DO YOU LIKE, NARUSE ?!
FWIP
?!
WELL...
SWIK
AHHHHHHHH
Myself!
THEN WHAT'S YOUR TYPE?
?!

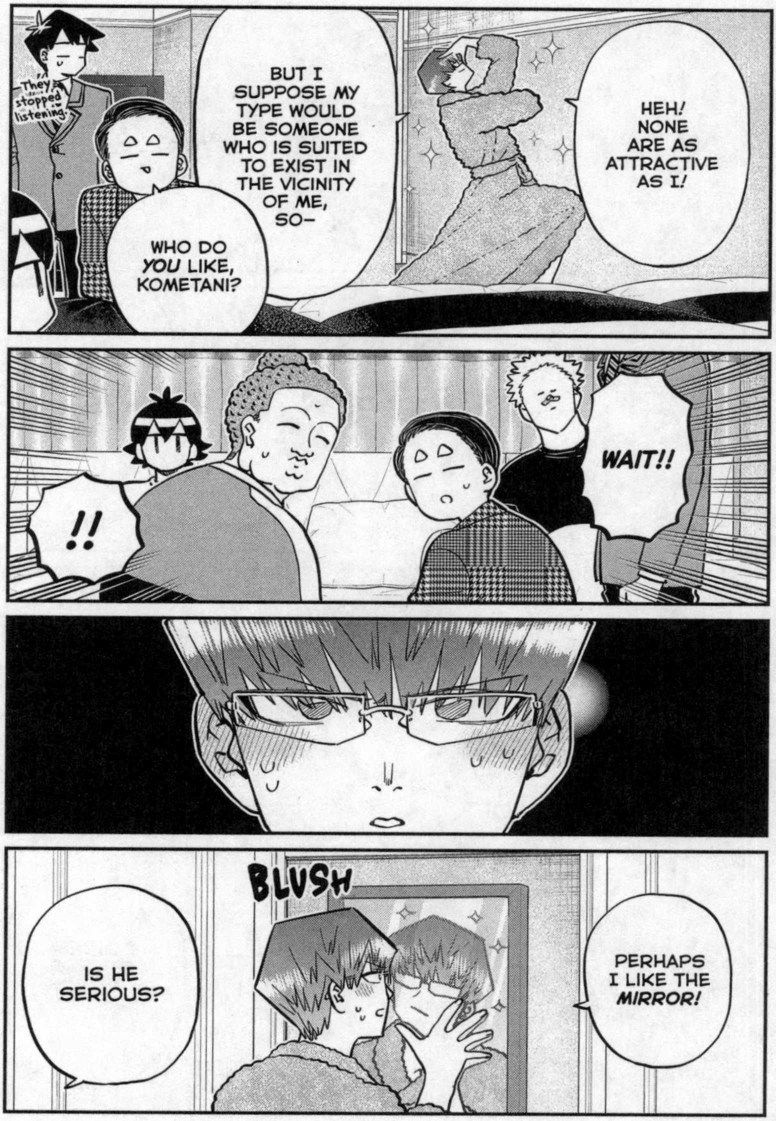
HEH! NONE ARE AS ATTRACTIVE AS I!
BUT I SUPPOSE MY TYPE WOULD BE SOMEONE WHO IS SUITED TO EXIST IN THE VICINITY OF ME, SO–
WHO DO *YOU* LIKE, KOMETANI?
They stopped listening.
WAIT!!
!!
PERHAPS I LIKE THE *MIRROR!*
BLUSH
IS HE SERIOUS?

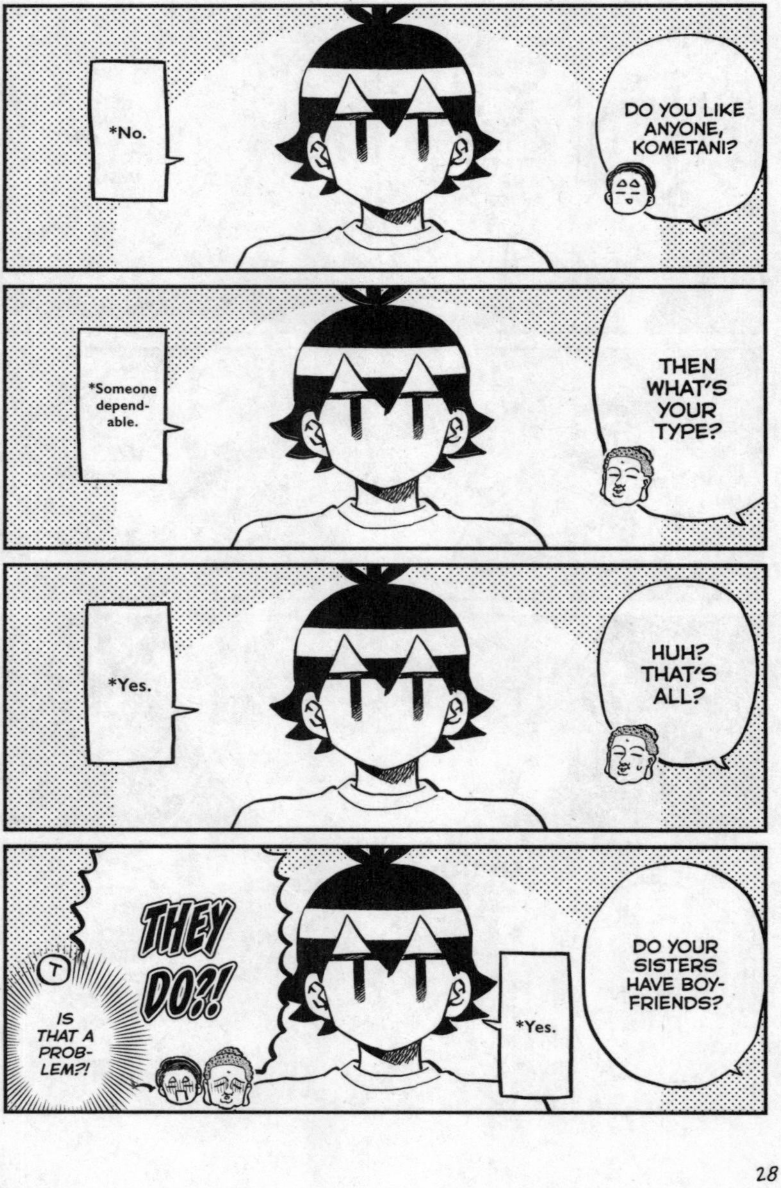
DO YOU LIKE ANYONE, KOMETANI?
*No.
THEN WHAT'S YOUR TYPE?
*Someone depend-able.
HUH? THAT'S ALL?
*Yes.
DO YOUR SISTERS HAVE BOY-FRIENDS?
*Yes.
THEY DO?!
IS THAT A PROB-LEM?!

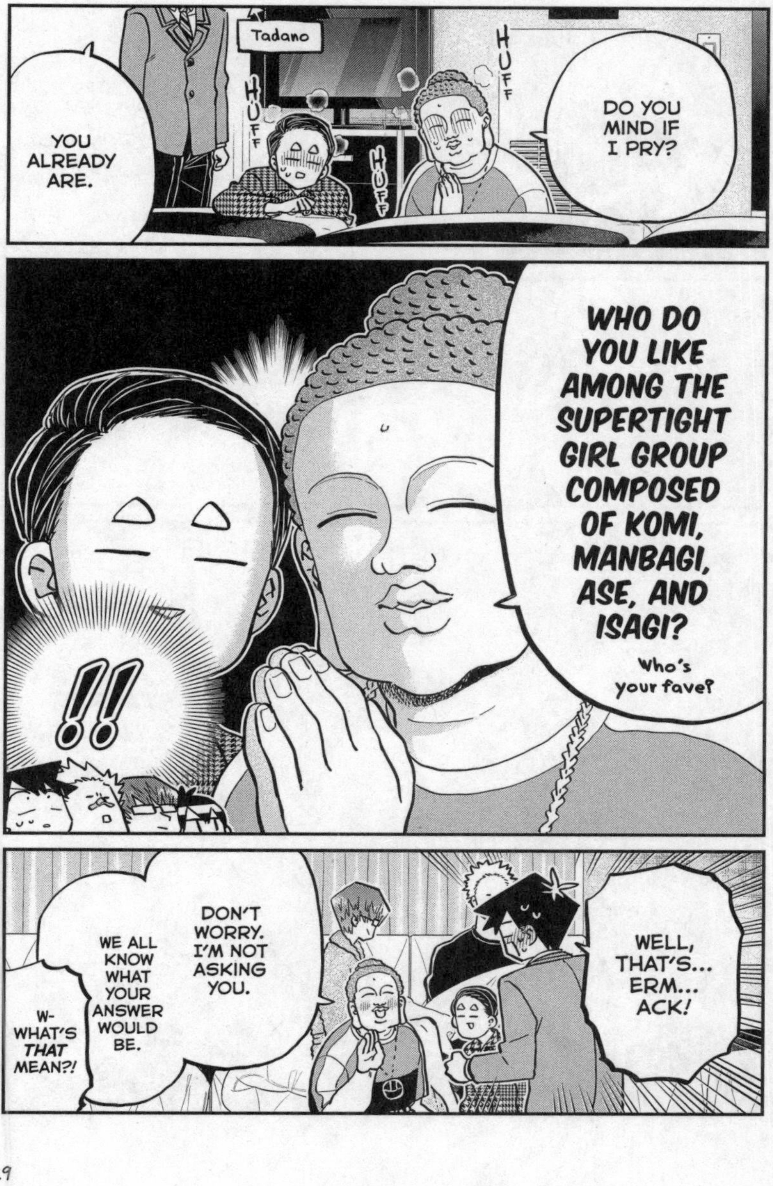
DO YOU MIND IF I PRY?
HUFF HUFF
Tadano
HUFF HUFF
HUFF HUFF
YOU ALREADY ARE.
WHO DO YOU LIKE AMONG THE SUPERTIGHT GIRL GROUP COMPOSED OF KOMI, MANBAGI, ASE, AND ISAGI?
Who's your fave?
!!
WELL, THAT'S... ERM... ACK!
DON'T WORRY. I'M NOT ASKING YOU.
WE ALL KNOW WHAT YOUR ANSWER WOULD BE.
W-WHAT'S *THAT* MEAN?!

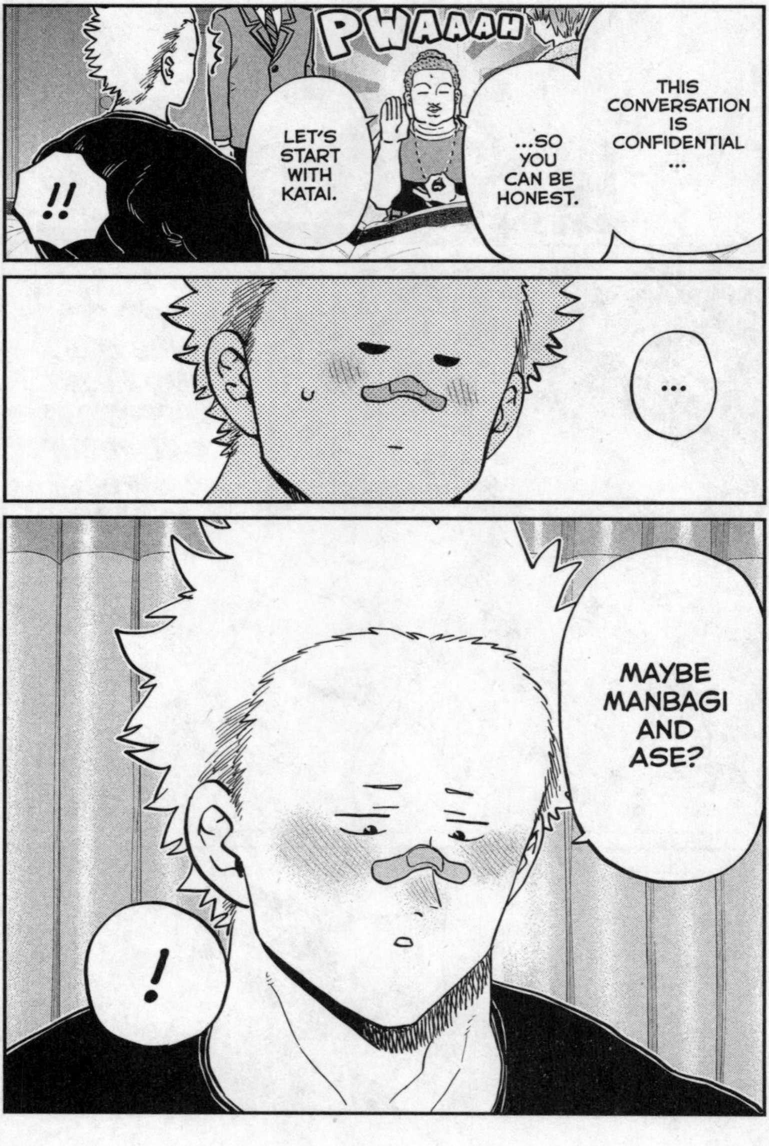

THIS CONVERSATION IS CONFIDENTIAL ...
...SO YOU CAN BE HONEST.
PWAAAH
LET'S START WITH KATAI.
!!
...
MAYBE MANBAGI AND ASE?
!

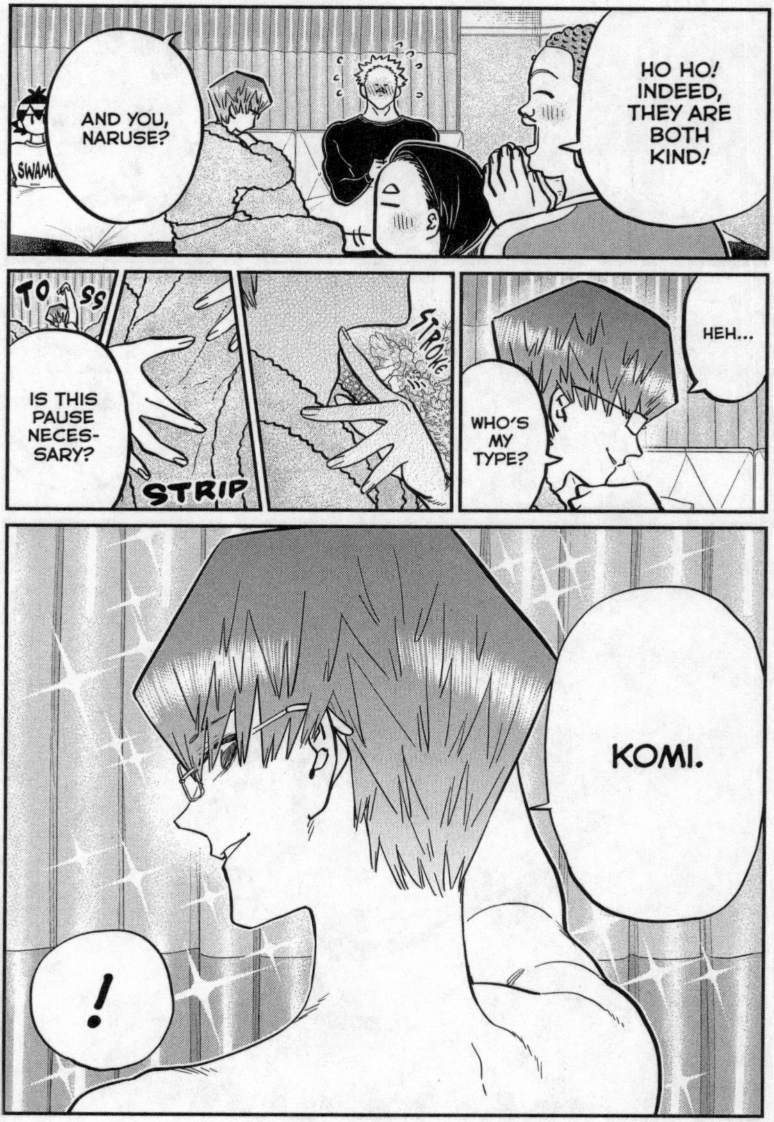
HO HO! INDEED, THEY ARE BOTH KIND!
AND YOU, NARUSE?
HEH...
WHO'S MY TYPE?
STROKE
TOSS
IS THIS PAUSE NECES-SARY?
STRIP
KOMI.
!

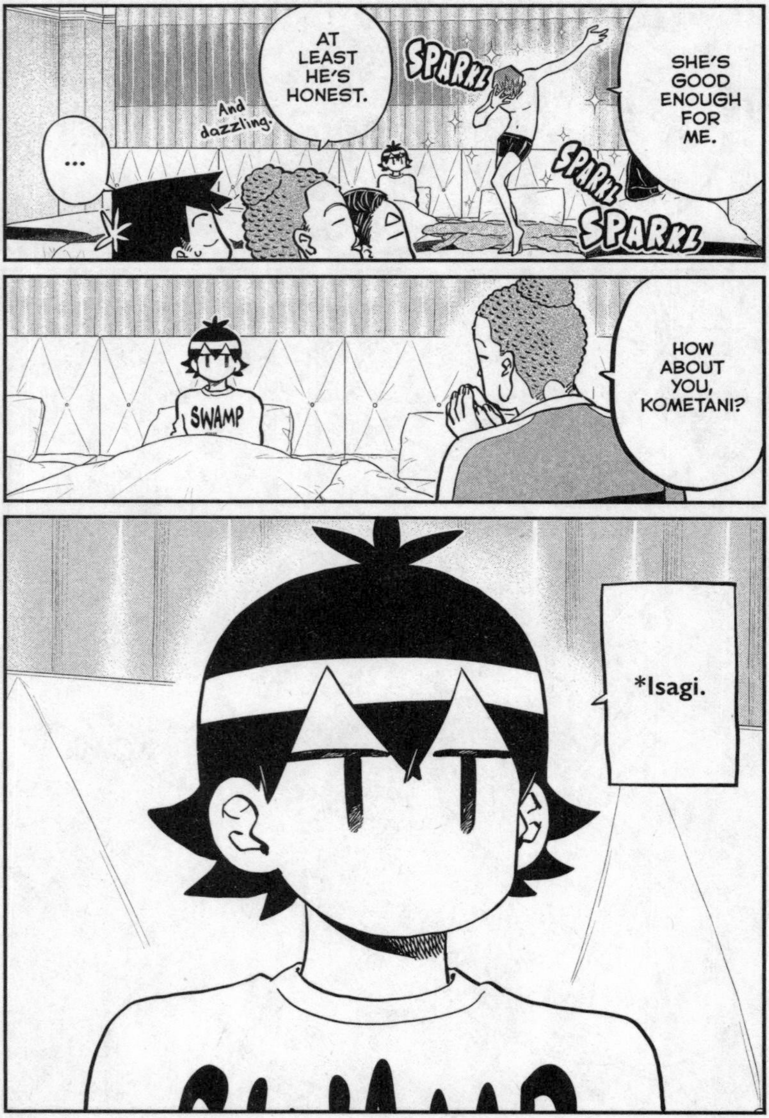
SHE'S GOOD ENOUGH FOR ME.
SPARKL
SPARKL
SPARKL
AT LEAST HE'S HONEST.
And dazzling.
...
HOW ABOUT YOU, KOMETANI?
SWAMP
*Isagi.

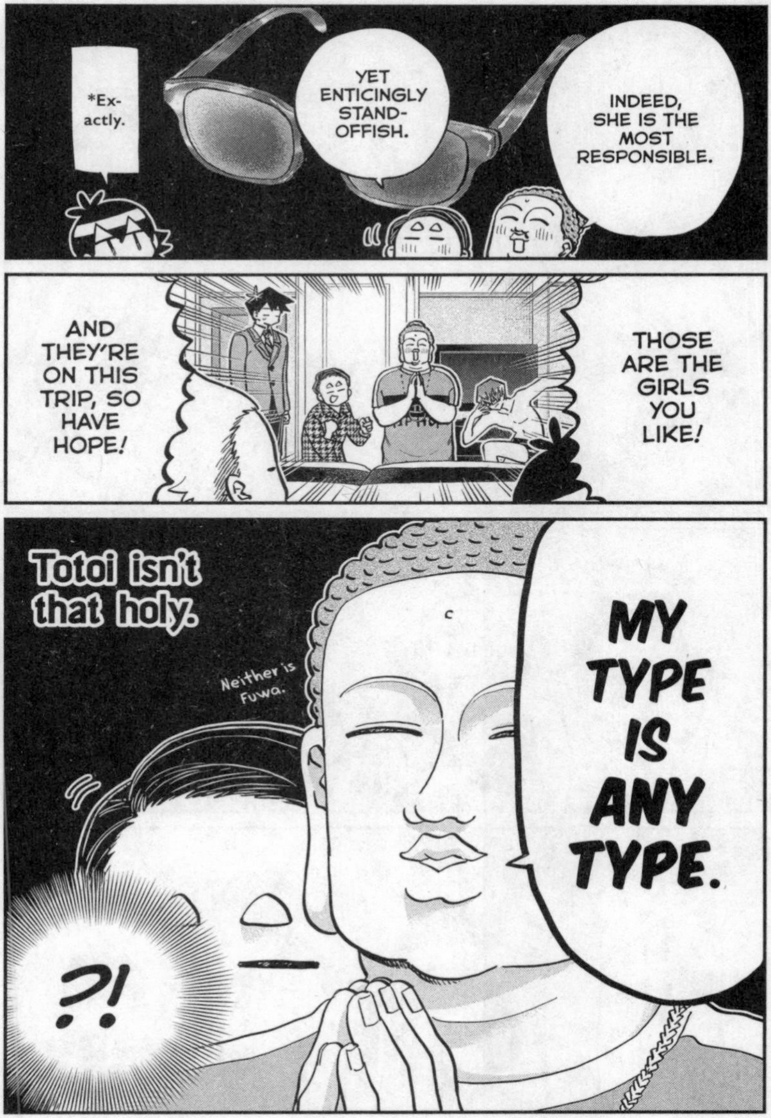
INDEED, SHE IS THE MOST RESPONSIBLE.
YET ENTICINGLY STAND-OFFISH.
*Ex-actly.
THOSE ARE THE GIRLS YOU LIKE!
AND THEY'RE ON THIS TRIP, SO HAVE HOPE!
MY TYPE IS ANY TYPE.
Totoi isn't that holy.
Neither is Fuwa.
?!

Communication 286 — The End

Communication 287: Splitting into Pairs

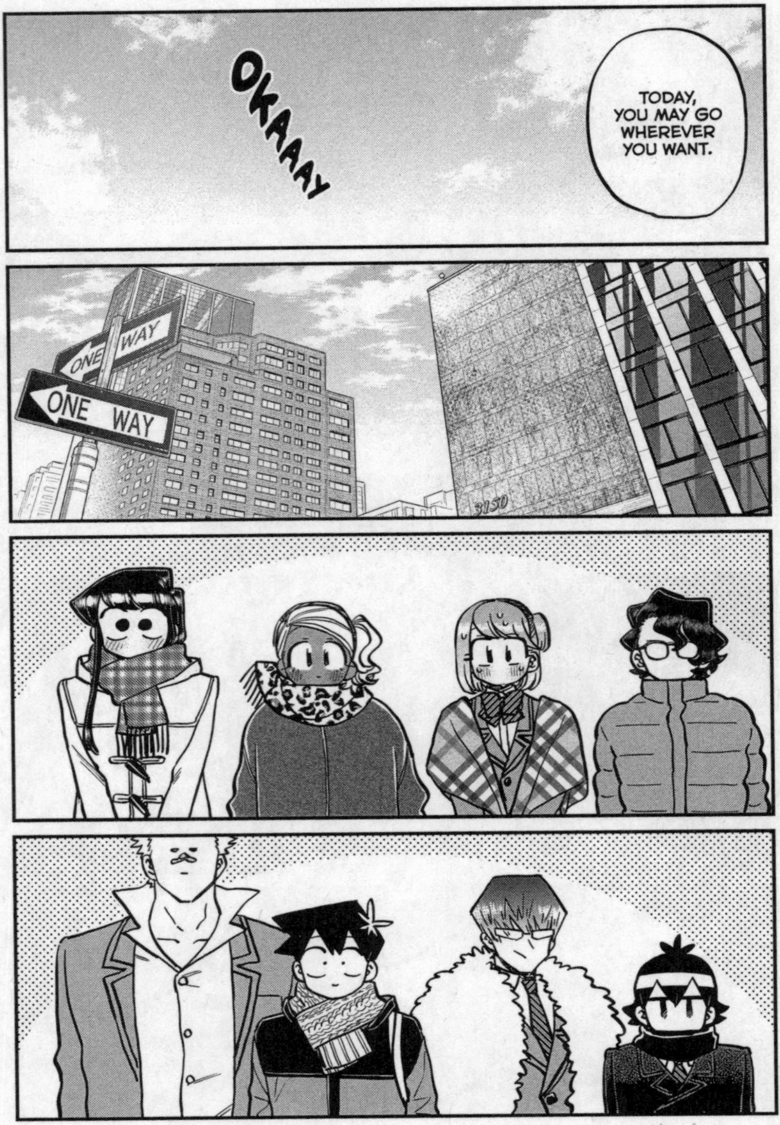
TODAY, YOU MAY GO WHEREVER YOU WANT.
OKAAAY
ONE WAY
ONE WAY
3150

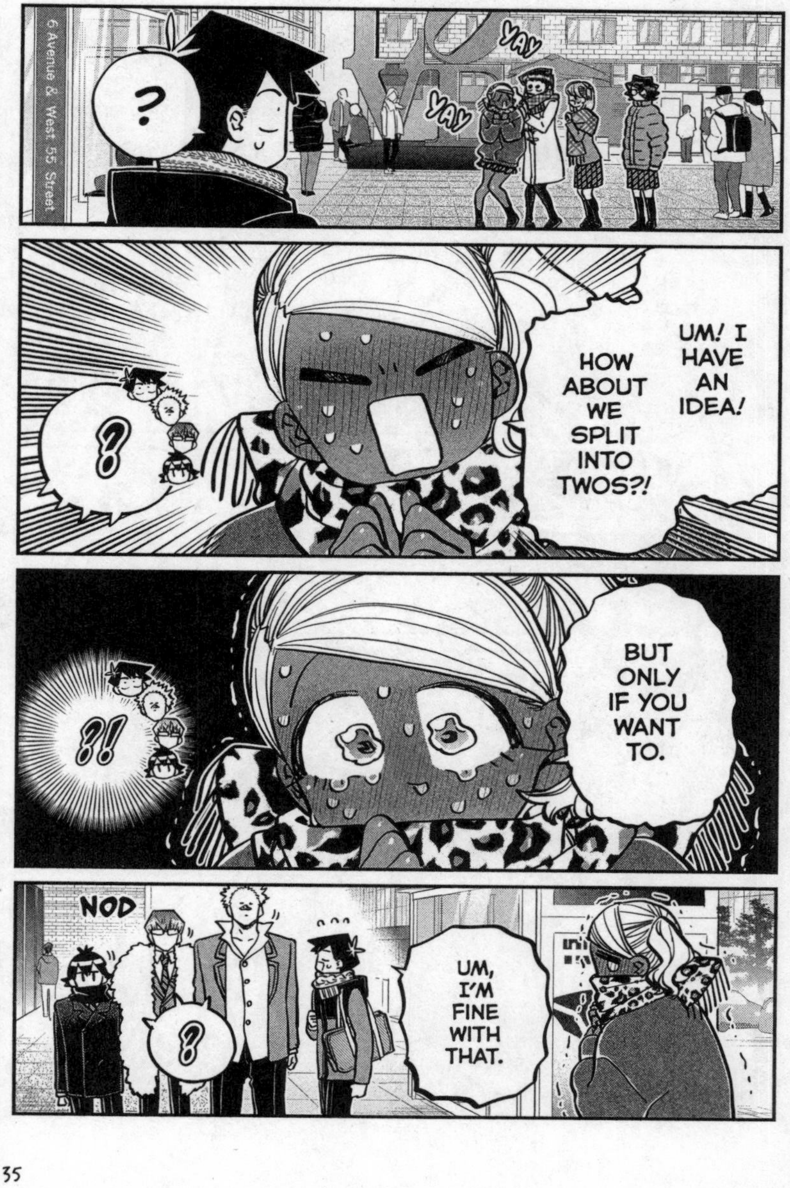
YAY
YAY
?
6 Avenue & West 55 Street
UM! I HAVE AN IDEA!
HOW ABOUT WE SPLIT INTO TWOS?!
?
BUT ONLY IF YOU WANT TO.
?!
UM, I'M FINE WITH THAT.
?
NOD

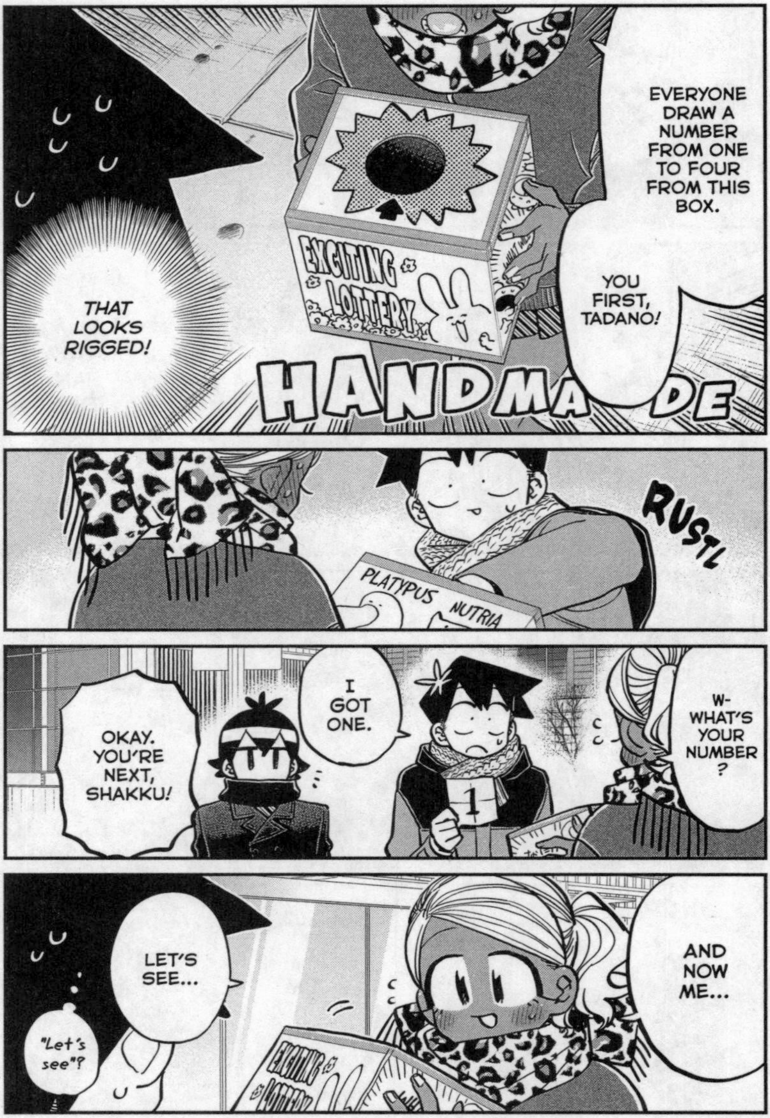
EVERYONE DRAW A NUMBER FROM ONE TO FOUR FROM THIS BOX.
YOU FIRST, TADANO!
EXCITING LOTTERY
THAT LOOKS RIGGED!
HANDMADE
RUSTL
PLATYPUS
NUTRIA
W-WHAT'S YOUR NUMBER?
I GOT ONE.
1
OKAY. YOU'RE NEXT, SHAKKU!
AND NOW ME...
LET'S SEE...
"Let's see"?

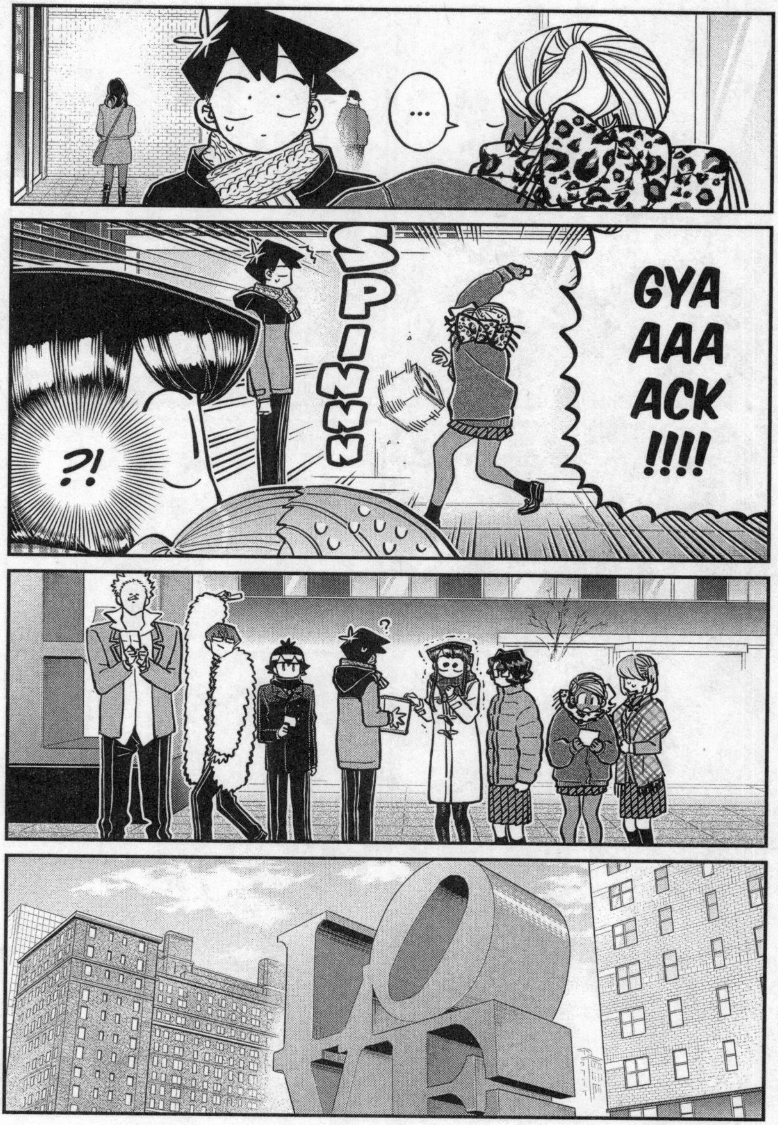
...
GYA AAA ACK !!!!
SPINNN
?!
?

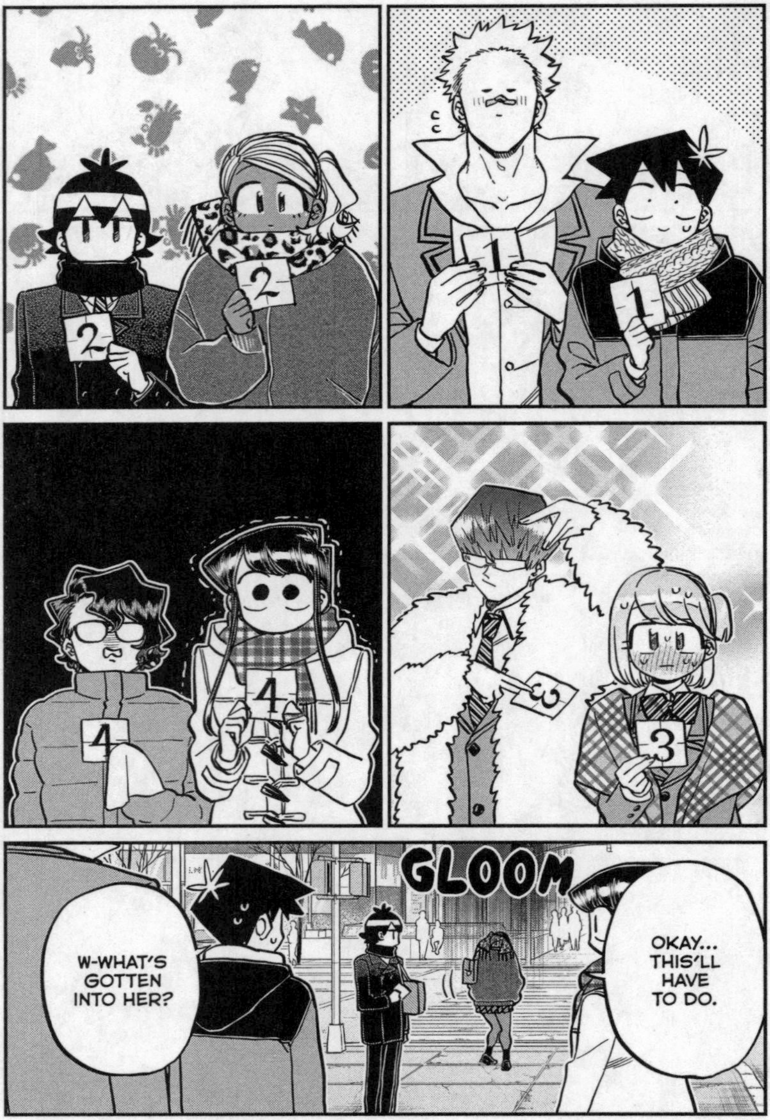
1
1
2
2
3
3
4
4
OKAY... THIS'LL HAVE TO DO.
GLOOM
W-WHAT'S GOTTEN INTO HER?

Communication 287 — The End

Komi Can't Communicate

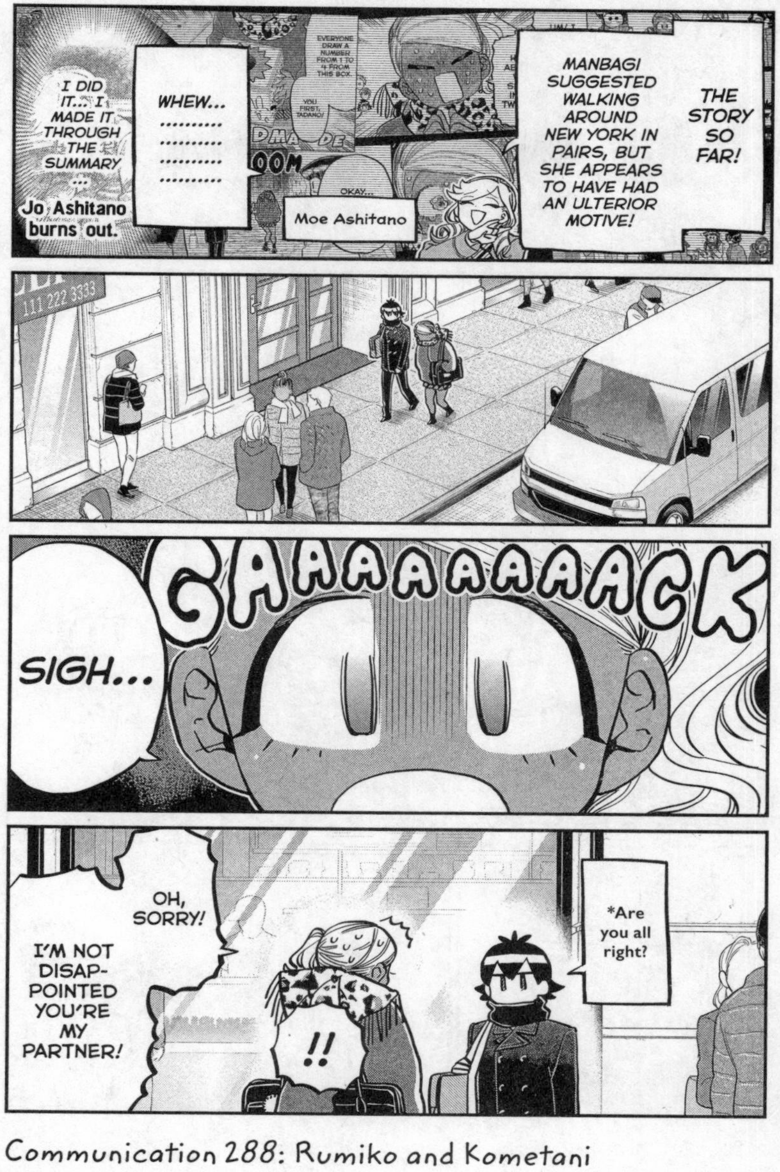
THE STORY SO FAR!
MANBAGI SUGGESTED WALKING AROUND NEW YORK IN PAIRS, BUT SHE APPEARS TO HAVE HAD AN ULTERIOR MOTIVE!
EVERYONE DRAW A NUMBER FROM 1 TO 4 FROM THIS BOX.
YOU FIRST, TADANO!
OKAY...
Moe Ashitano
WHEW... ....
I DID IT... I MADE IT THROUGH THE SUMMARY...
Jo Ashitano burns out.
111 222 3333
GAAAAAAAACK
SIGH...
*Are you all right?
OH, SORRY!
!!
I'M NOT DISAP-POINTED YOU'RE MY PARTNER!

Communication 288: Rumiko and Kometani

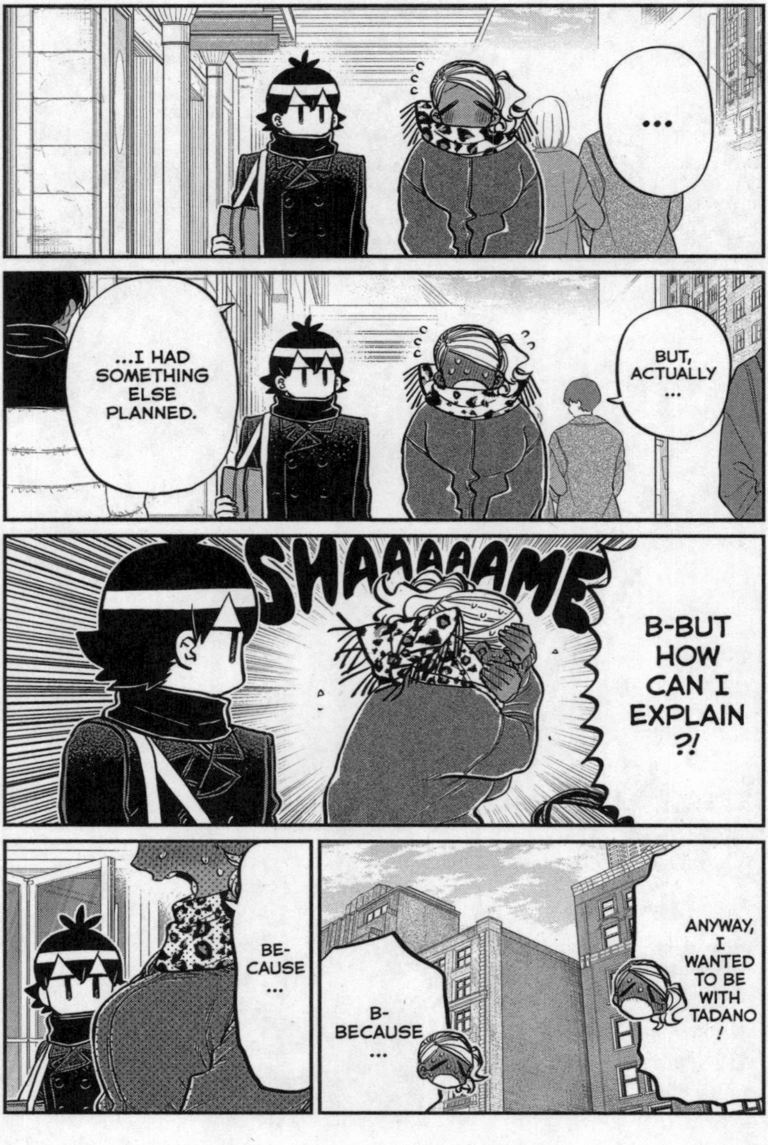
...
BUT, ACTUALLY ...
...I HAD SOMETHING ELSE PLANNED.
SHAAAAAME
B-BUT HOW CAN I EXPLAIN ?!
ANYWAY, I WANTED TO BE WITH TADANO !
B-BECAUSE ...
BE-CAUSE ...

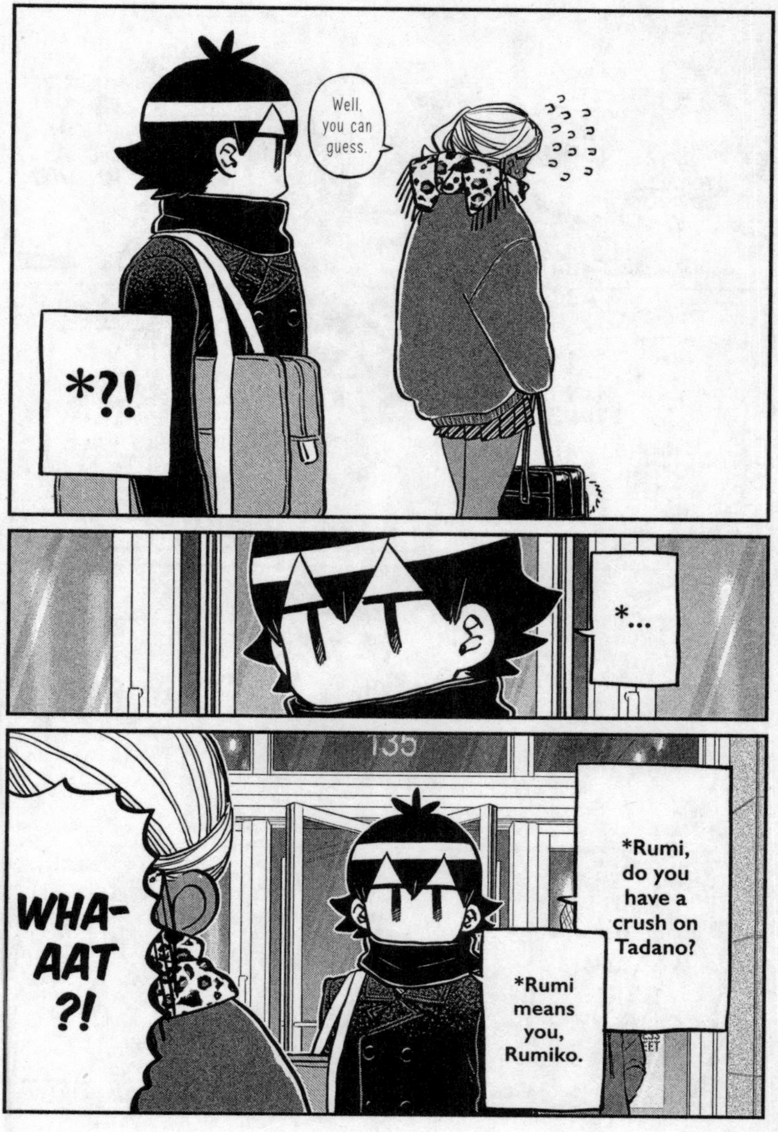
Well, you can guess.
*?!
*...
135
*Rumi, do you have a crush on Tadano?
*Rumi means you, Rumiko.
WHA-AAT ?!

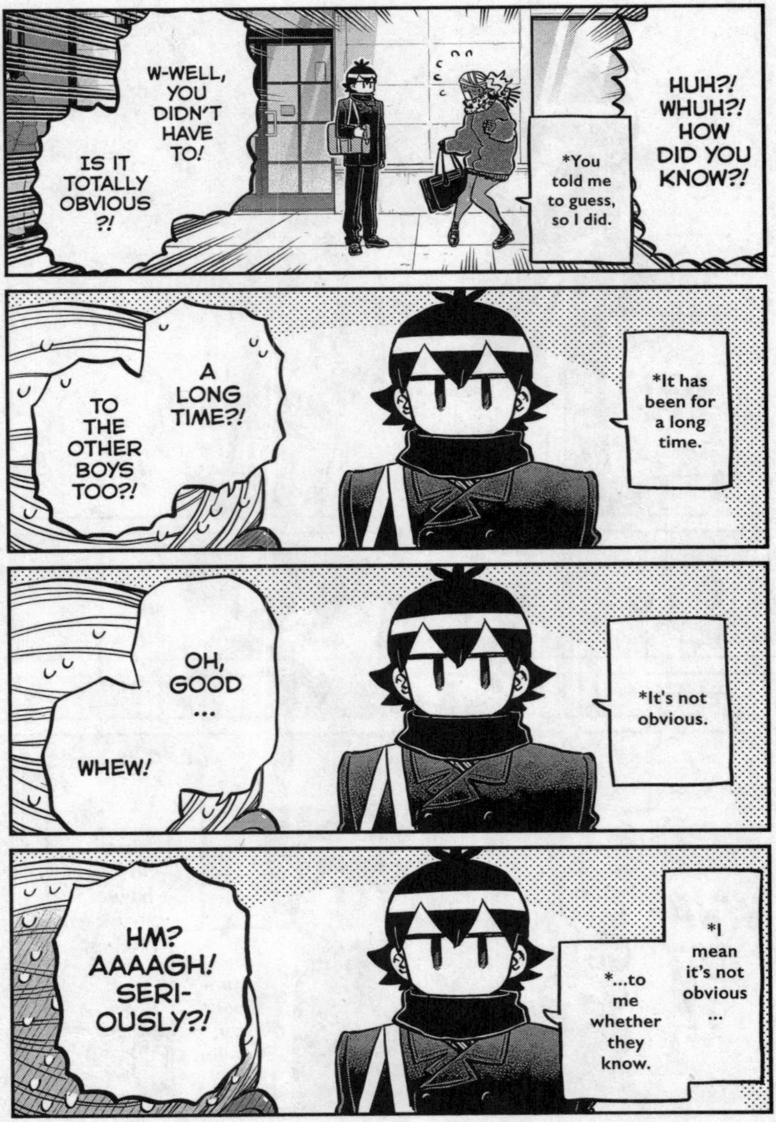
HUH?! WHUH?! HOW DID YOU KNOW?!
*You told me to guess, so I did.
W-WELL, YOU DIDN'T HAVE TO!
IS IT TOTALLY OBVIOUS?!
*It has been for a long time.
A LONG TIME?!
TO THE OTHER BOYS TOO?!
*It's not obvious.
OH, GOOD ...
WHEW!
*I mean it's not obvious ...
*...to me whether they know.
HM? AAAAGH! SERI-OUSLY?!

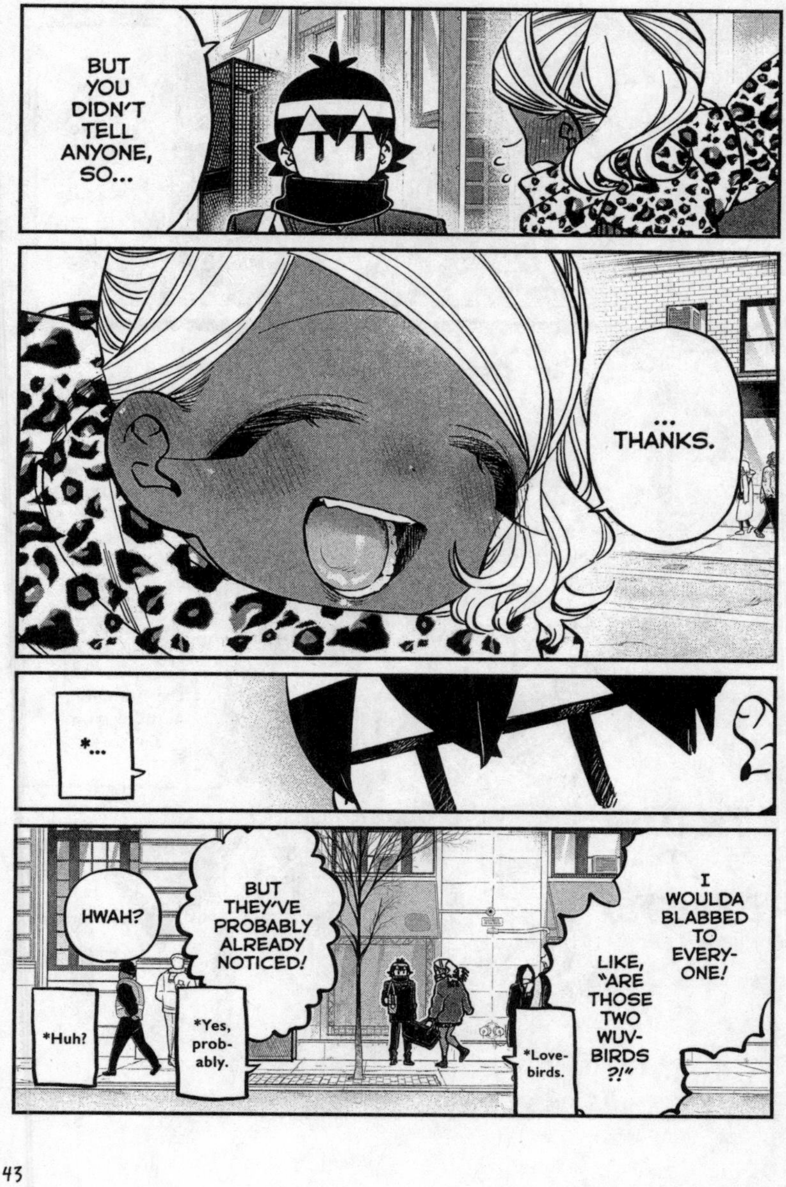
BUT YOU DIDN'T TELL ANYONE, SO...
...THANKS.
*...
I WOULDA BLABBED TO EVERY-ONE!
LIKE, "ARE THOSE TWO WUV-BIRDS?!"
*Love-birds.
BUT THEY'VE PROBABLY ALREADY NOTICED!
*Yes, probably.
HWAH?
*Huh?

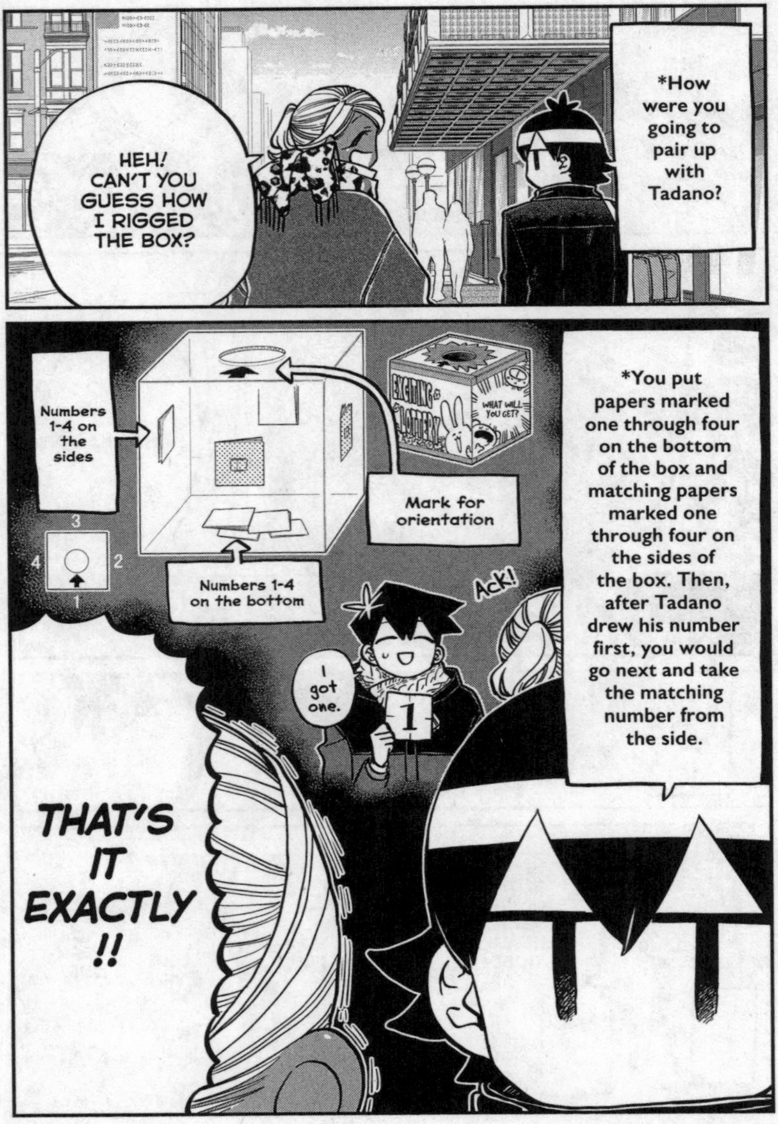
*How were you going to pair up with Tadano?
HEH! CAN'T YOU GUESS HOW I RIGGED THE BOX?
*You put papers marked one through four on the bottom of the box and matching papers marked one through four on the sides of the box. Then, after Tadano drew his number first, you would go next and take the matching number from the side.
EXCITING LOTTERY
WHAT WILL YOU GET?
Mark for orientation
Numbers 1-4 on the sides
3
4
2
1
Numbers 1-4 on the bottom
Ack!
I got one.
1
THAT'S IT EXACTLY!!

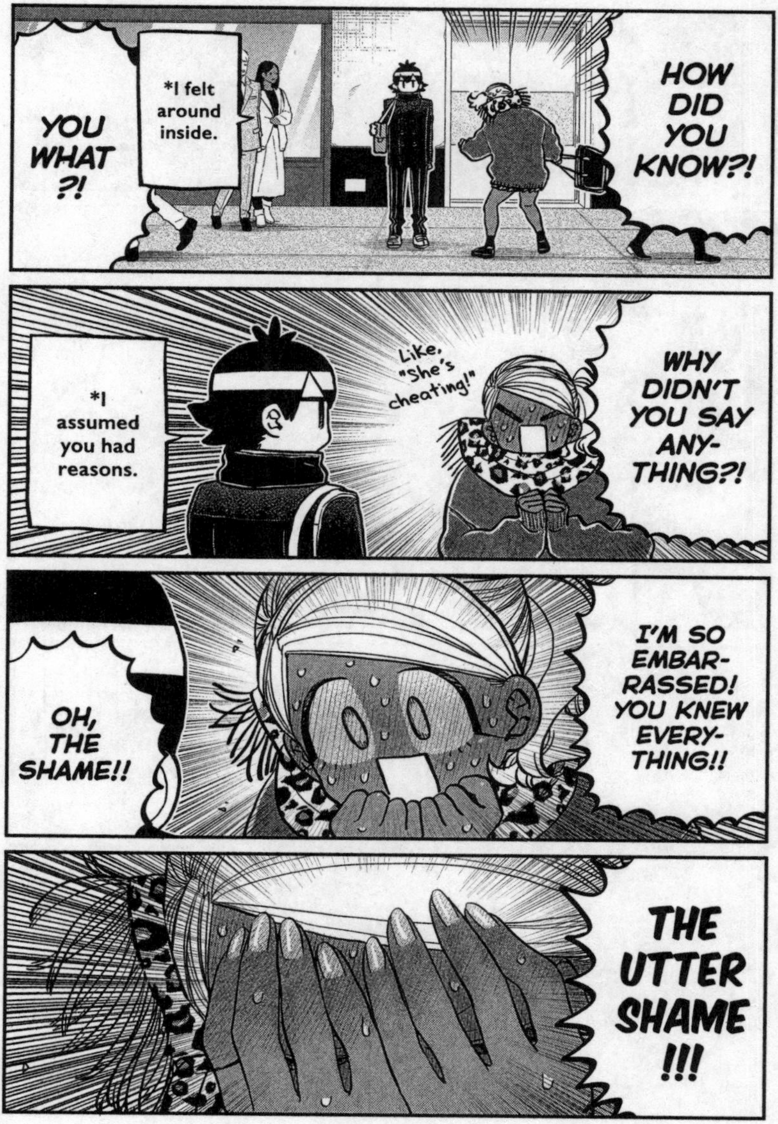

HOW DID YOU KNOW?!
*I felt around inside.
YOU WHAT?!
WHY DIDN'T YOU SAY ANY-THING?!
Like, "She's cheating!"
*I assumed you had reasons.
I'M SO EMBAR-RASSED! YOU KNEW EVERY-THING!!
OH, THE SHAME!!
THE UTTER SHAME !!!

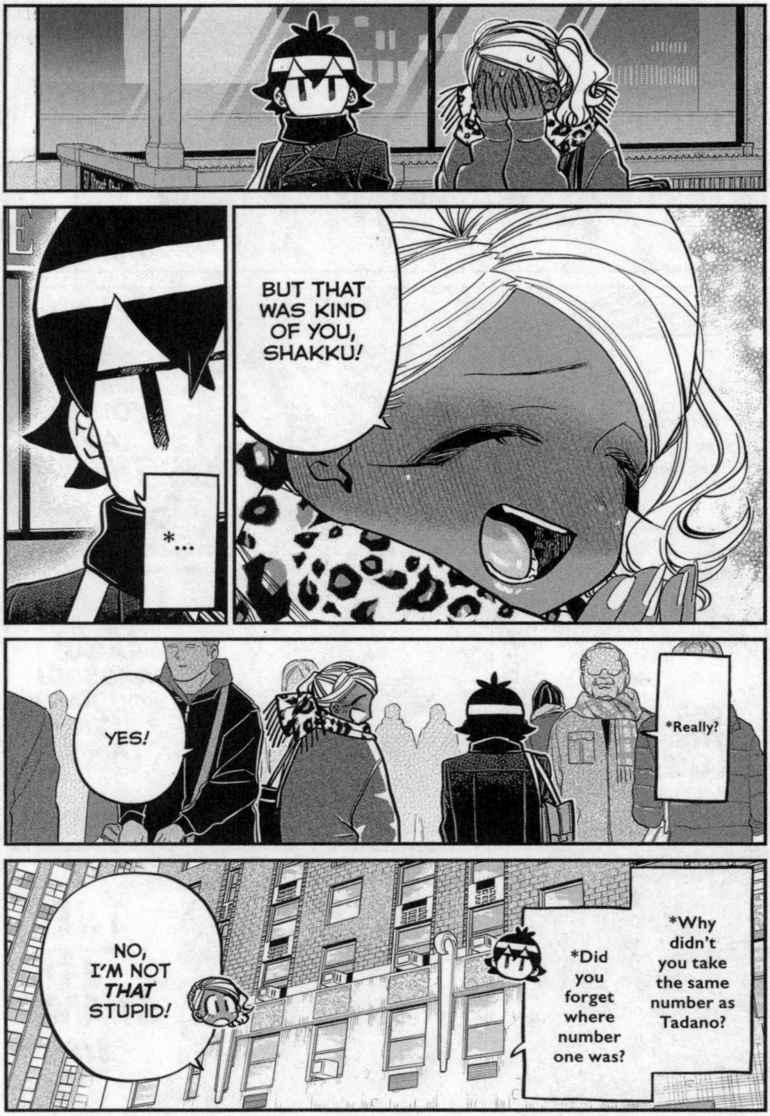
BUT THAT WAS KIND OF YOU, SHAKKU!
*...
*Really?
YES!
*Why didn't you take the same number as Tadano?
*Did you forget where number one was?
NO, I'M NOT *THAT* STUPID!

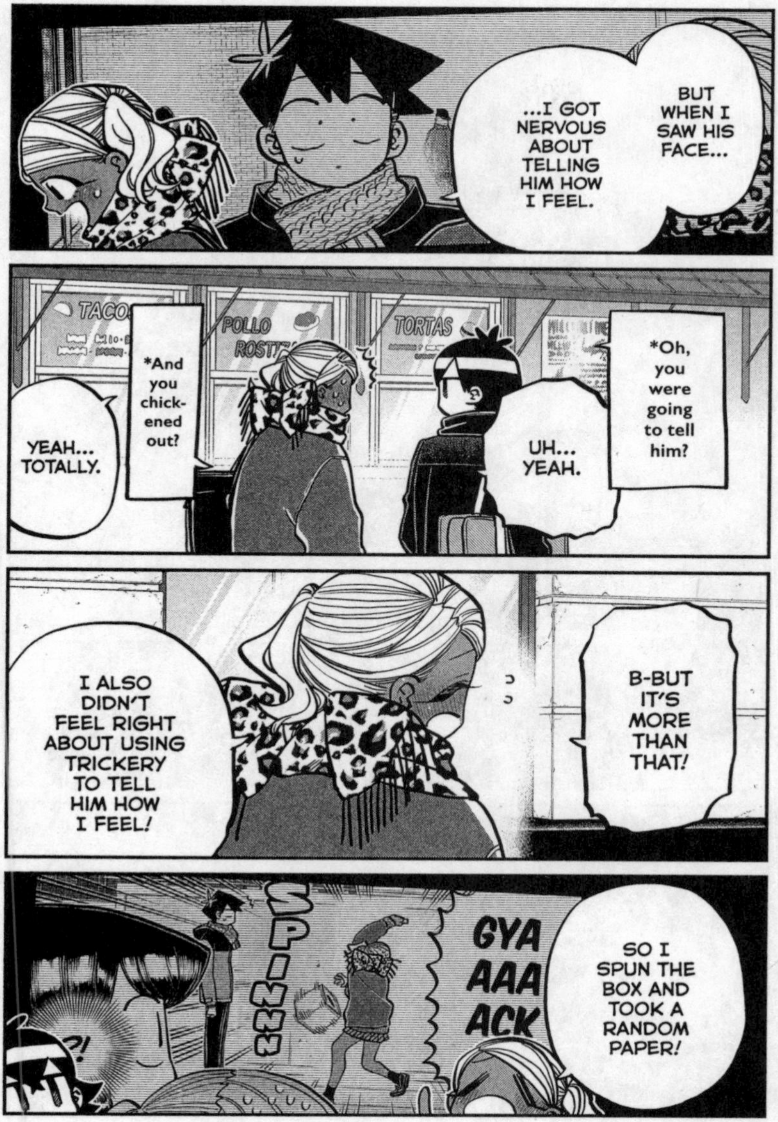
BUT WHEN I SAW HIS FACE...
...I GOT NERVOUS ABOUT TELLING HIM HOW I FEEL.
*Oh, you were going to tell him?
UH... YEAH.
*And you chickened out?
YEAH... TOTALLY.
B-BUT IT'S MORE THAN THAT!
I ALSO DIDN'T FEEL RIGHT ABOUT USING TRICKERY TO TELL HIM HOW I FEEL!
SO I SPUN THE BOX AND TOOK A RANDOM PAPER!
GYA AAA ACK
SPINNN
?!

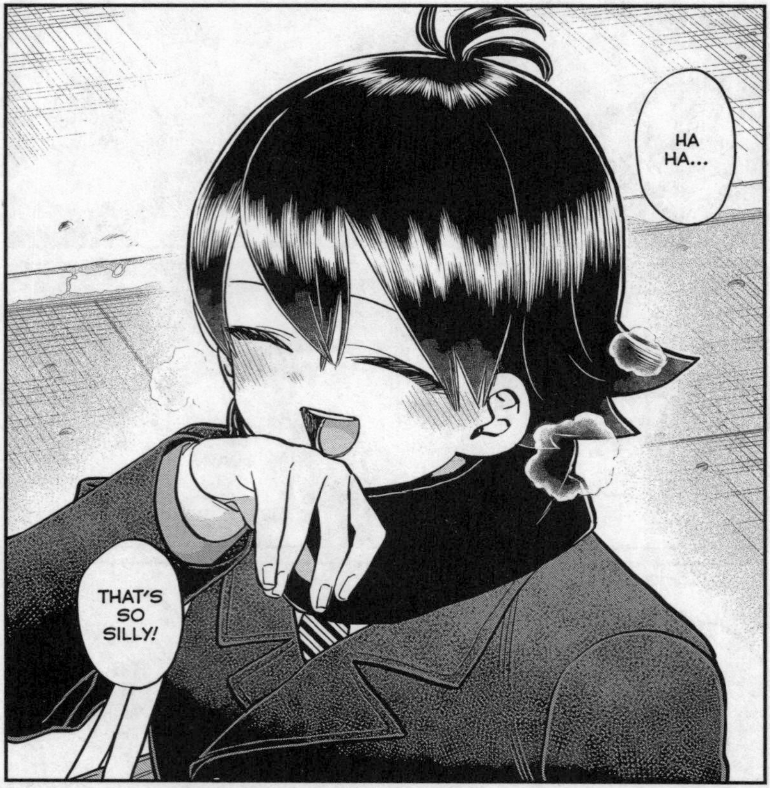
HA HA...
THAT'S SO SILLY!
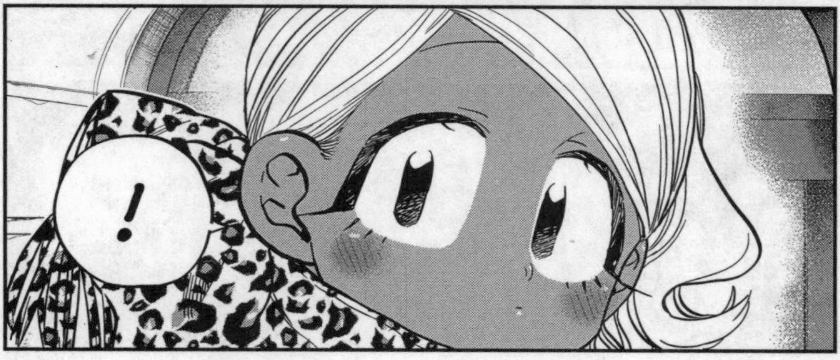
!

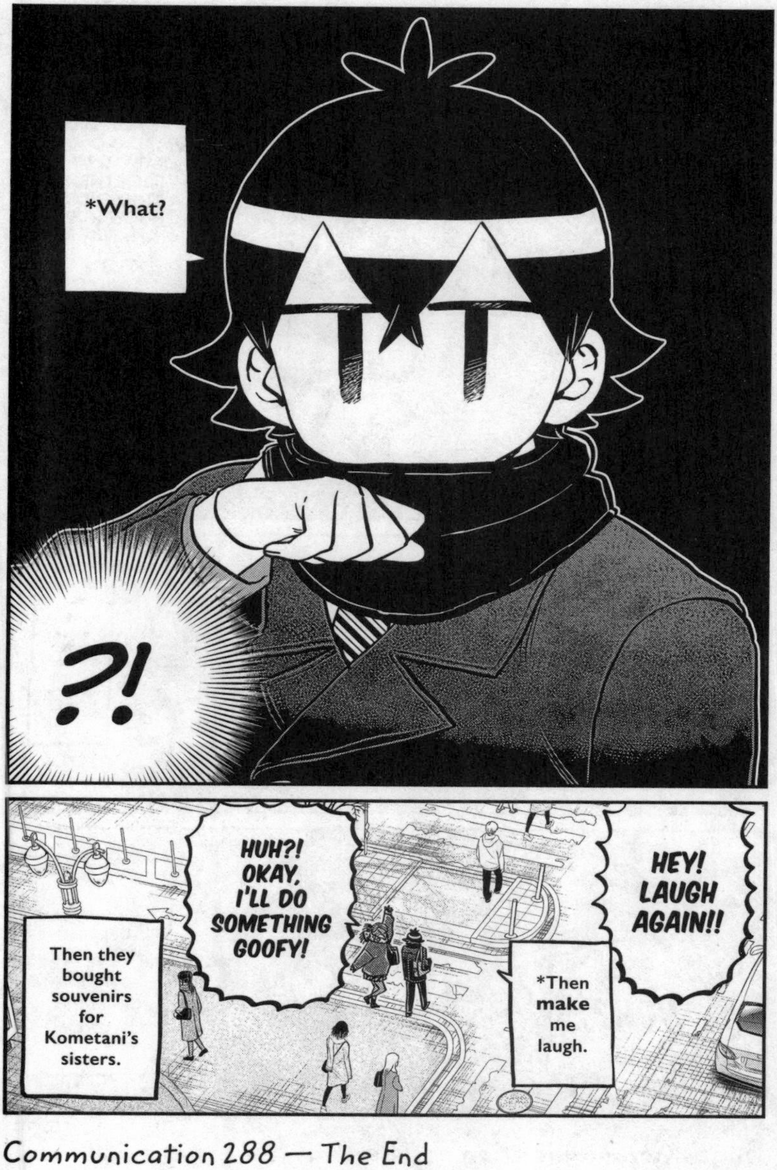
*What?
?!
HEY! LAUGH AGAIN!!
*Then make me laugh.
HUH?! OKAY, I'LL DO SOMETHING GOOFY!
Then they bought souvenirs for Kometani's sisters.

Communication 288 — The End

Bonus

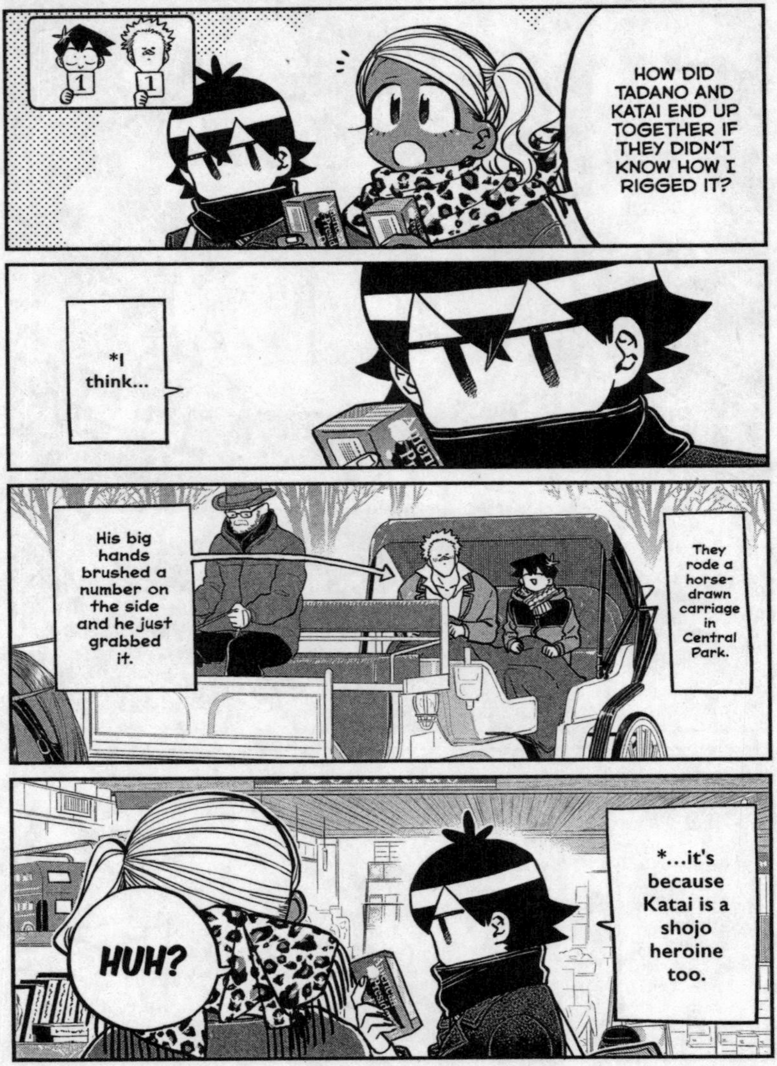
HOW DID TADANO AND KATAI END UP TOGETHER IF THEY DIDN'T KNOW HOW I RIGGED IT?
1
1
*I think...
They rode a horse-drawn carriage in Central Park.
His big hands brushed a number on the side and he just grabbed it.
*...it's because Katai is a shojo heroine too.
HUH?

Bonus Communication — The End

Communication 289: Naruse and Ase, Part 1

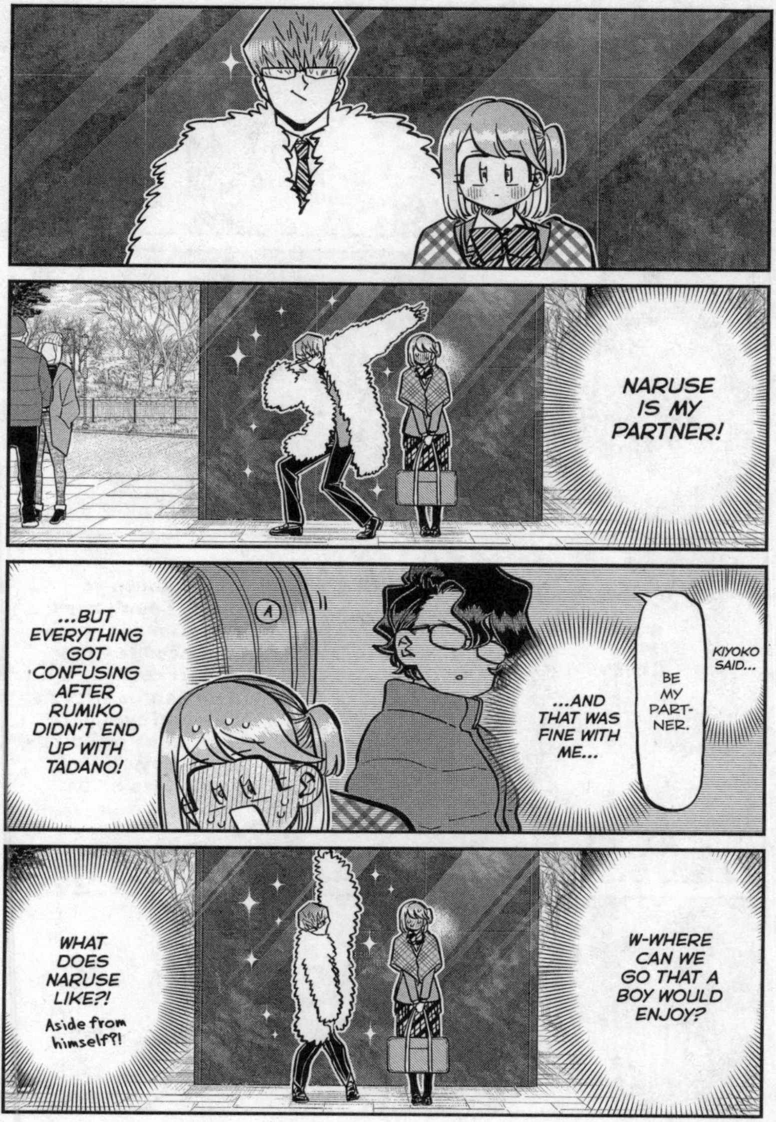
NARUSE IS MY PARTNER!
KIYOKO SAID...
BE MY PART-NER.
...AND THAT WAS FINE WITH ME...
...BUT EVERYTHING GOT CONFUSING AFTER RUMIKO DIDN'T END UP WITH TADANO!
W-WHERE CAN WE GO THAT A BOY WOULD ENJOY?
WHAT DOES NARUSE LIKE?!
Aside from himself?!

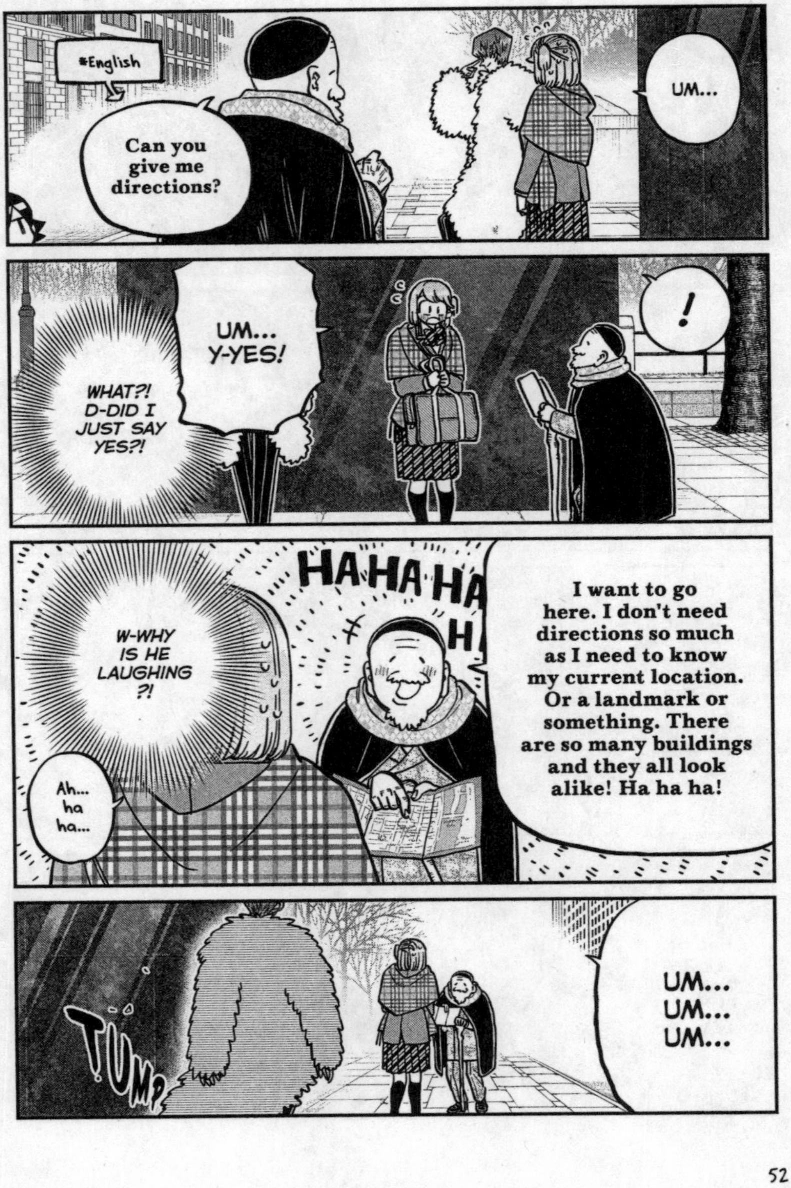

UM...
#English
Can you give me directions?
!
UM... Y-YES!
WHAT?! D-DID I JUST SAY YES?!
I want to go here. I don't need directions so much as I need to know my current location. Or a landmark or something. There are so many buildings and they all look alike! Ha ha ha!
HAHAHA HA
W-WHY IS HE LAUGHING?!
Ah... ha ha...
UM... UM... UM...
TUMP

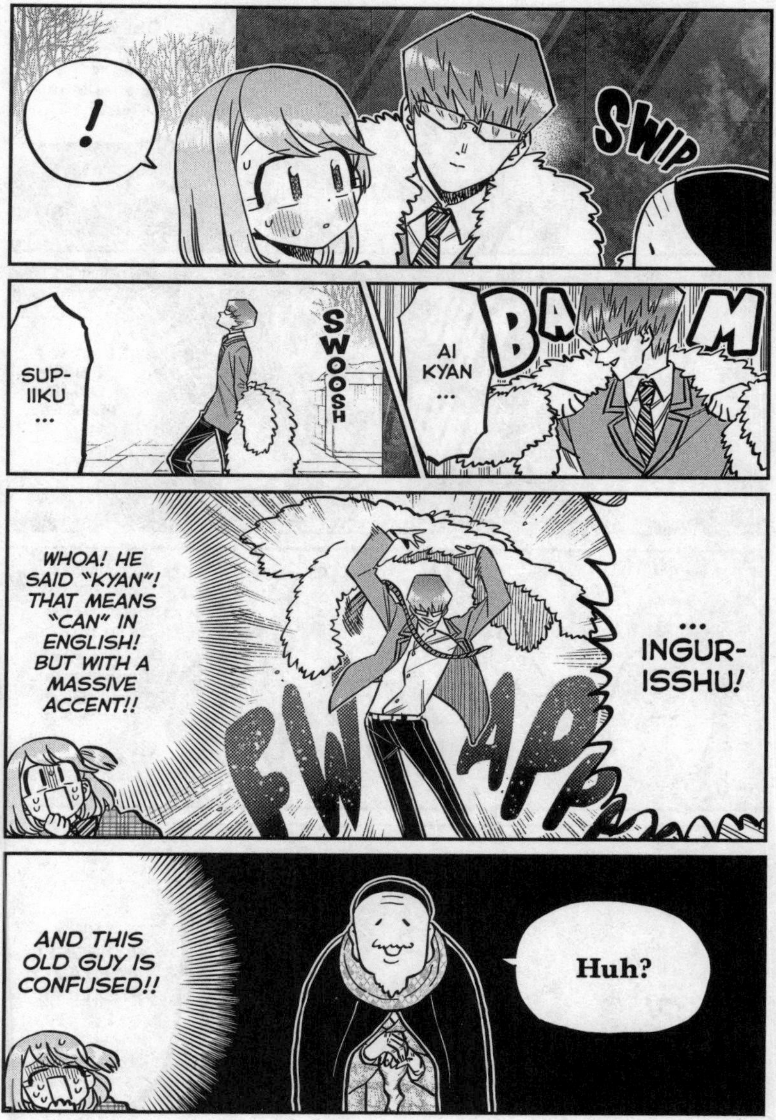
SWIP
!
BAM
AI KYAN ...
SWOOSH
SUP-IIKU ...
... INGUR-ISSHU!
FWAPP
WHOA! HE SAID "KYAN"! THAT MEANS "CAN" IN ENGLISH! BUT WITH A MASSIVE ACCENT!!
Huh?
AND THIS OLD GUY IS CONFUSED!!

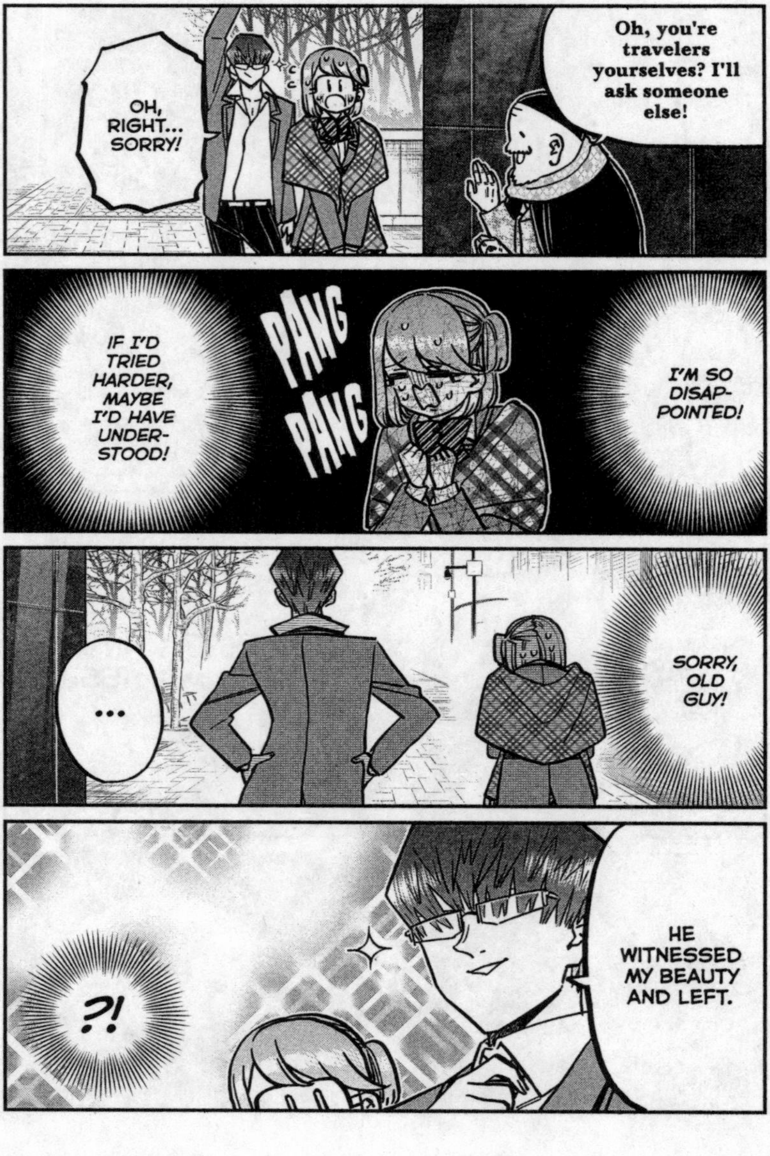
Oh, you're travelers yourselves? I'll ask someone else!
OH, RIGHT... SORRY!
I'M SO DISAP-POINTED!
PANG PANG
IF I'D TRIED HARDER, MAYBE I'D HAVE UNDER-STOOD!
SORRY, OLD GUY!
...
HE WITNESSED MY BEAUTY AND LEFT.
?!

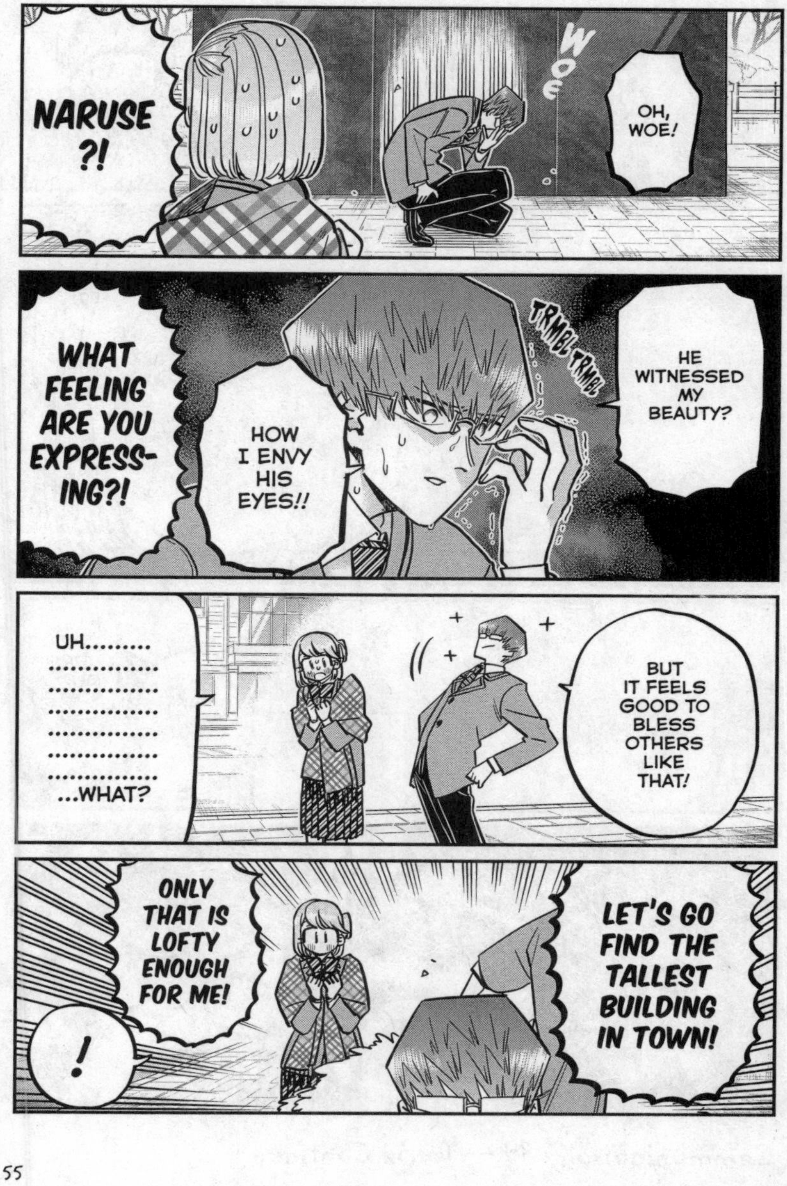

OH, WOE!
WOE
NARUSE ?!
HE WITNESSED MY BEAUTY?
TRMBL TRMBL
HOW I ENVY HIS EYES!!
WHAT FEELING ARE YOU EXPRESSING?!
BUT IT FEELS GOOD TO BLESS OTHERS LIKE THAT!
UH.. ...WHAT?
LET'S GO FIND THE TALLEST BUILDING IN TOWN!
ONLY THAT IS LOFTY ENOUGH FOR ME!
!

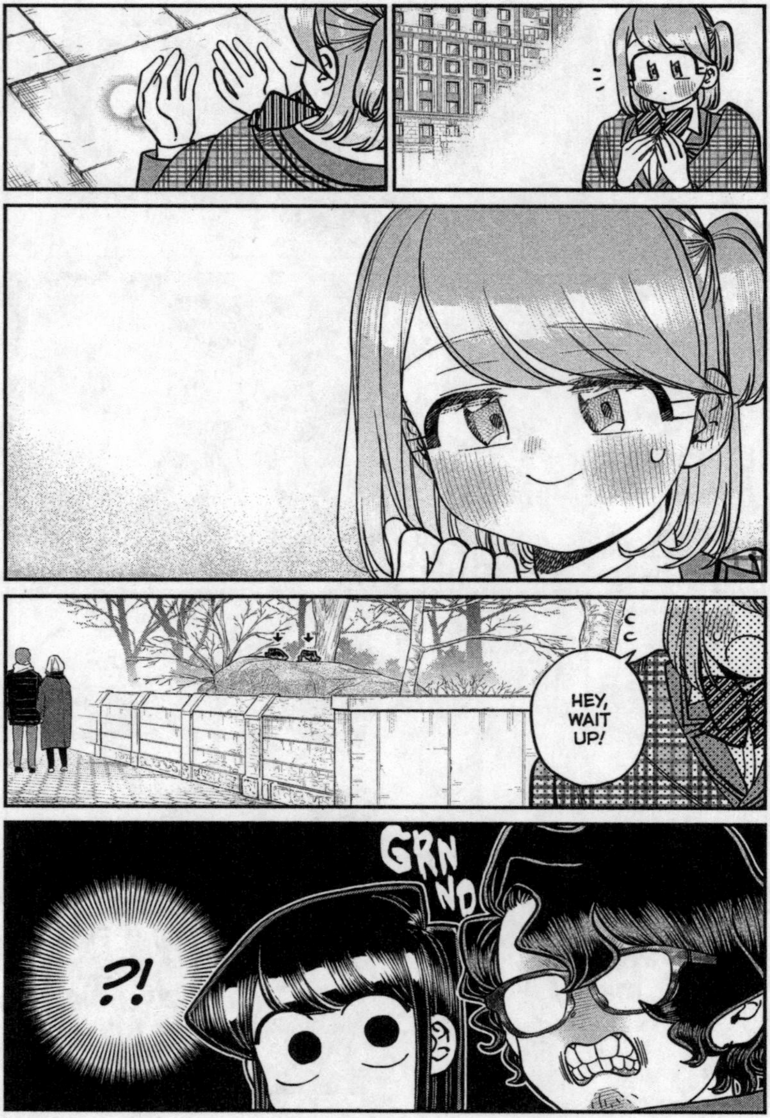
HEY, WAIT UP!
GRN ND
?!

Communication 289 — To Be Continued

Komi Can't Communicate

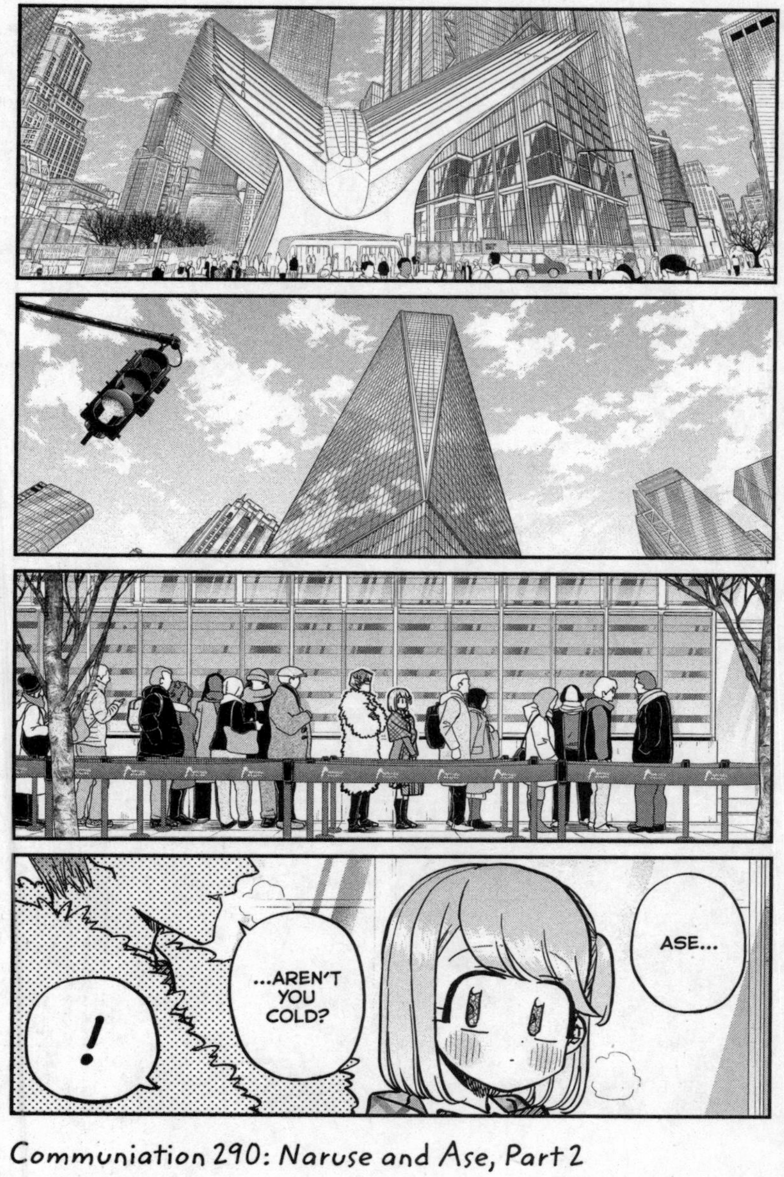
ASE...
...AREN'T YOU COLD?
!

Communiation 290: Naruse and Ase, Part 2

NO, NOT AT—
SHIVR SHIVR SHIVR SHIVR SHIVR SHIVR SHIVR SHIVR
?!
ON NO! ARE YOU COLD?!
ANYWAY, WE'LL BE INSIDE SOON!
...
NEW YORK OBSERVATO
Welcome to New York Observ

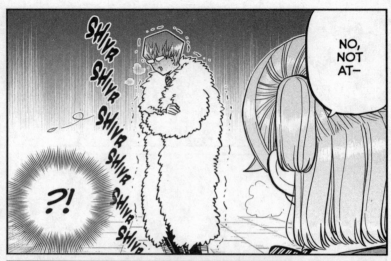

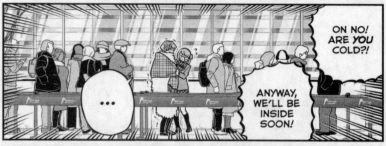

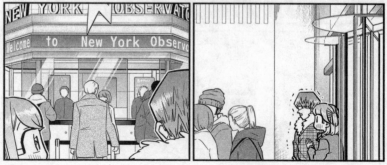

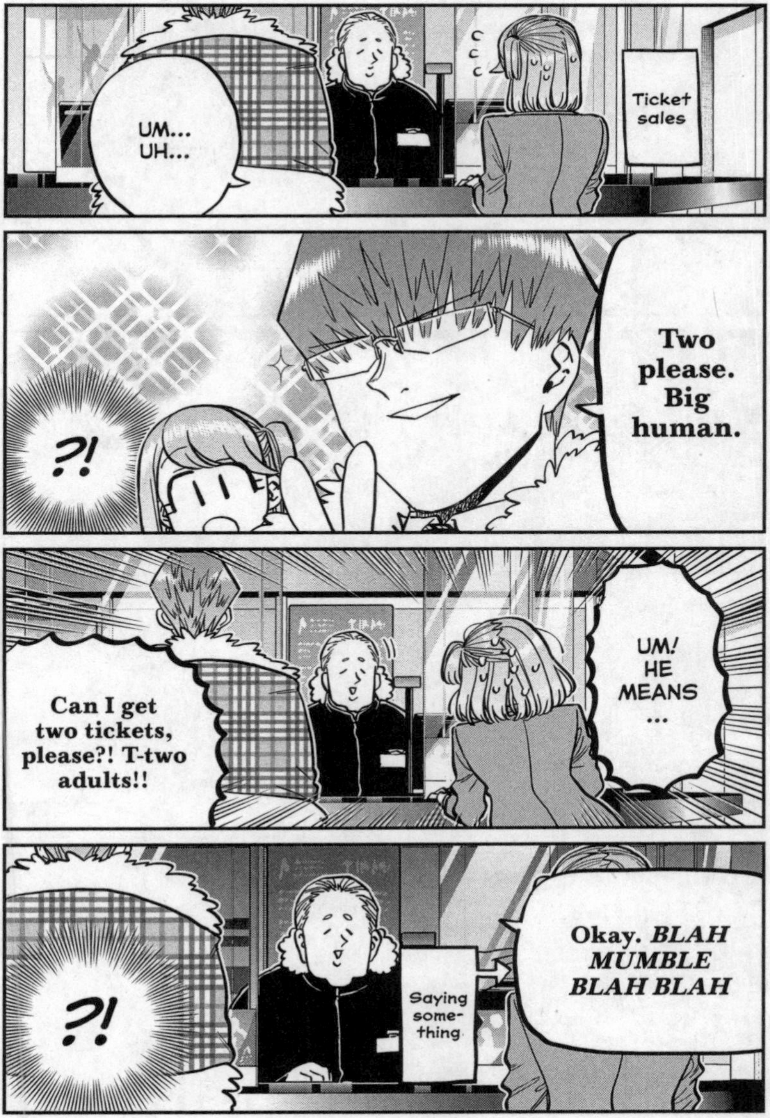
Ticket sales
UM... UH...
Two please. Big human.
?!
UM! HE MEANS ...
Can I get two tickets, please?! T-two adults!!
Okay. *BLAH MUMBLE BLAH BLAH*
Saying some-thing
?!

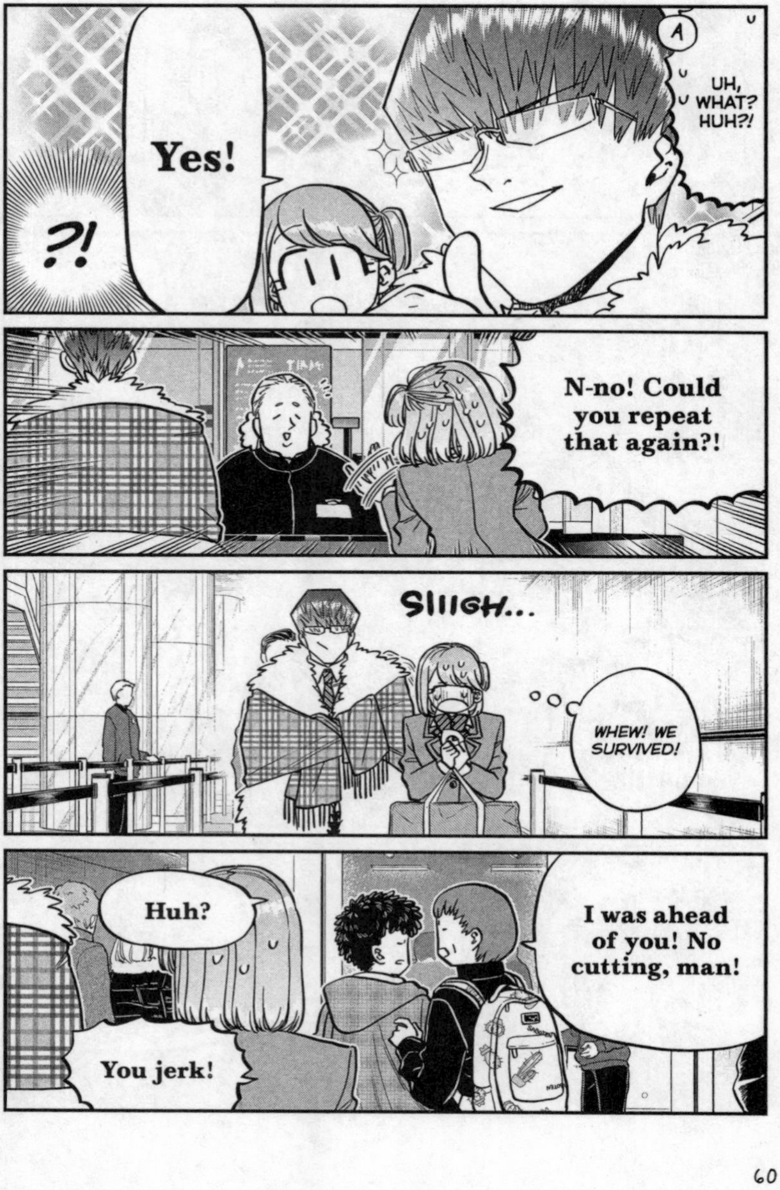

A
UH, WHAT? HUH?!
Yes!
?!
N-no! Could you repeat that again?!
SIIIGH...
WHEW! WE SURVIVED!
I was ahead of you! No cutting, man!
Huh?
You jerk!

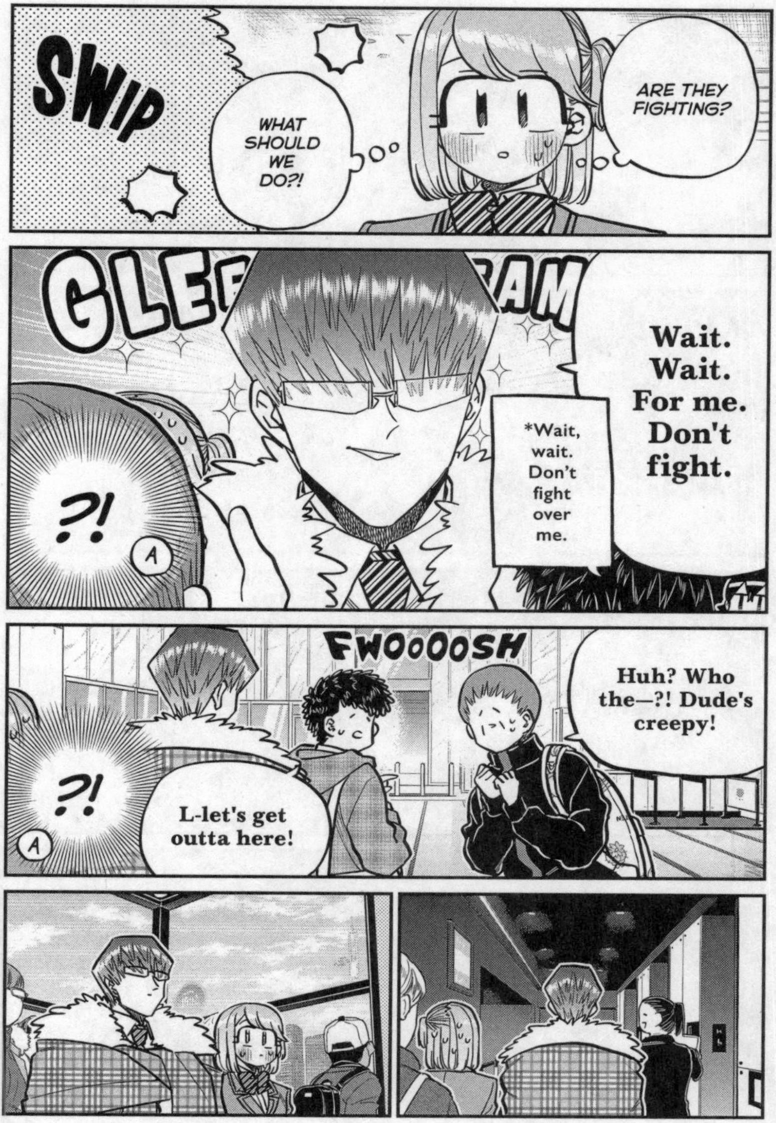
ARE THEY FIGHTING?
WHAT SHOULD WE DO?!
SWIP
Wait. Wait. For me. Don't fight.
*Wait, wait. Don't fight over me.
?!
A
Huh? Who the—?! Dude's creepy!
FWOOOOSH
?!
L-let's get outta here!
A

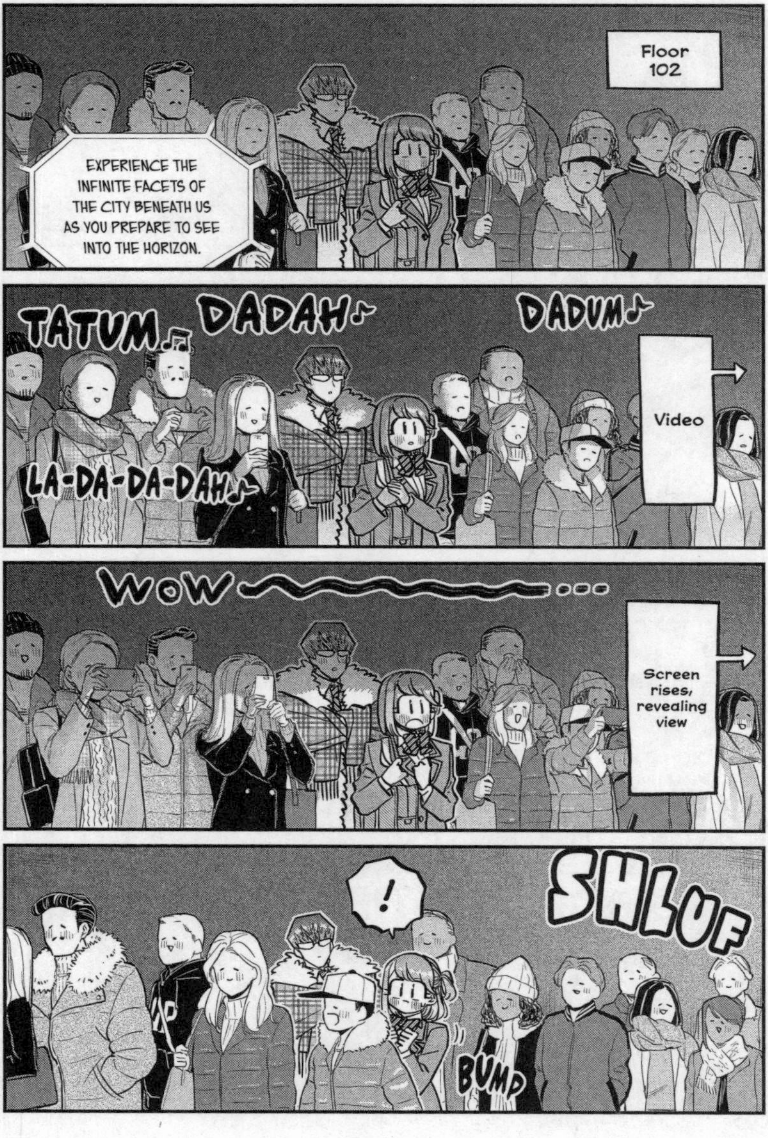
Floor 102
EXPERIENCE THE INFINITE FACETS OF THE CITY BENEATH US AS YOU PREPARE TO SEE INTO THE HORIZON.
DADUM♪
Video
DADAH♪
TATUM♫
LA-DA-DA-DAH♪
Screen rises, revealing view
WOW~~...
SHLUF
!
BUMP

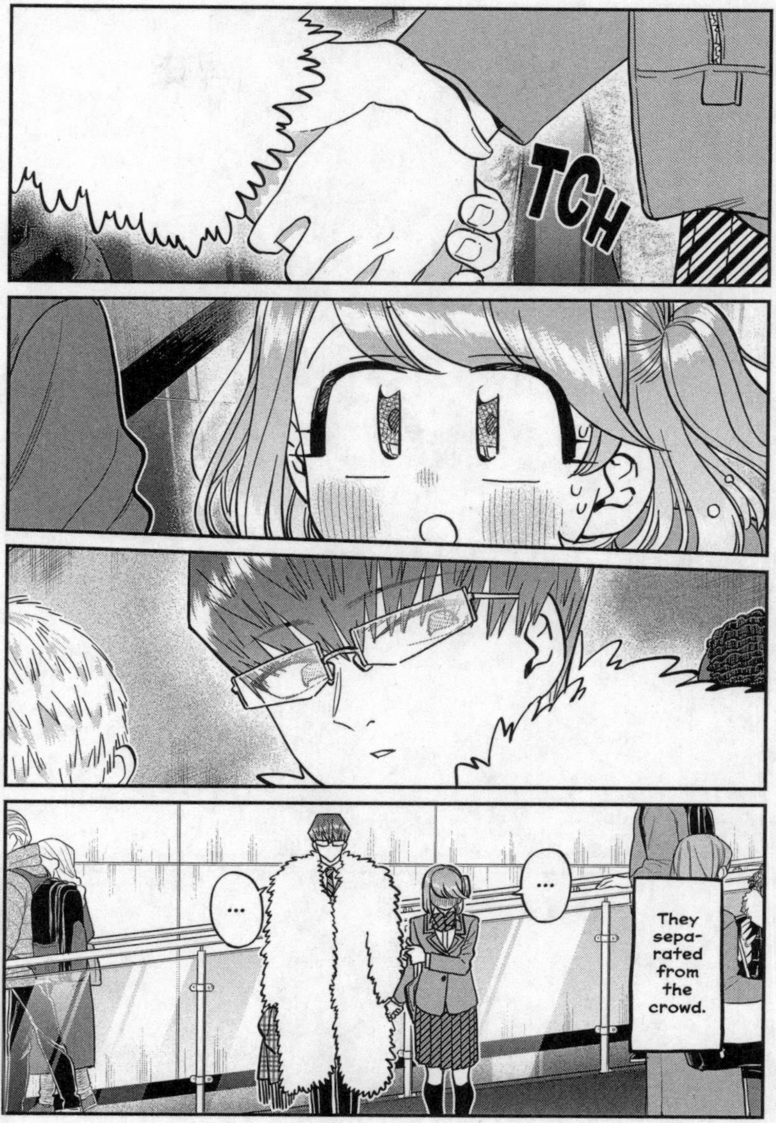
TCH
They separated from the crowd.
...
...

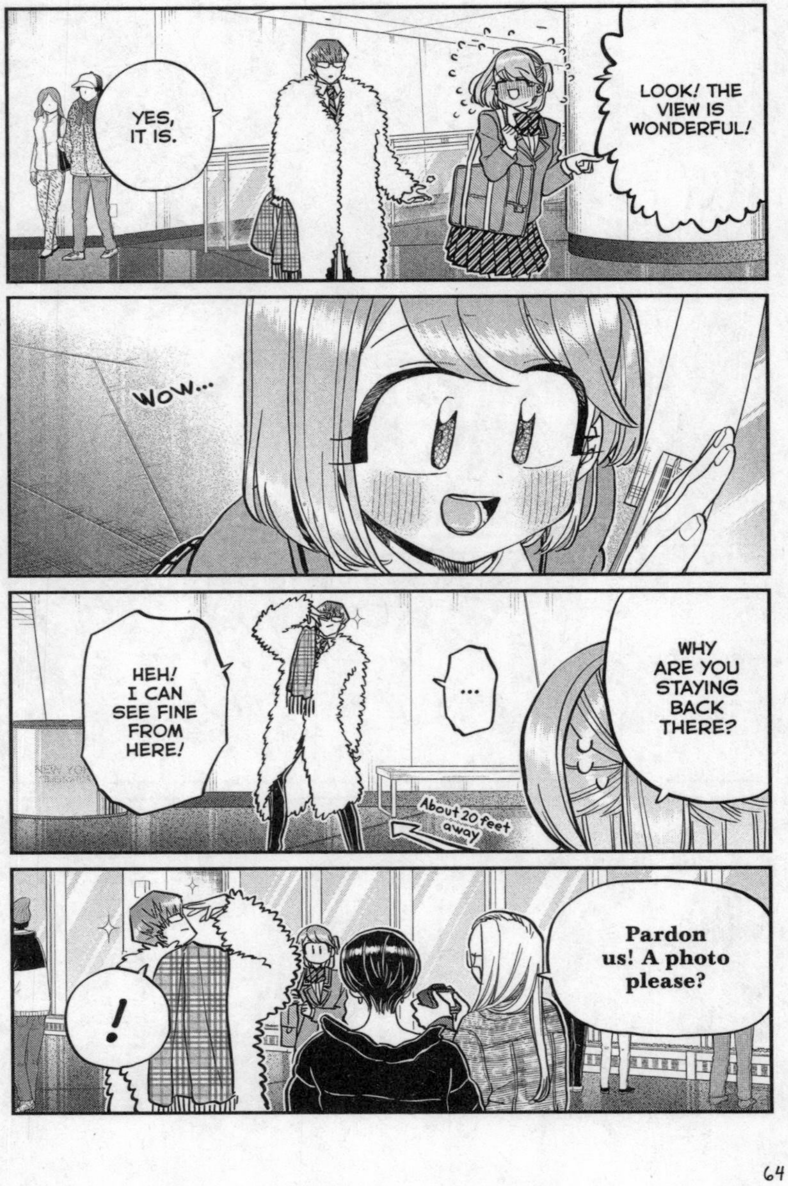
LOOK! THE VIEW IS WONDERFUL!
YES, IT IS.
WOW...
WHY ARE YOU STAYING BACK THERE?
...
HEH! I CAN SEE FINE FROM HERE!
About 20 feet away
Pardon us! A photo please?
!

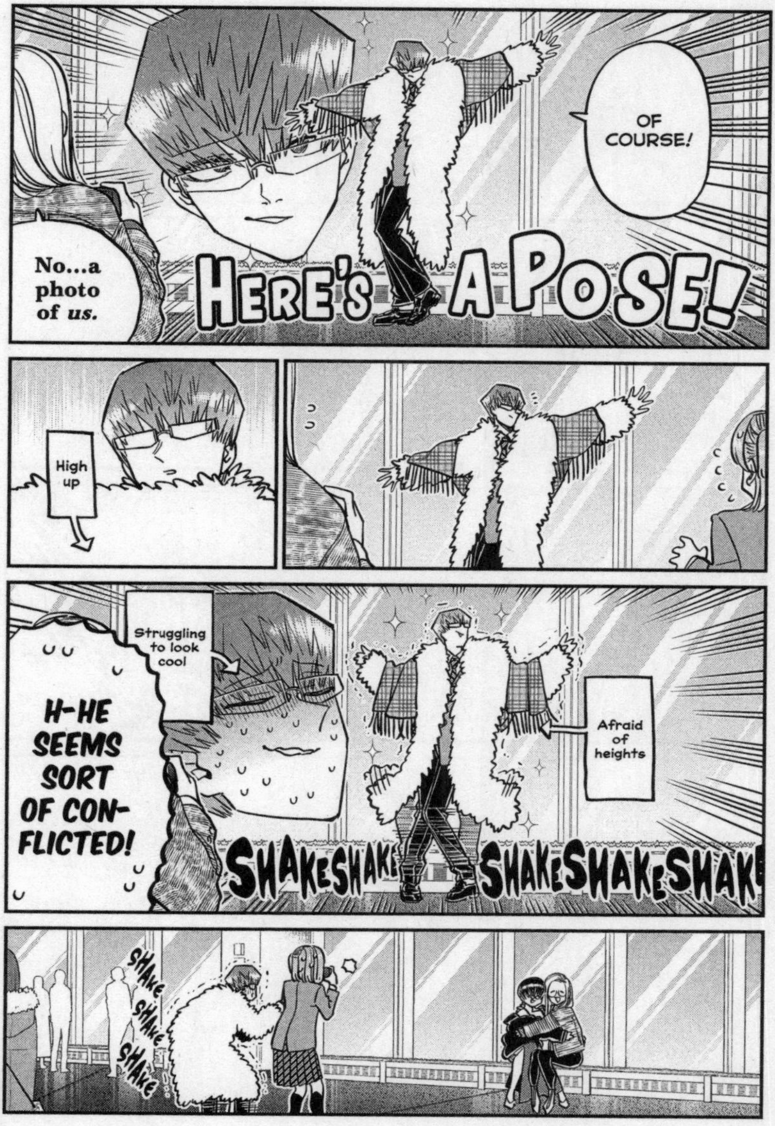

OF COURSE!
HERE'S A POSE!
No...a photo of *us.*
High up
Afraid of heights
SHAKESHAKESHAK
SHAKESHAKE
Struggling to look cool
H-HE SEEMS SORT OF CON-FLICTED!
SHAKE SHAKE SHAKE

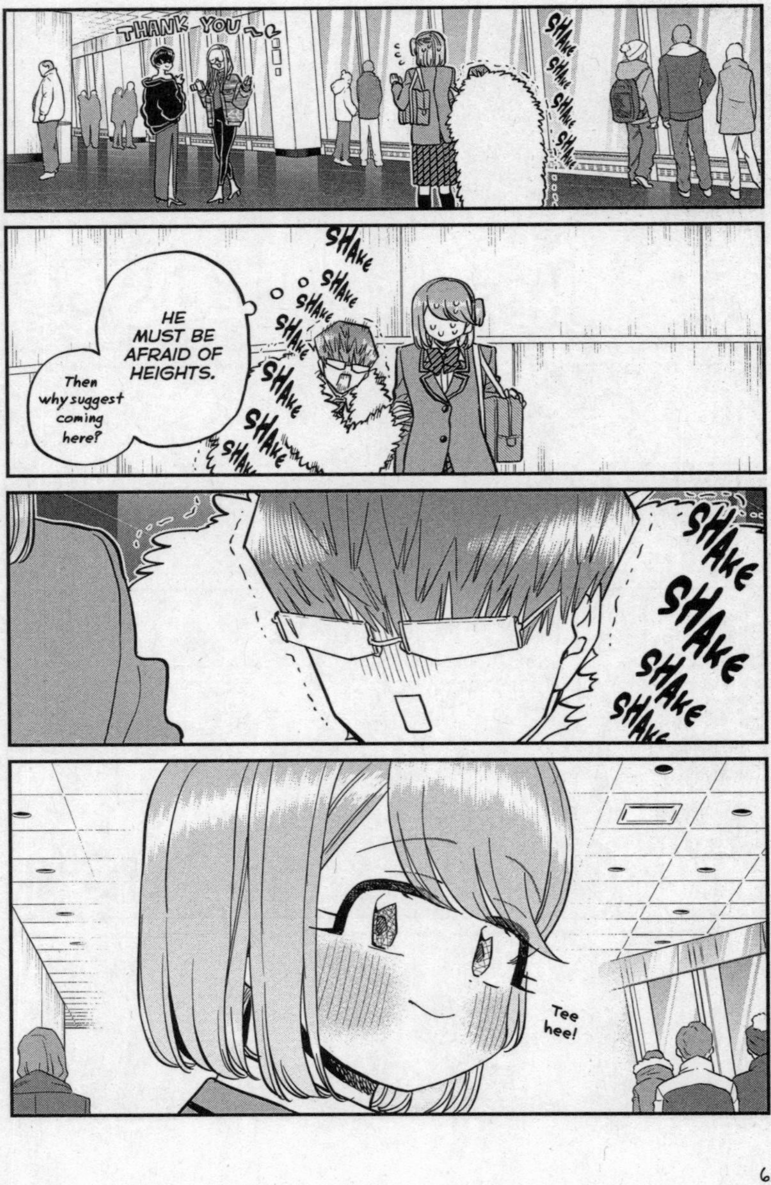
SHAKE SHAKE SHAKE SHAKE
THANK YOU~
SHAKE SHAKE SHAKE SHAKE SHAKE SHAKE SHAKE
HE MUST BE AFRAID OF HEIGHTS.
Then why suggest coming here?
SHAKE SHAKE SHAKE SHAKE SHAKE
Tee hee!

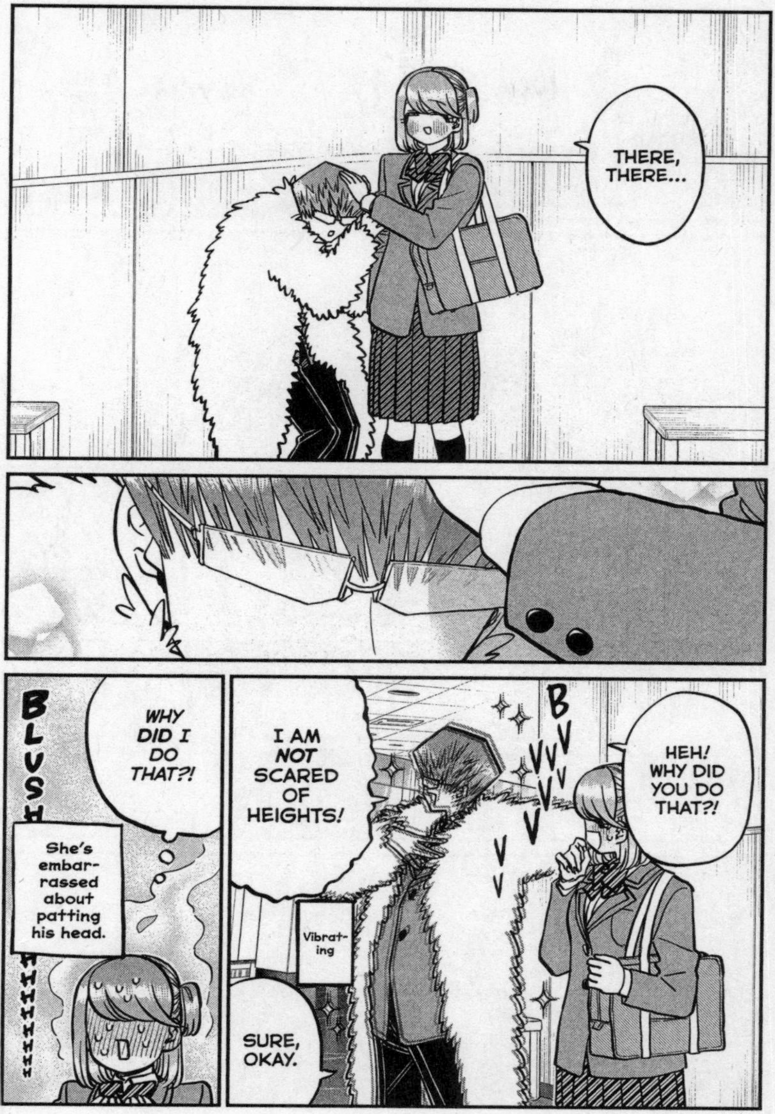
THERE, THERE...
HEH! WHY DID YOU DO THAT?!
BVVVVVVVVV
I AM *NOT* SCARED OF HEIGHTS!
Vibrating
SURE, OKAY.
WHY DID I DO THAT?!
BLUSHHHHHHHHHHH
She's embarrassed about patting his head.

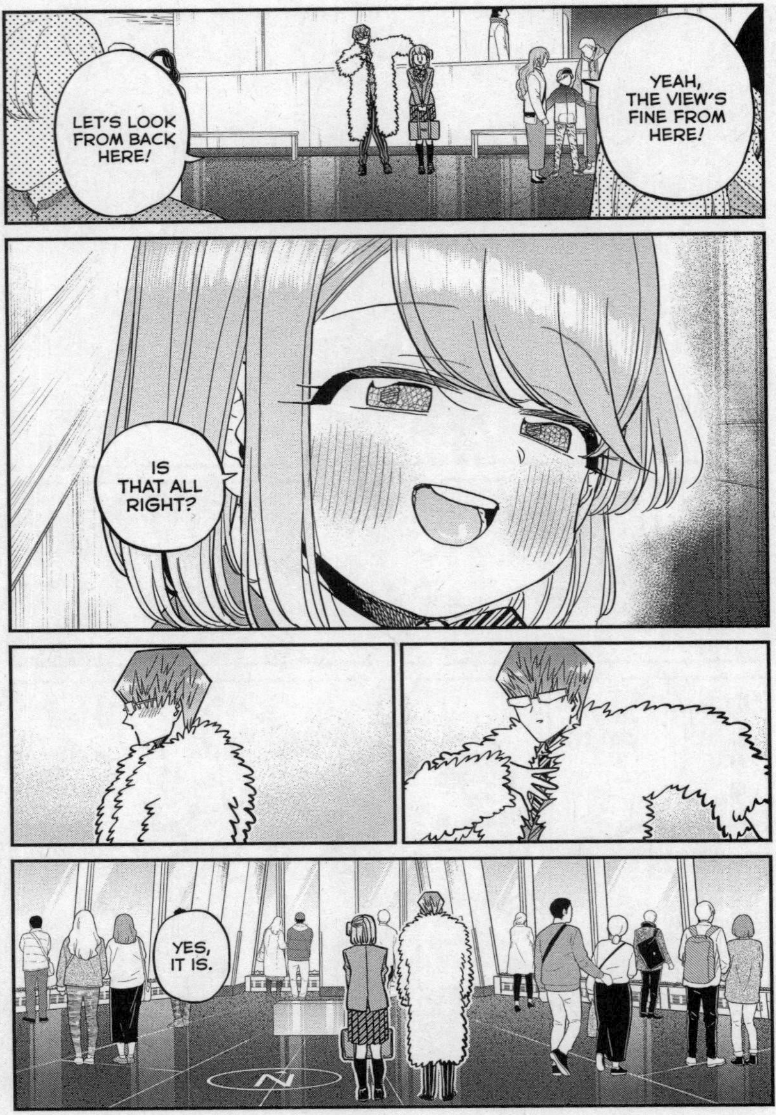
YEAH, THE VIEW'S FINE FROM HERE!
LET'S LOOK FROM BACK HERE!
IS THAT ALL RIGHT?
YES, IT IS.

Communication 290 — The End

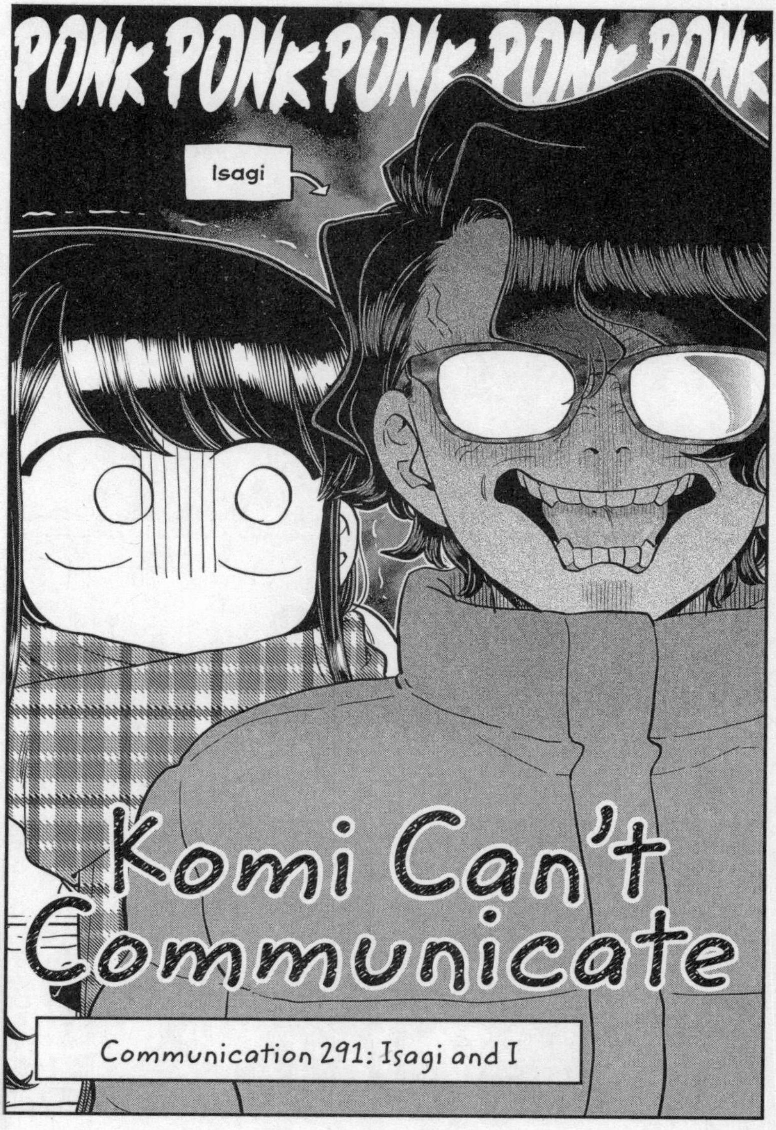
PONK PONK PONK PONK PONK
Isagi
Komi Can't Communicate
Communication 291: Isagi and I

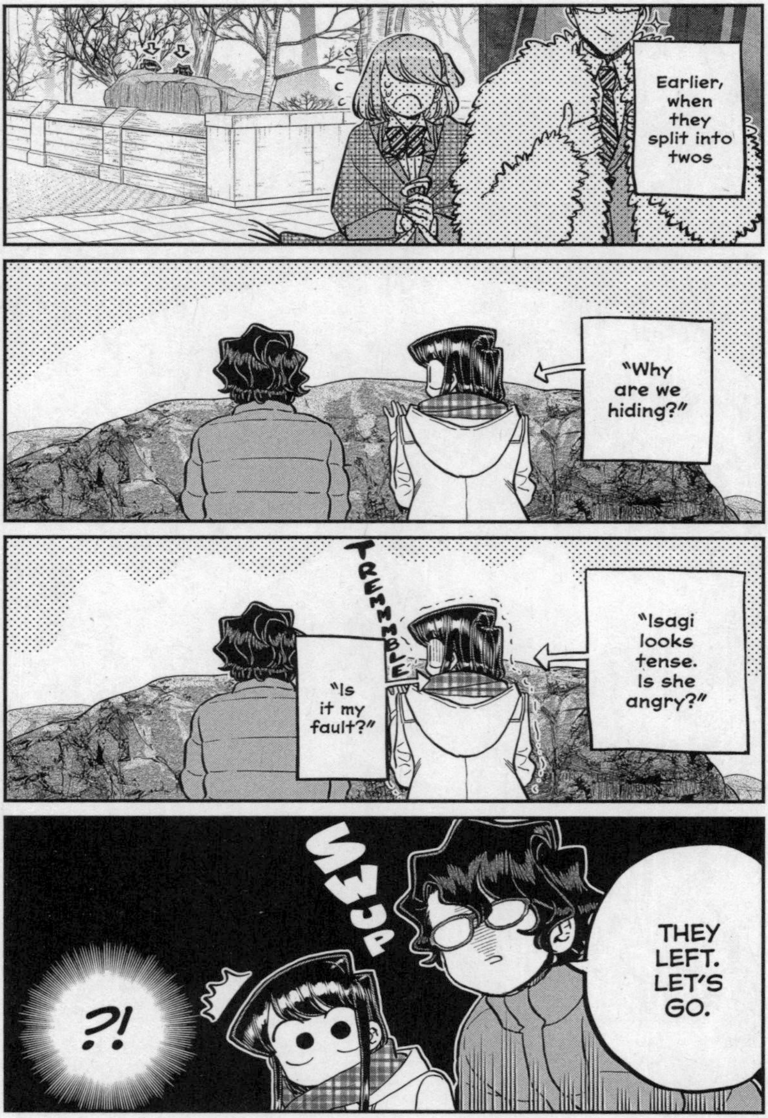
Earlier, when they split into twos
"Why are we hiding?"
"Isagi looks tense. Is she angry?"
TREMMBLE
"Is it my fault?"
THEY LEFT. LET'S GO.
SWUP
?!

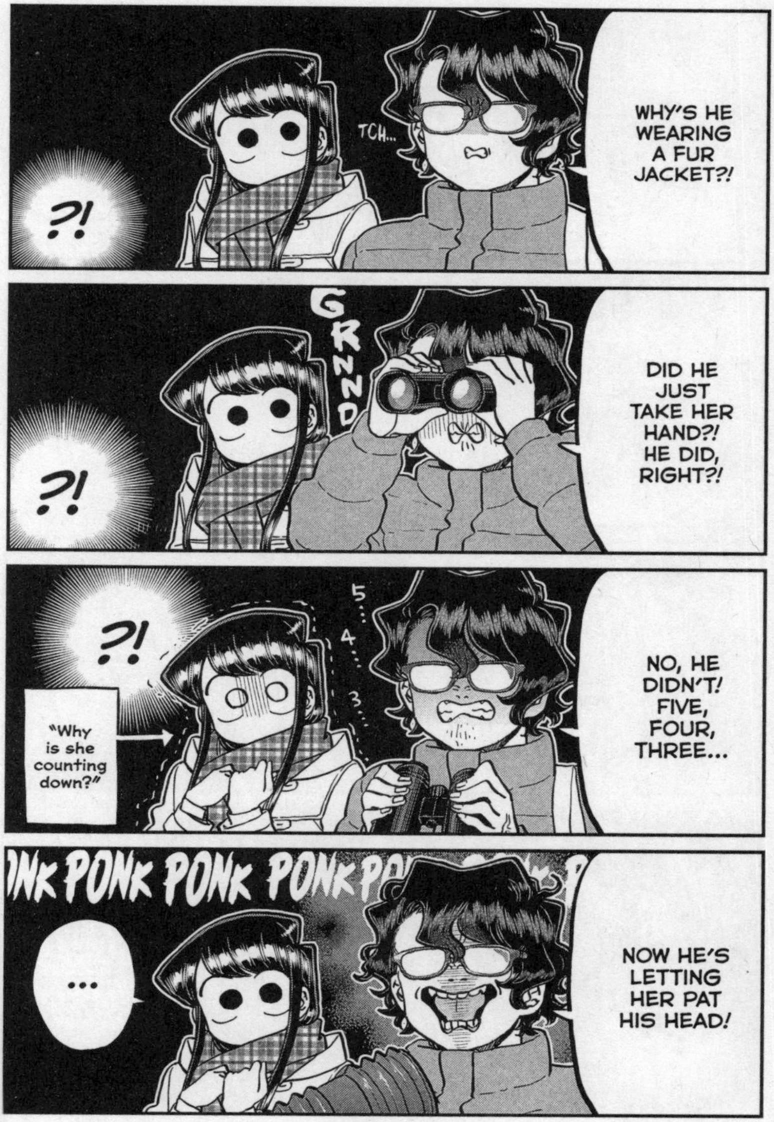
WHY'S HE WEARING A FUR JACKET?!
TCH...
?!
DID HE JUST TAKE HER HAND?! HE DID, RIGHT?!
GRNND
?!
NO, HE DIDN'T! FIVE, FOUR, THREE...
5... 4... 3...
?!
"Why is she counting down?"
PONK PONK PONK PONK
NOW HE'S LETTING HER PAT HIS HEAD!
...

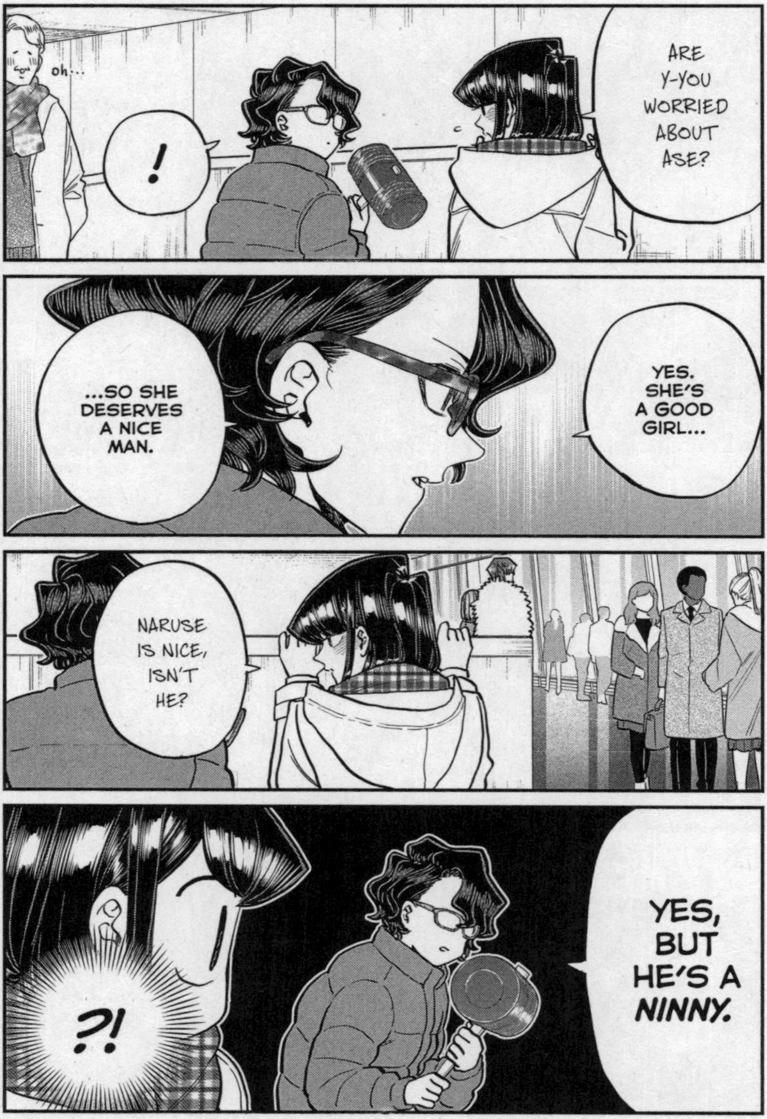
ARE Y-YOU WORRIED ABOUT ASE?
!
oh...
YES. SHE'S A GOOD GIRL...
...SO SHE DESERVES A NICE MAN.
NARUSE IS NICE, ISN'T HE?
YES, BUT HE'S A NINNY.
?!

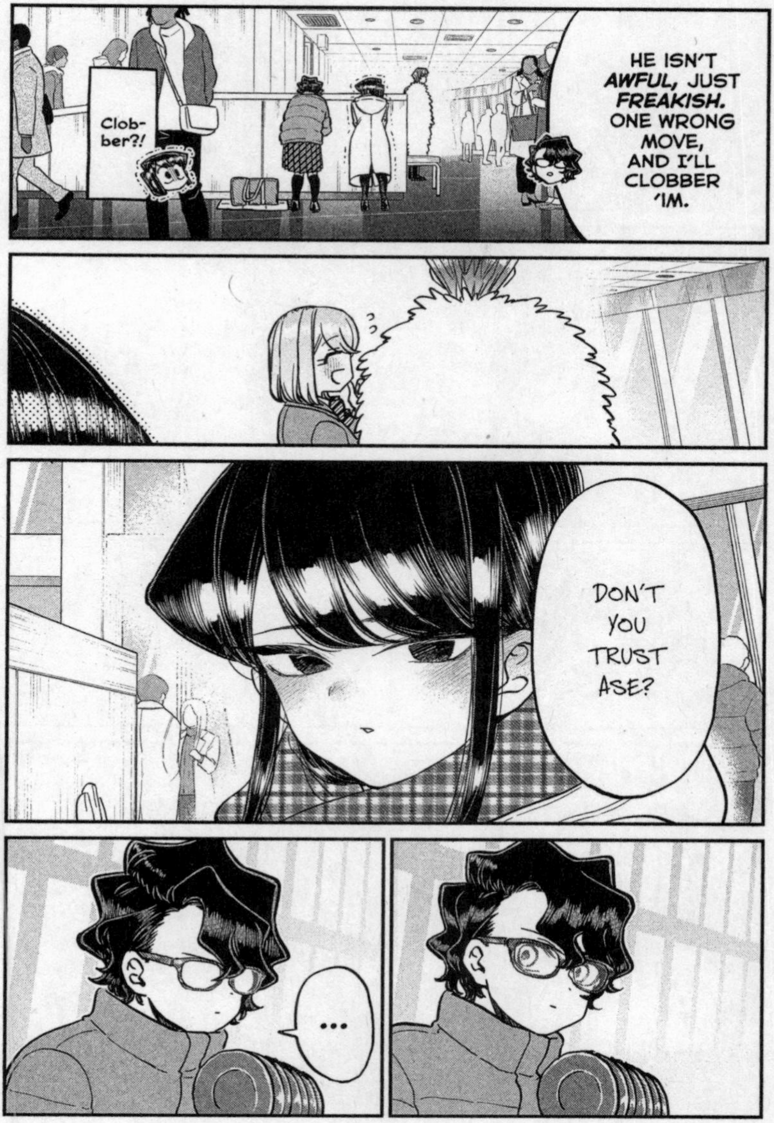
HE ISN'T *AWFUL,* JUST *FREAKISH.* ONE WRONG MOVE, AND I'LL CLOBBER 'IM.
Clob-ber?!
DON'T YOU TRUST ASE?
...

STOMP STOMP STOMP STOMP
I DISIN-FECTED IT.
SWUP
KIYOKO ?!
LET'S GO FOR COFFEE.
NOD
!
SORRY TO PUT YOU THROUGH THAT.
SHAKE SHAKE
!!

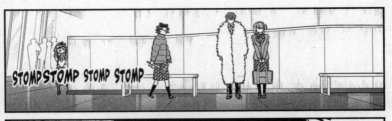

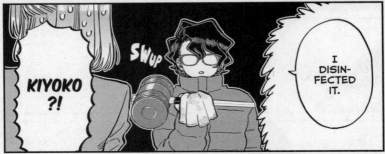

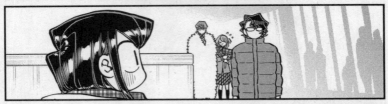

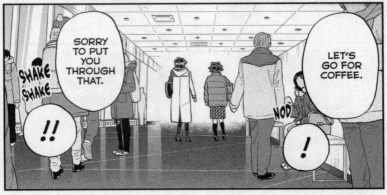

Communication 291 — The End

They enjoy their coffee in
a comfortable silence.

Komi Can't
Communicate

Komi Can't Communicate

An Altercation While Traveling Darkens the Mood

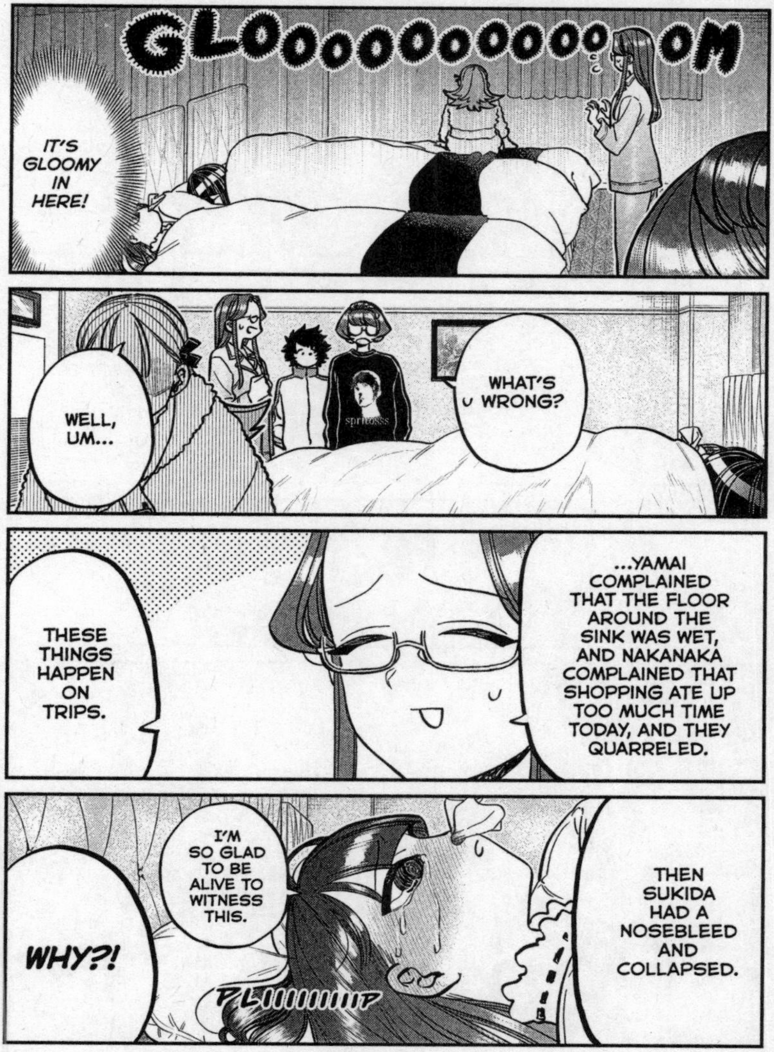
GLOOOOOOOOOOM
IT'S GLOOMY IN HERE!
WHAT'S WRONG?
WELL, UM...
...YAMAI COMPLAINED THAT THE FLOOR AROUND THE SINK WAS WET, AND NAKANAKA COMPLAINED THAT SHOPPING ATE UP TOO MUCH TIME TODAY, AND THEY QUARRELED.
THESE THINGS HAPPEN ON TRIPS.
THEN SUKIDA HAD A NOSEBLEED AND COLLAPSED.
I'M SO GLAD TO BE ALIVE TO WITNESS THIS.
WHY?!
PLIIIIIIIIIP

Communication 292: School-Trip Happenings

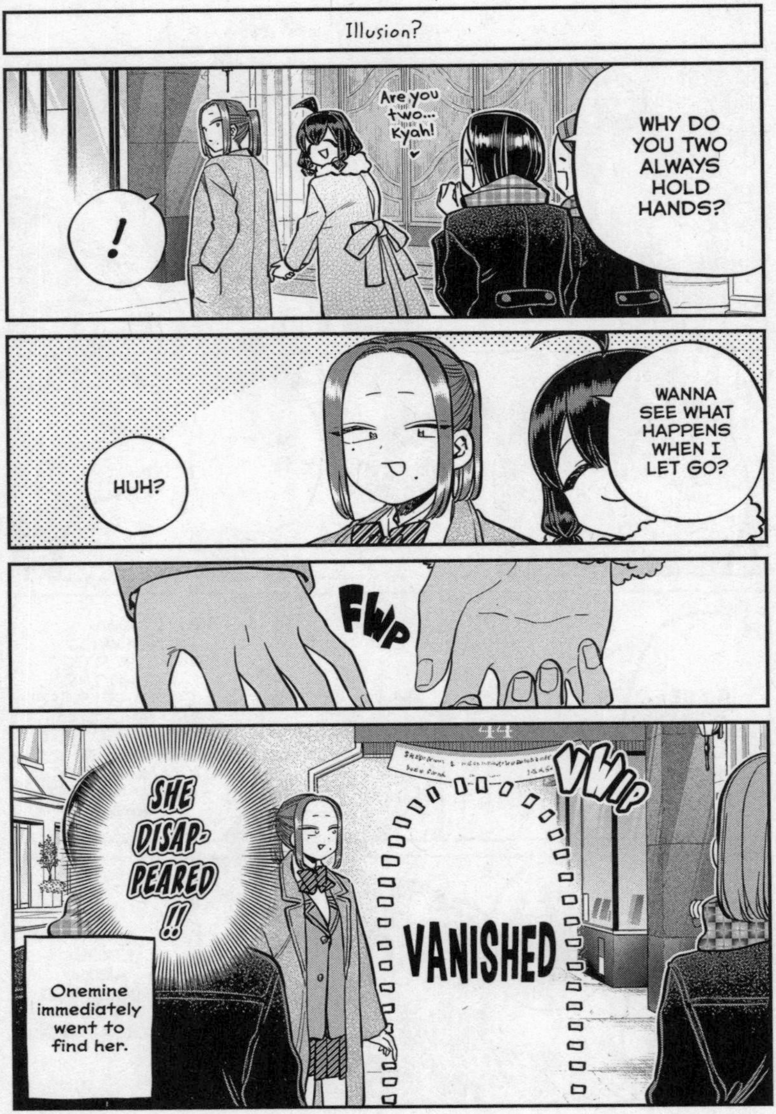
Illusion?
WHY DO YOU TWO ALWAYS HOLD HANDS?
Are you two... Kyah! ♥
!
WANNA SEE WHAT HAPPENS WHEN I LET GO?
HUH?
FWP
VWIP
VANISHED
SHE DISAP-PEARED !!
Onemine immediately went to find her.

Becoming a New Yorker

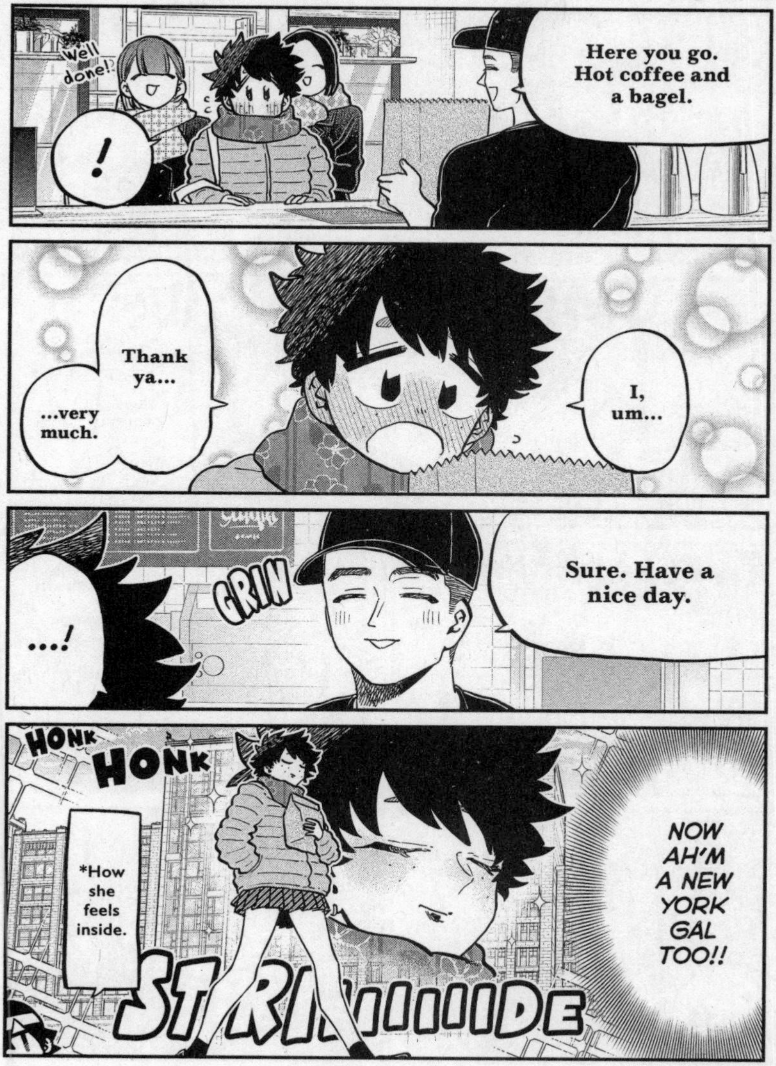
Here you go. Hot coffee and a bagel.
Well done!?
!
I, um...
Thank ya...
...very much.
Sure. Have a nice day.
GRIN
...!
NOW AH'M A NEW YORK GAL TOO!!
HONK
HONK
*How she feels inside.
STRIIIIIIDE

Game Devices While Traveling

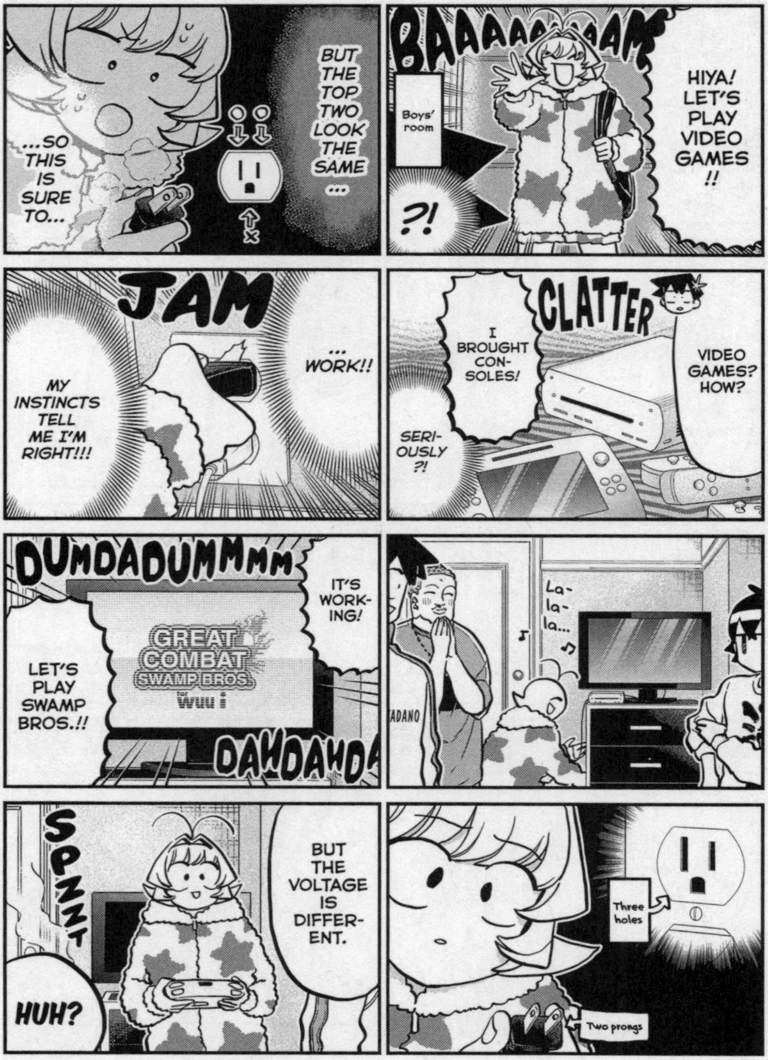
BAAAAAAAAM
Boys' room
HIYA! LET'S PLAY VIDEO GAMES!!
?!
BUT THE TOP TWO LOOK THE SAME...
...SO THIS IS SURE TO...
CLATTER
VIDEO GAMES? HOW?
I BROUGHT CONSOLES!
SERIOUSLY?!
JAM
...WORK!!
MY INSTINCTS TELL ME I'M RIGHT!!!
La-la-la...
DUMDADUMMMM
IT'S WORKING!
GREAT COMBAT SWAMP BROS. for Wuu i
LET'S PLAY SWAMP BROS.!!
DAHDAHDA
Three holes
Two prongs
SPZZZT
BUT THE VOLTAGE IS DIFFERENT.
HUH?

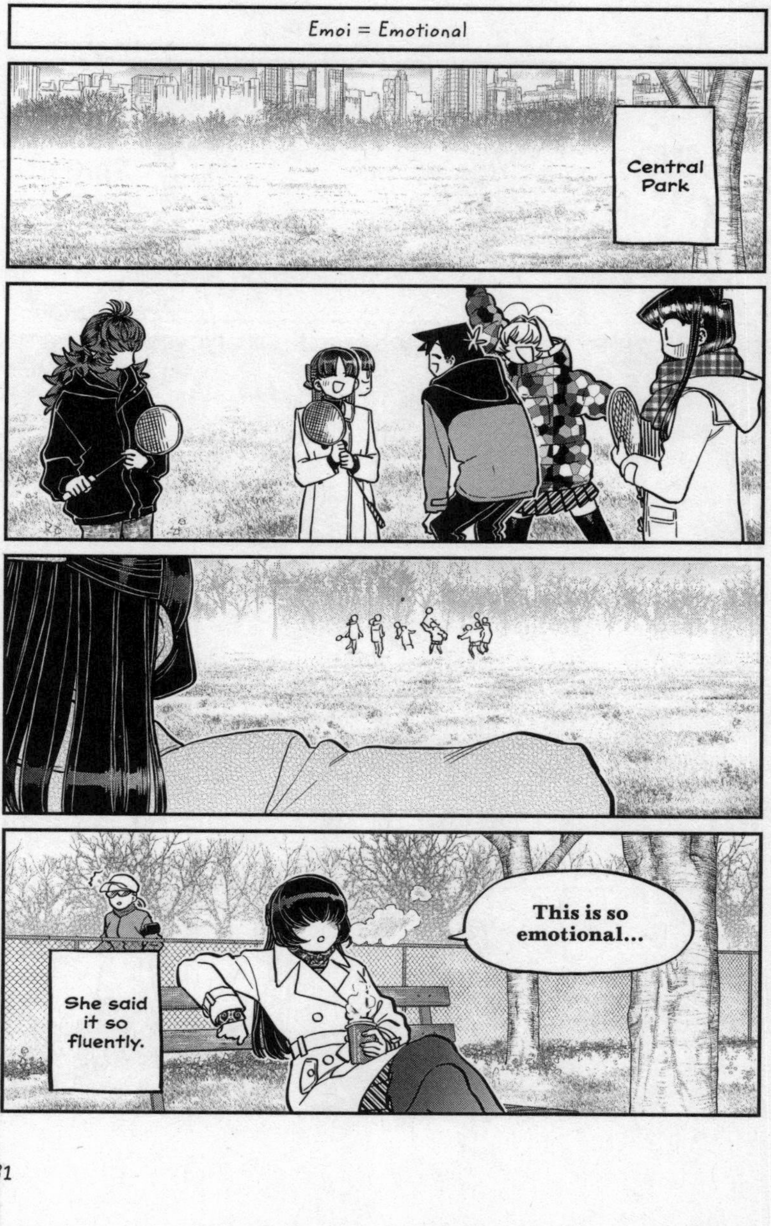
Emoi = Emotional
Central Park
This is so emotional...
She said it so fluently.

Y.Y. Hannya Visits New York

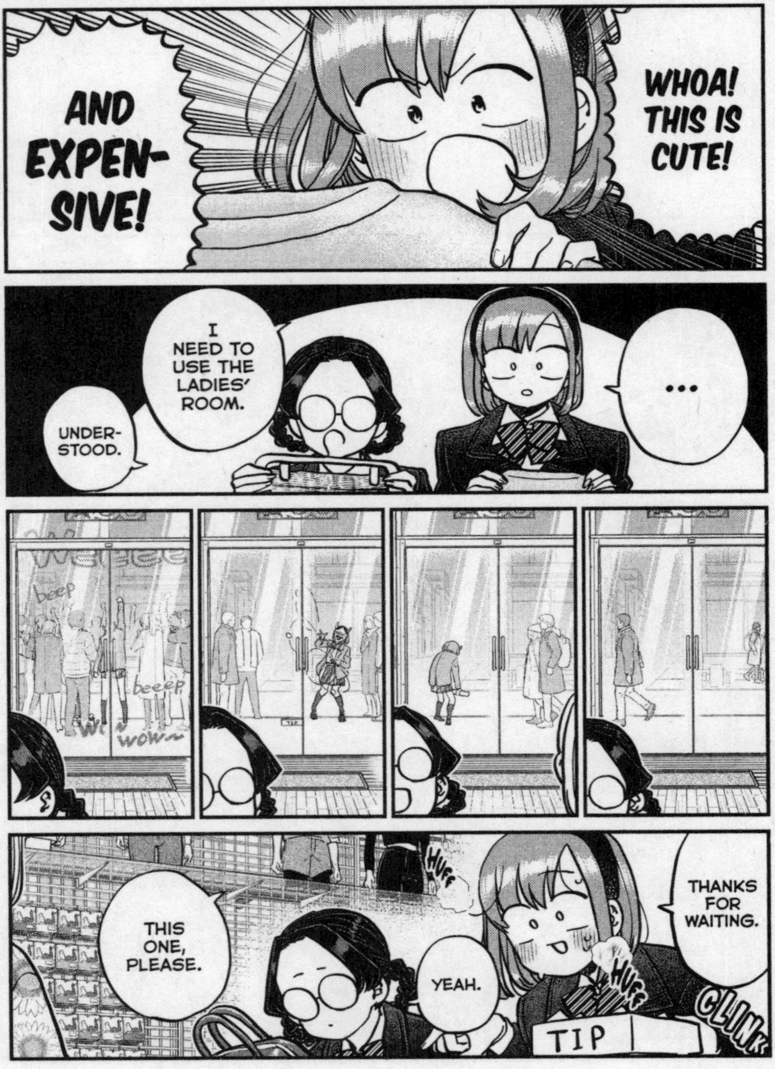
WHOA! THIS IS CUTE!
AND EXPEN-SIVE!
...
I NEED TO USE THE LADIES' ROOM.
UNDER-STOOD.
beep
beeep
wow~
THANKS FOR WAITING.
HUFF
HUFF
CLINK
TIP
YEAH.
THIS ONE, PLEASE.

The Ideal New York Date

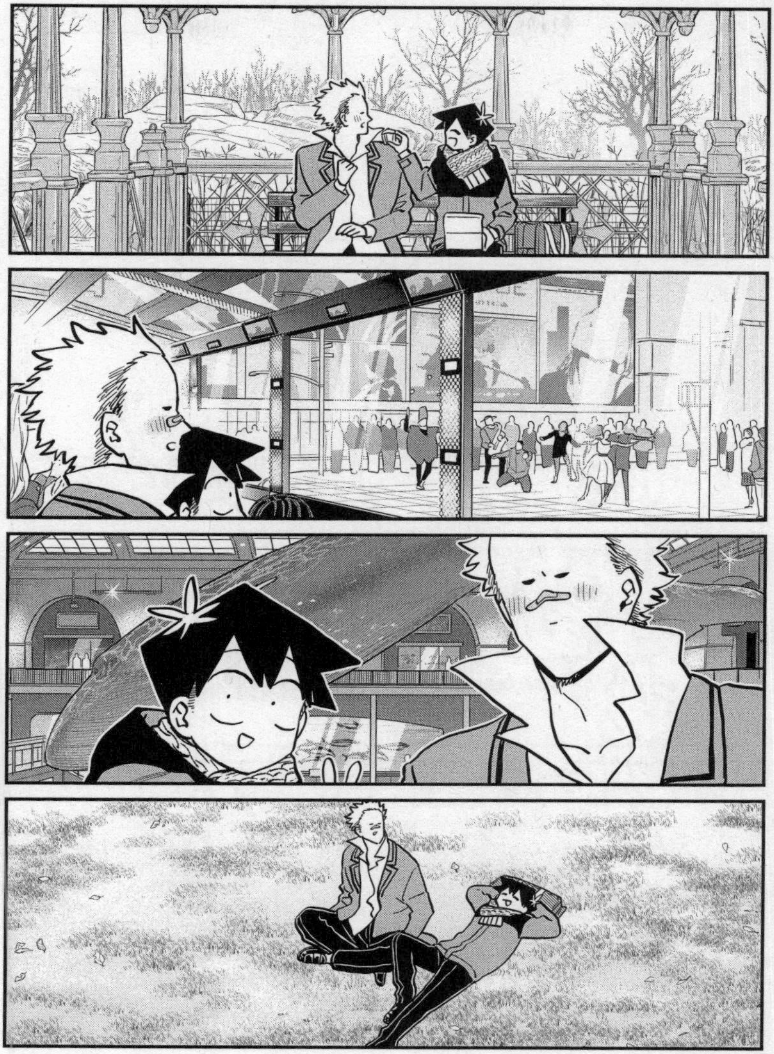

Never Do This

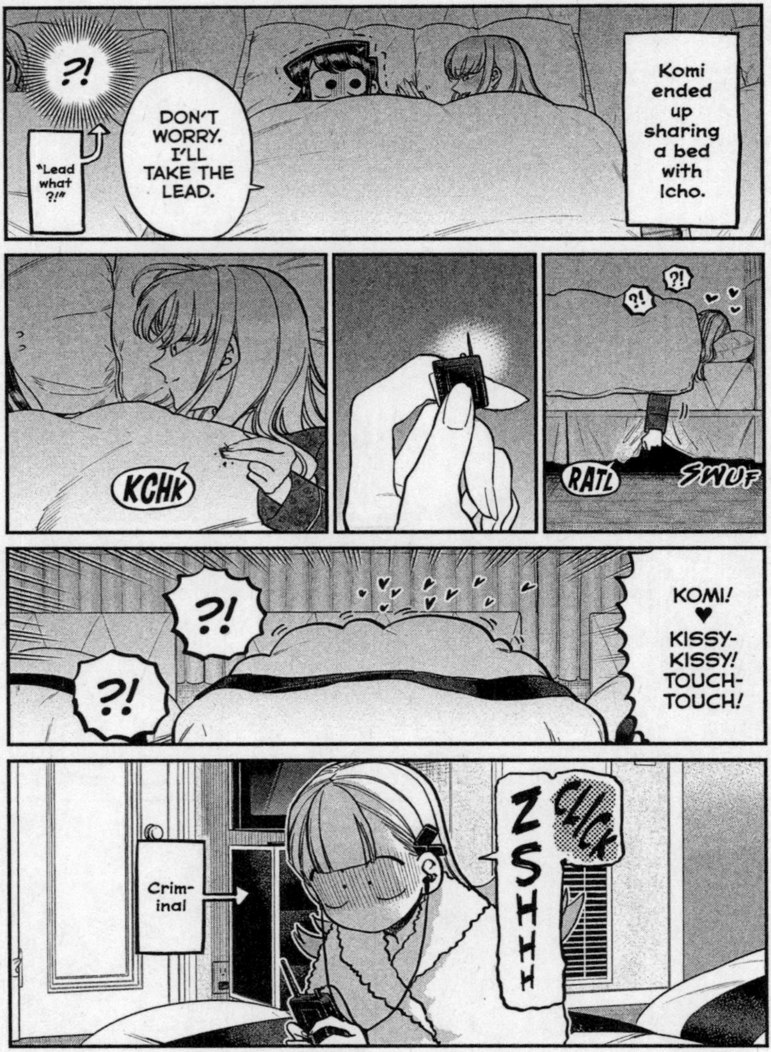
Komi ended up sharing a bed with Icho.
DON'T WORRY. I'LL TAKE THE LEAD.
?!
"Lead what ?!"
?!
?!
RATL
SWUF
KCHK
KOMI! ♥ KISSY-KISSY! TOUCH-TOUCH!
?!
?!
CLICK
ZSHHH
Criminal

Communication 292 — The End

Komi Can't Communicate

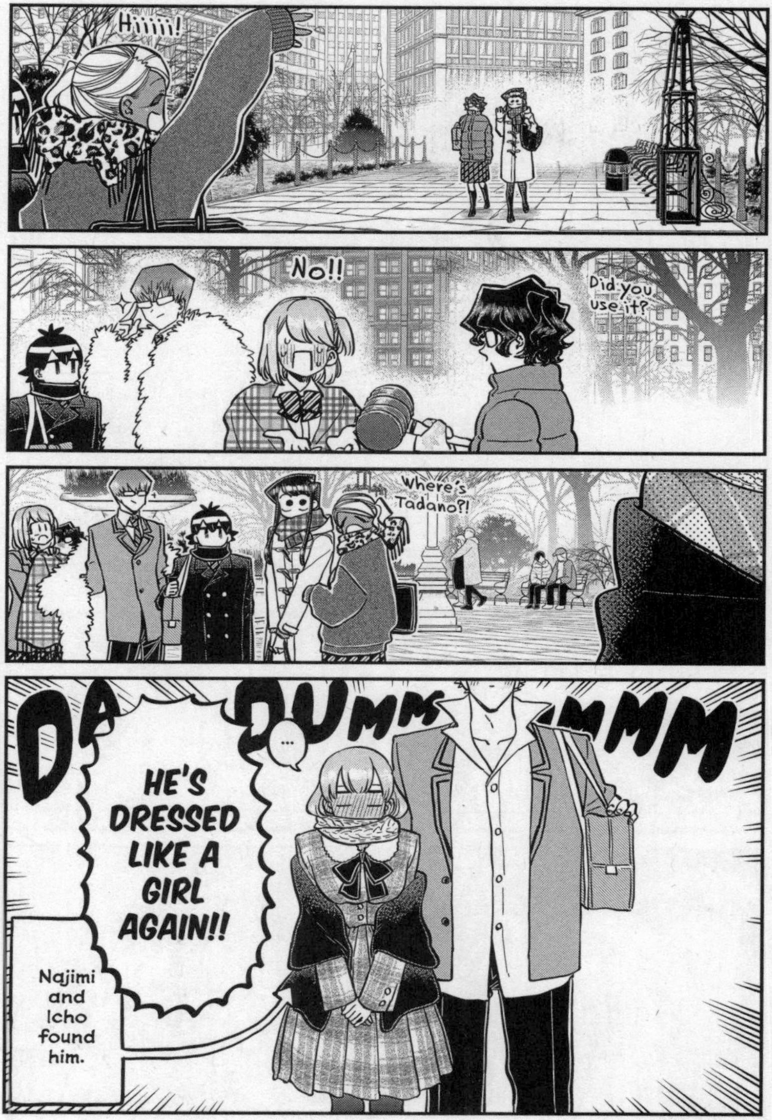
Hiiiiii!
Did you use it?
No!!
Where's Tadano?!
DA
DUMM
MMMM
...
HE'S DRESSED LIKE A GIRL AGAIN!!
Najimi and Icho found him.

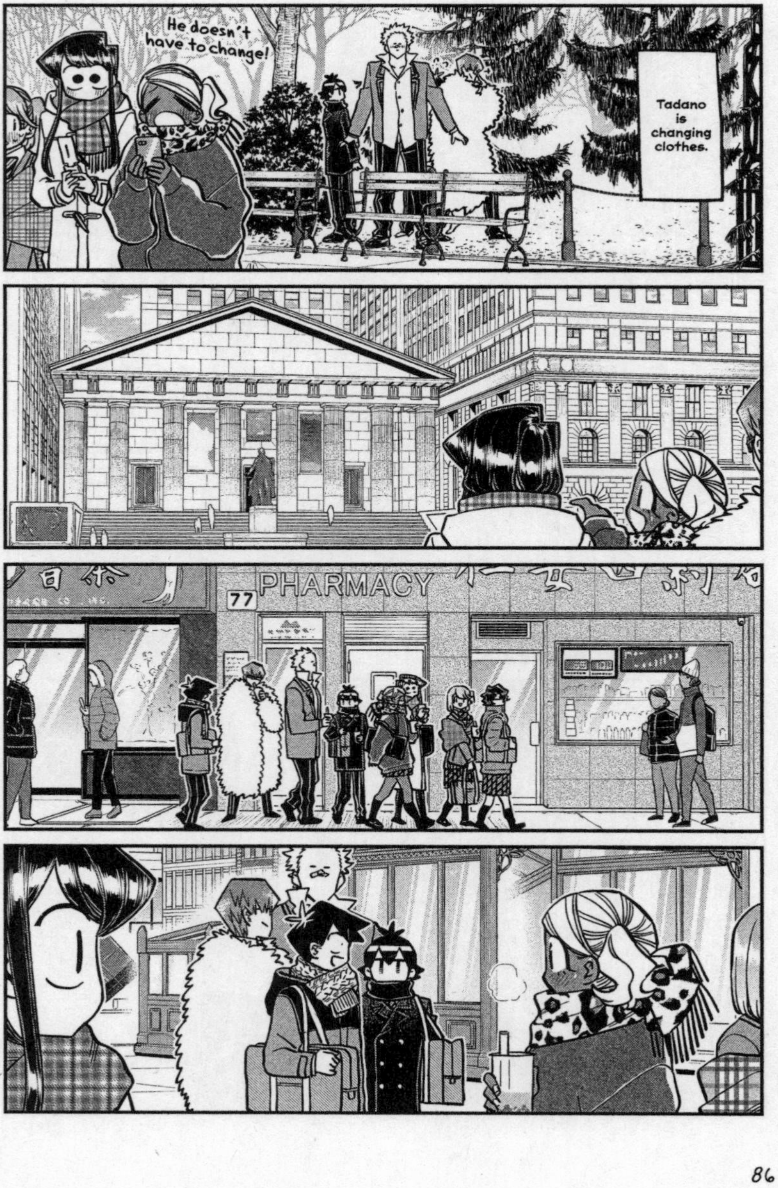
Tadano is changing clothes.
He doesn't have to change!
PHARMACY
77

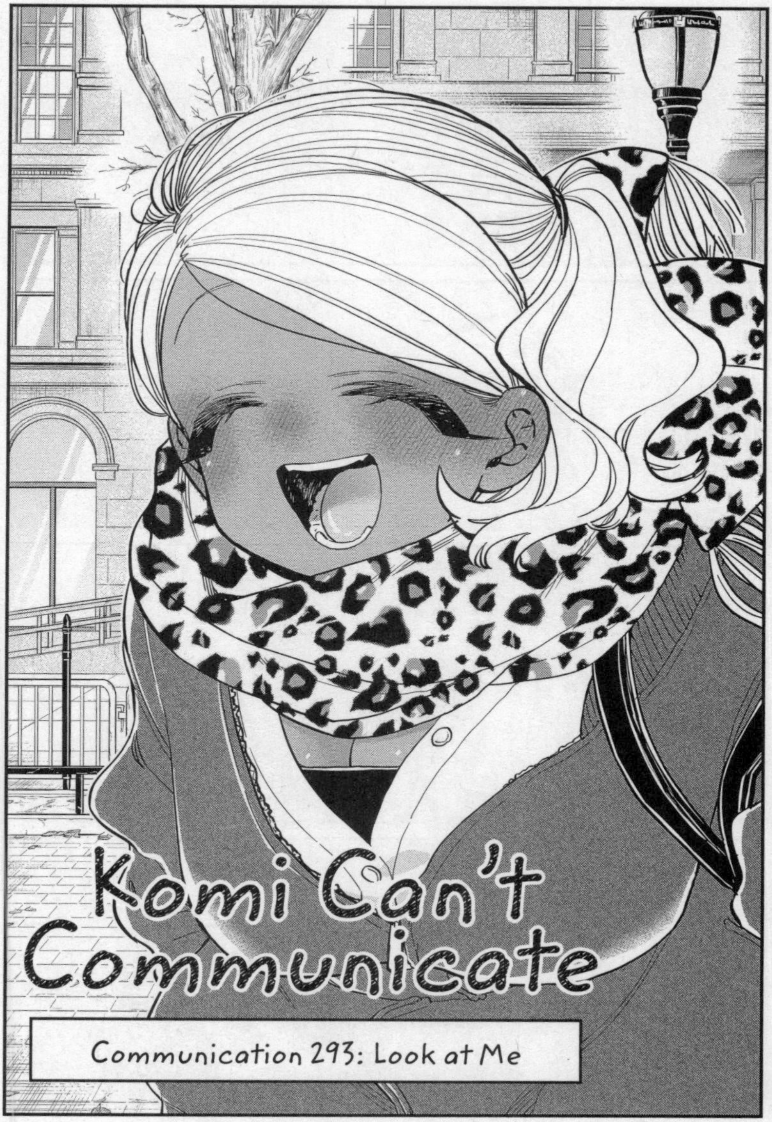
Komi Can't Communicate
Communication 293: Look at Me

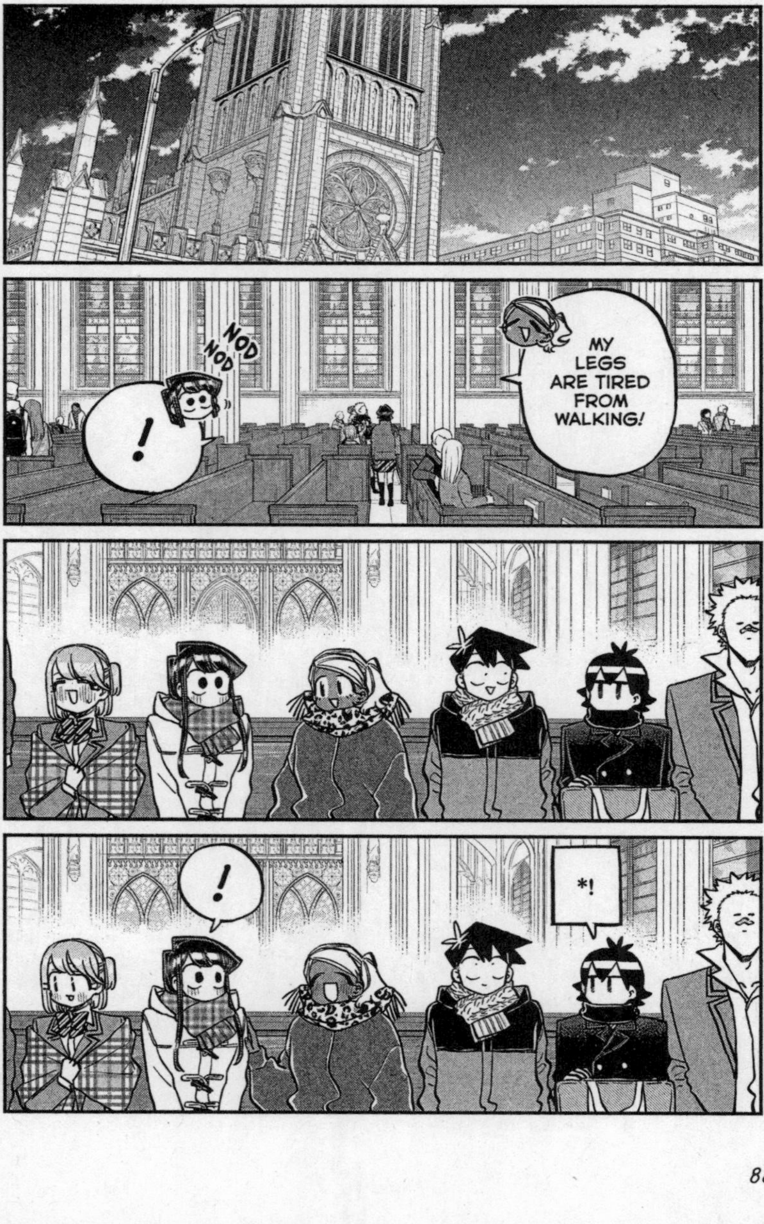
MY LEGS ARE TIRED FROM WALKING!
NOD NOD
!
*!
!

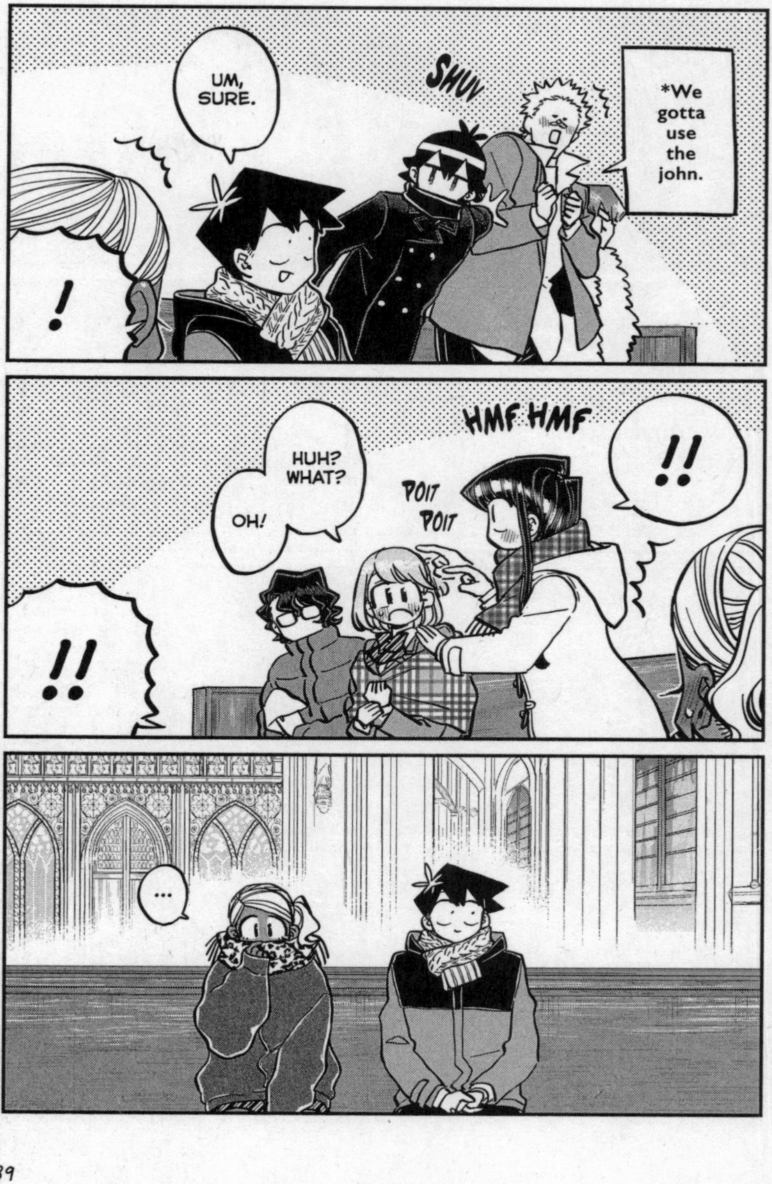
*We gotta use the john.
SHUV
UM, SURE.
!
!!
HMF HMF
POIT POIT
HUH? WHAT?
OH!
!!
...

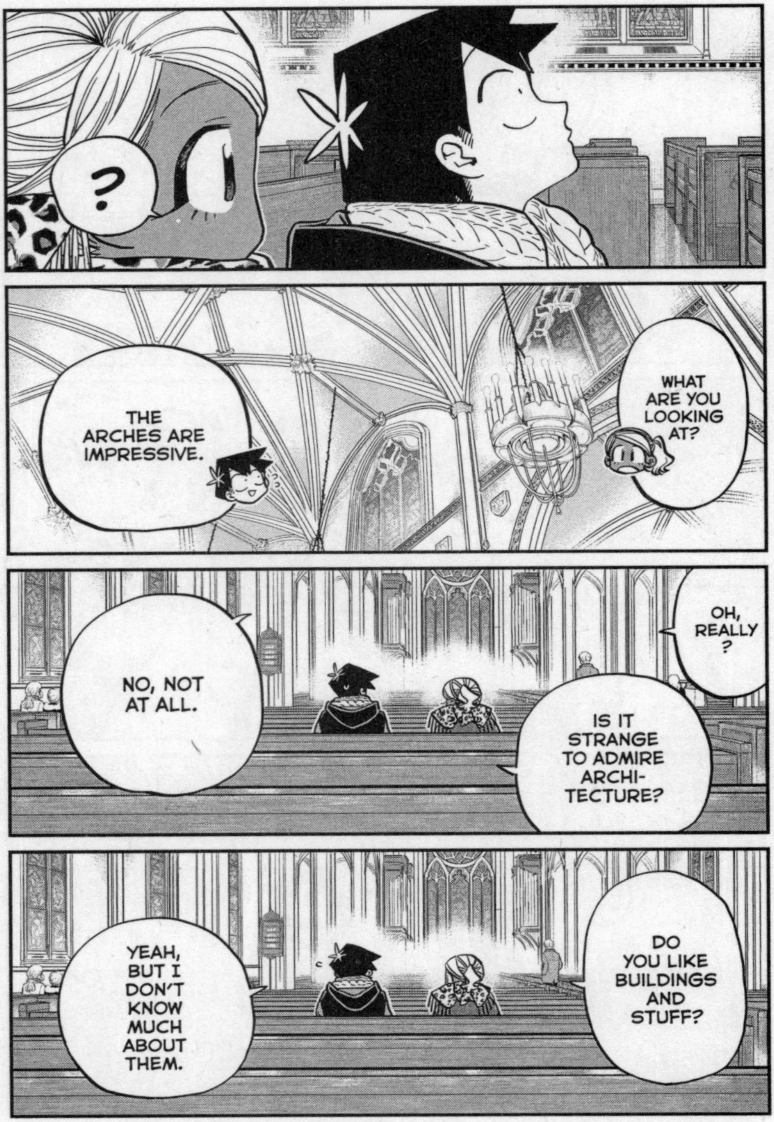
?
WHAT ARE YOU LOOKING AT?
THE ARCHES ARE IMPRESSIVE.
OH, REALLY?
IS IT STRANGE TO ADMIRE ARCHI-TECTURE?
NO, NOT AT ALL.
DO YOU LIKE BUILDINGS AND STUFF?
YEAH, BUT I DON'T KNOW MUCH ABOUT THEM.

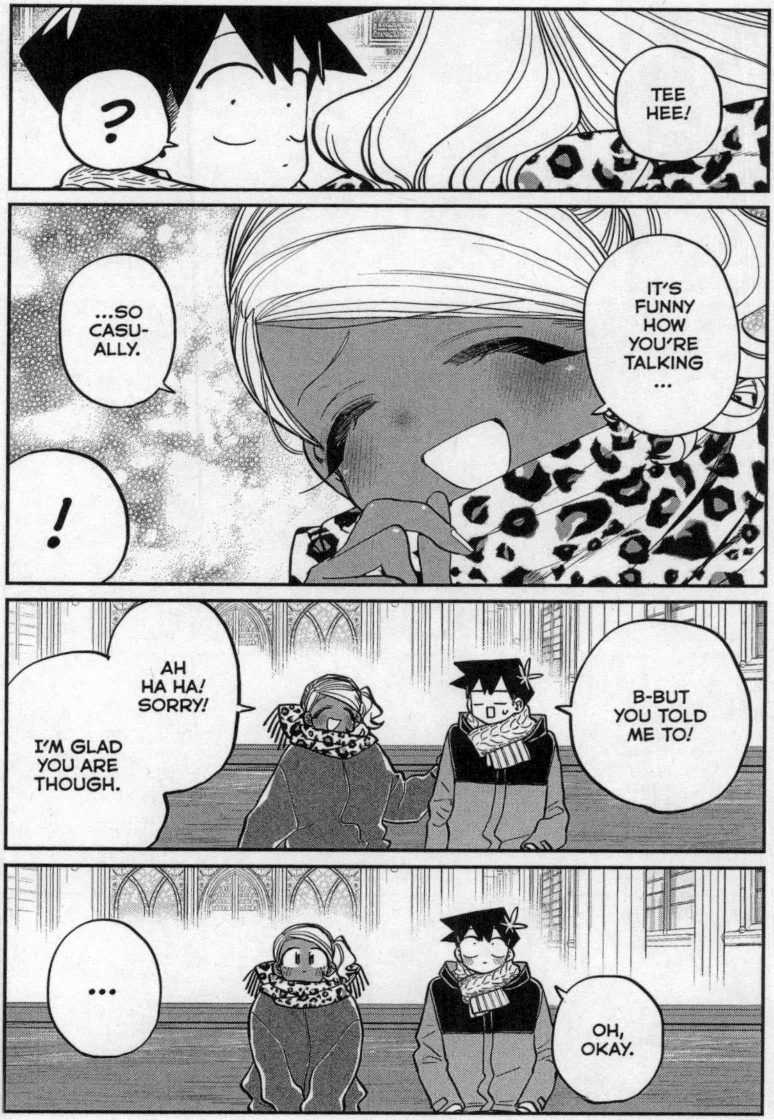
TEE HEE!
?
IT'S FUNNY HOW YOU'RE TALKING ...
...SO CASU-ALLY.
!
B-BUT YOU TOLD ME TO!
AH HA HA! SORRY!
I'M GLAD YOU ARE THOUGH.
OH, OKAY.
...

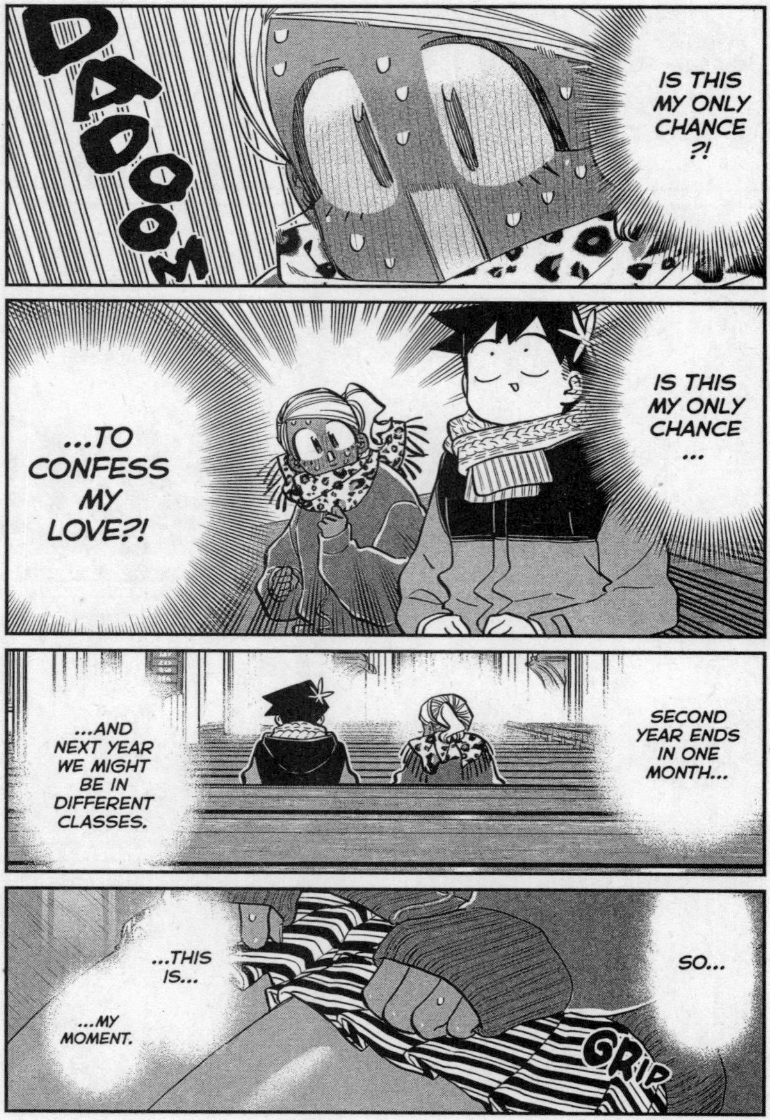
IS THIS MY ONLY CHANCE ?!
DADOOM
IS THIS MY ONLY CHANCE ...
...TO CONFESS MY LOVE?!
SECOND YEAR ENDS IN ONE MONTH...
...AND NEXT YEAR WE MIGHT BE IN DIFFERENT CLASSES.
SO...
GRIP
...THIS IS...
...MY MOMENT.

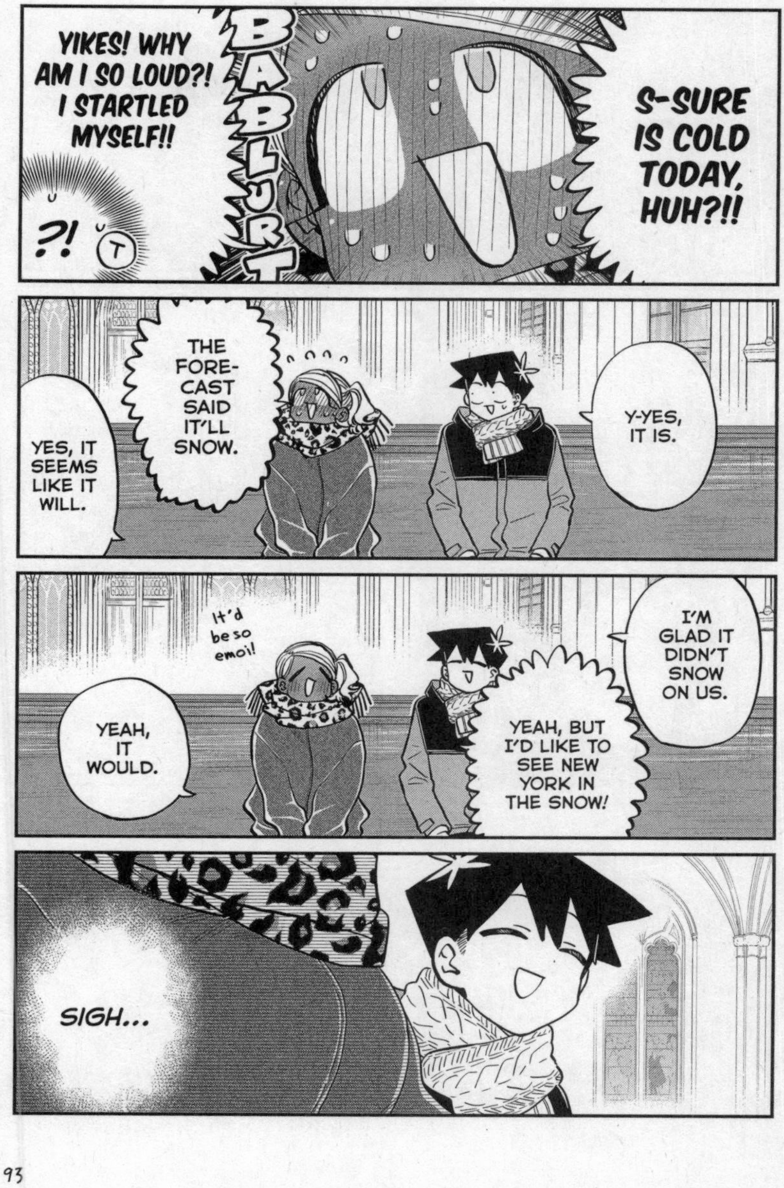
S-SURE IS COLD TODAY, HUH?!!
BABLURT
YIKES! WHY AM I SO LOUD?! I STARTLED MYSELF!!
?!
T
Y-YES, IT IS.
THE FORE-CAST SAID IT'LL SNOW.
YES, IT SEEMS LIKE IT WILL.
I'M GLAD IT DIDN'T SNOW ON US.
YEAH, BUT I'D LIKE TO SEE NEW YORK IN THE SNOW!
It'd be so emoi!
YEAH, IT WOULD.
SIGH...

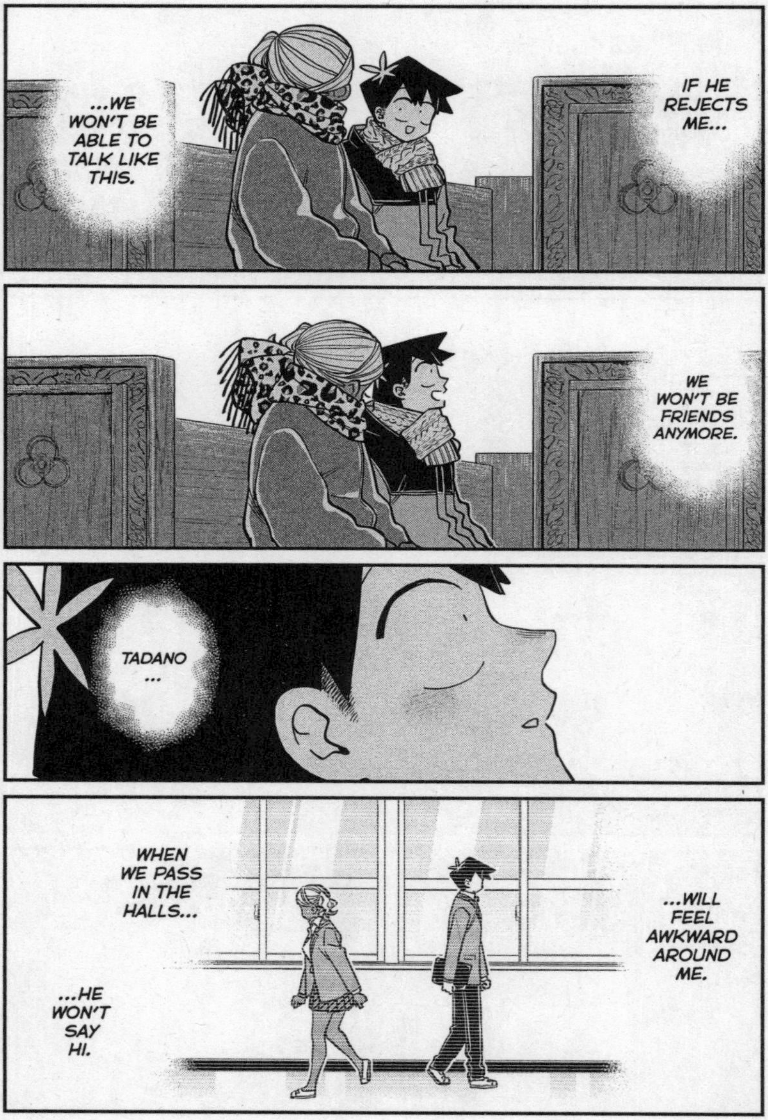
IF HE REJECTS ME...
...WE WON'T BE ABLE TO TALK LIKE THIS.
WE WON'T BE FRIENDS ANYMORE.
TADANO ...
WHEN WE PASS IN THE HALLS...
...HE WON'T SAY HI.
...WILL FEEL AWKWARD AROUND ME.

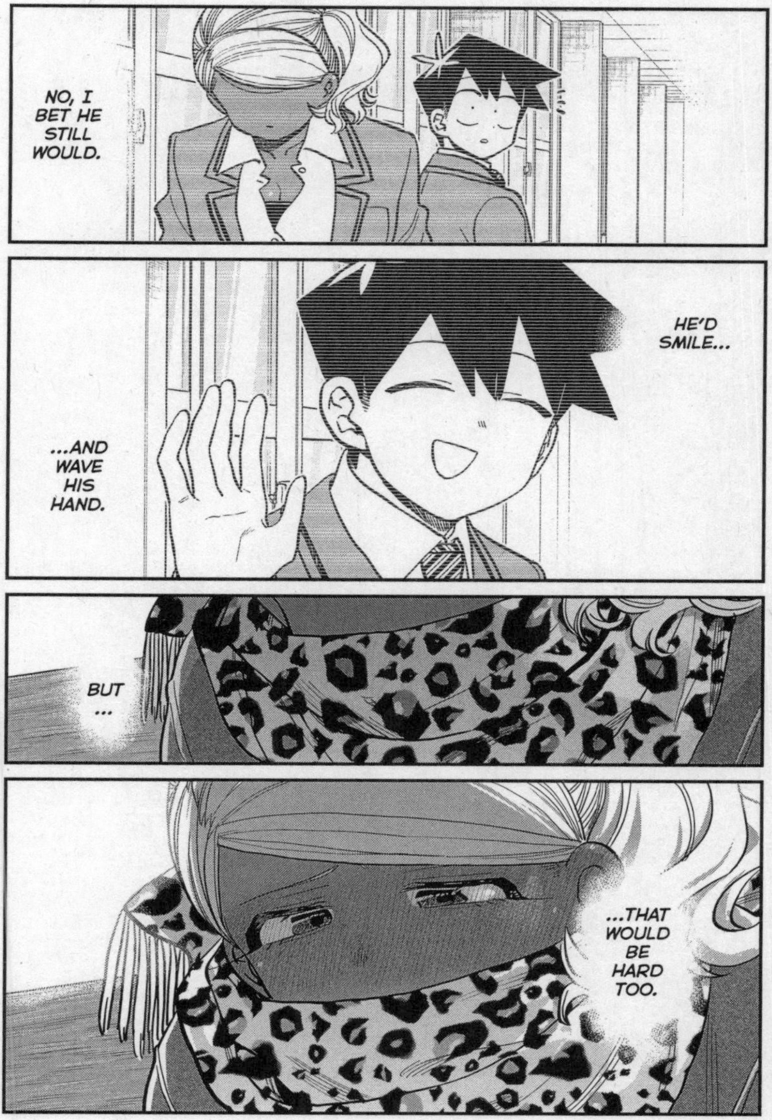
NO, I BET HE STILL WOULD.
HE'D SMILE...
...AND WAVE HIS HAND.
BUT ...
...THAT WOULD BE HARD TOO.

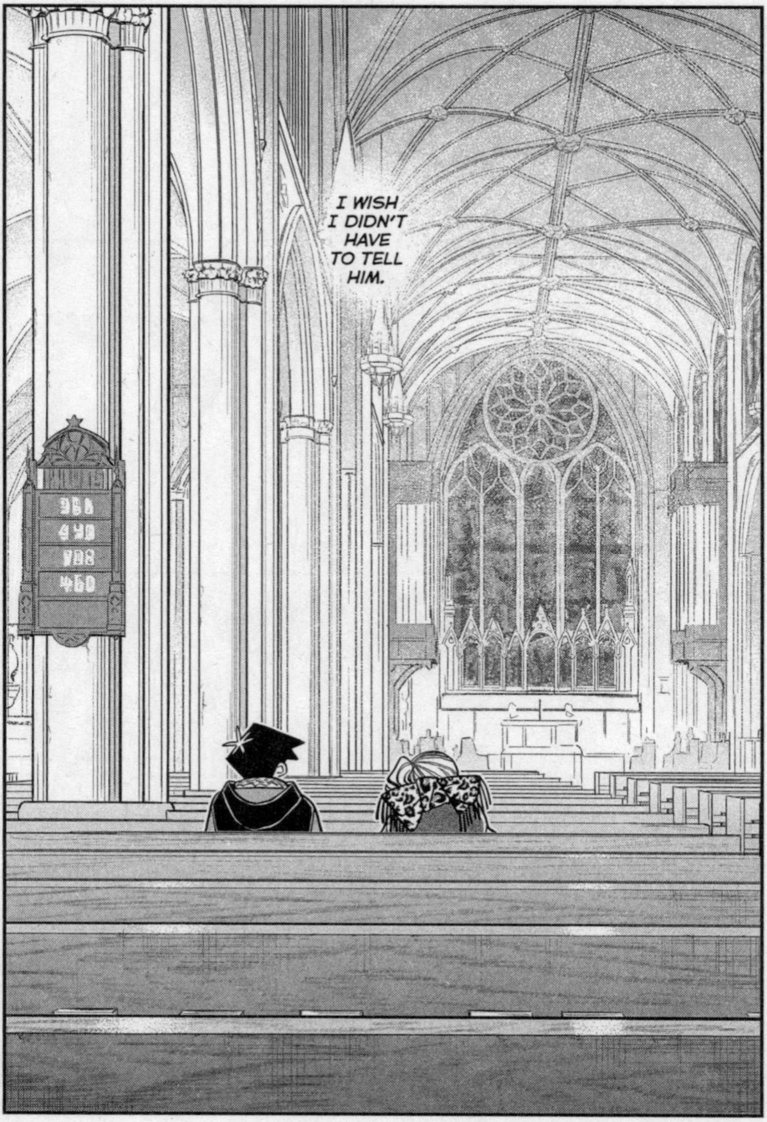
I WISH I DIDN'T HAVE TO TELL HIM.

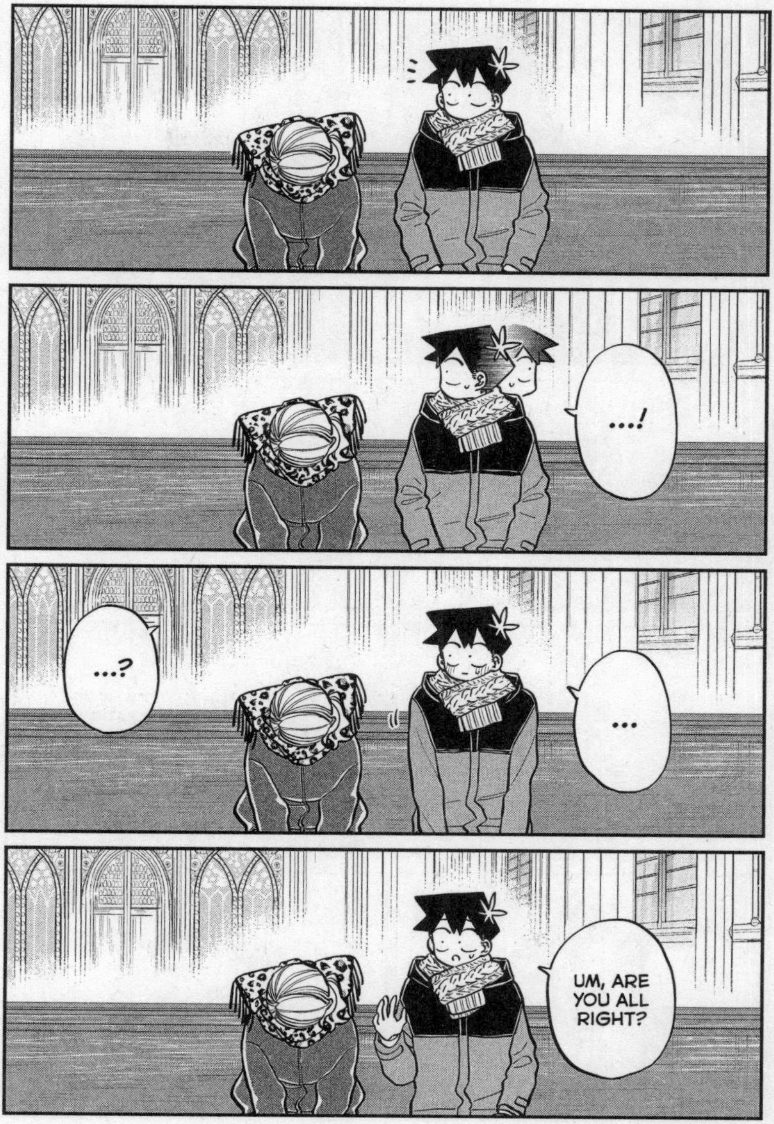

...!
...
...?
UM, ARE YOU ALL RIGHT?

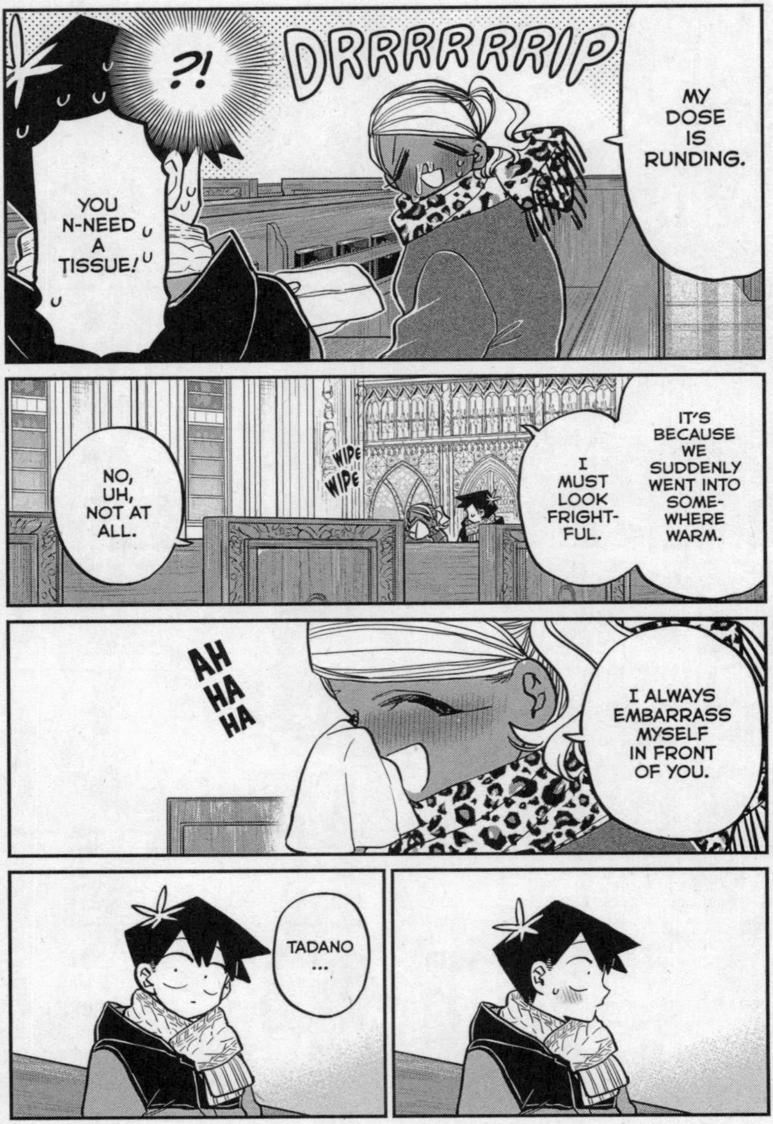
MY DOSE IS RUNDING.
DRRRRRRIP
?!
YOU N-NEED A TISSUE!
IT'S BECAUSE WE SUDDENLY WENT INTO SOME-WHERE WARM.
I MUST LOOK FRIGHT-FUL.
WIPE WIPE
NO, UH, NOT AT ALL.
I ALWAYS EMBARRASS MYSELF IN FRONT OF YOU.
AH HA HA
TADANO ...

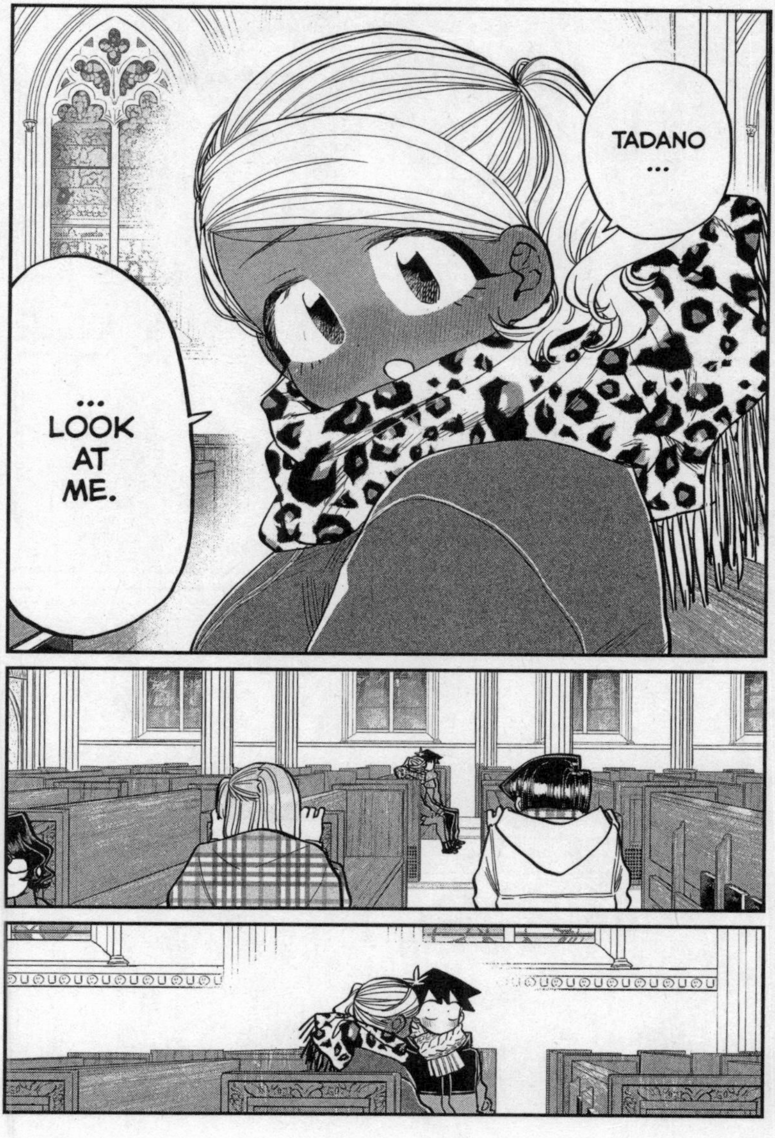
TADANO ...
... LOOK AT ME.

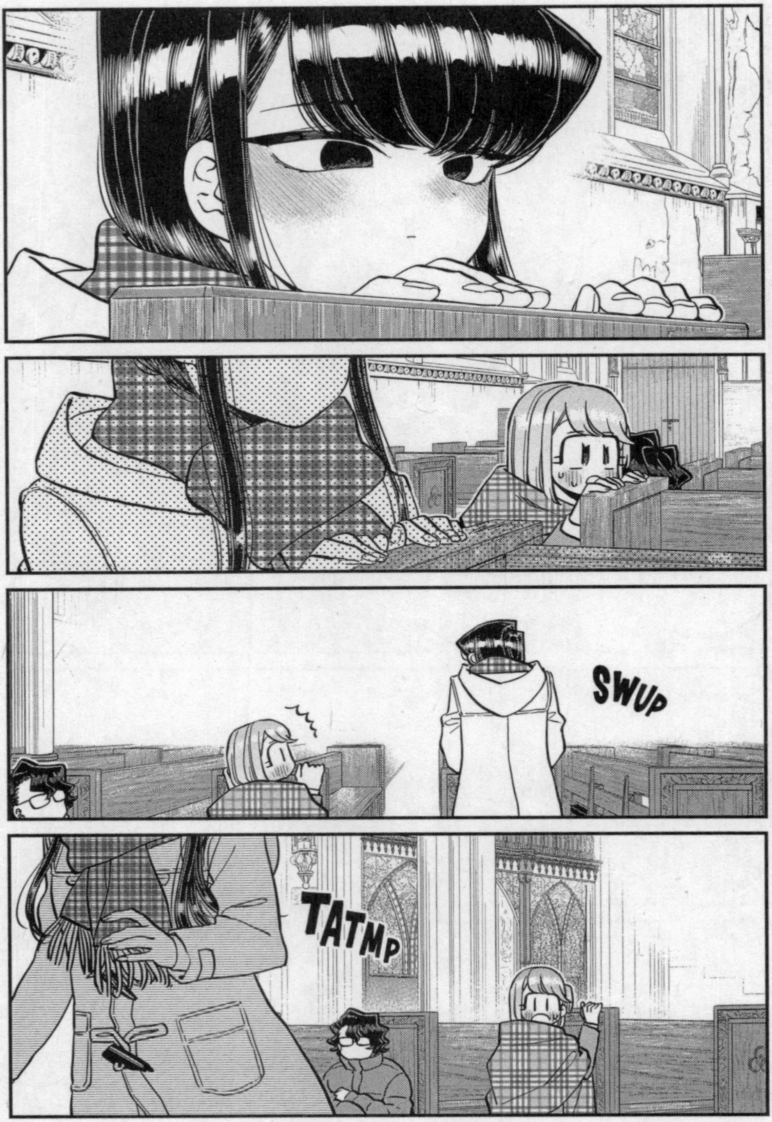
SWUP
TATMP

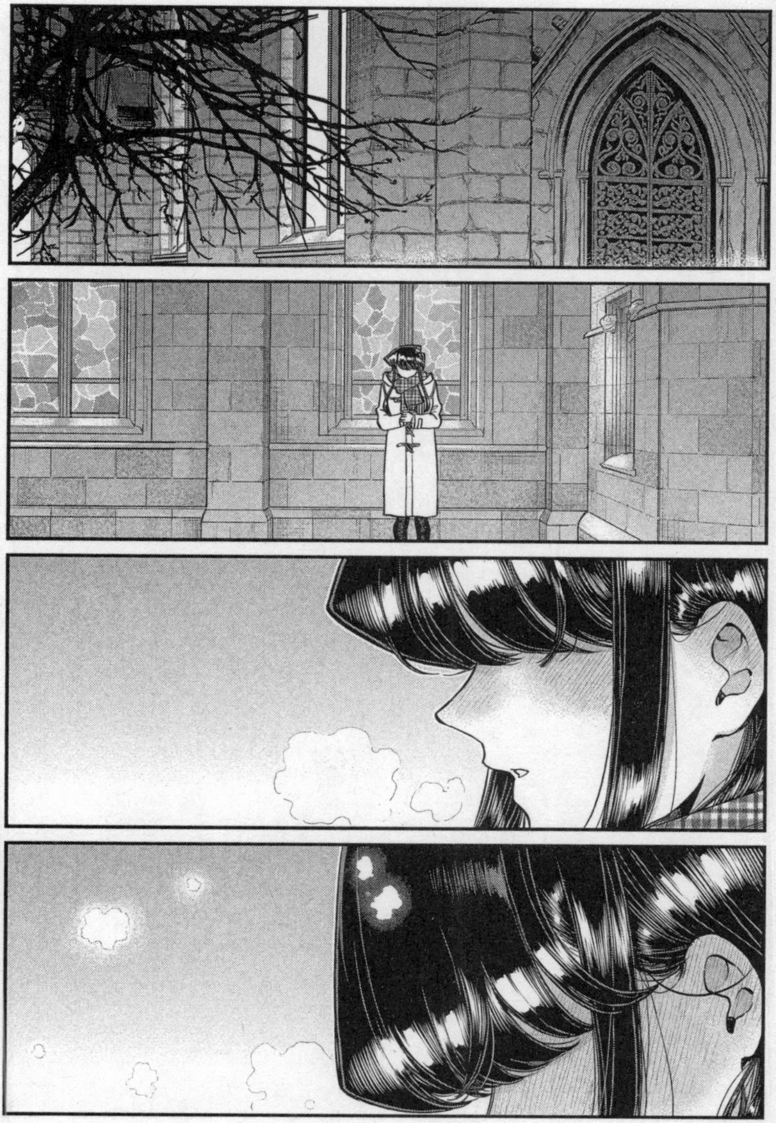

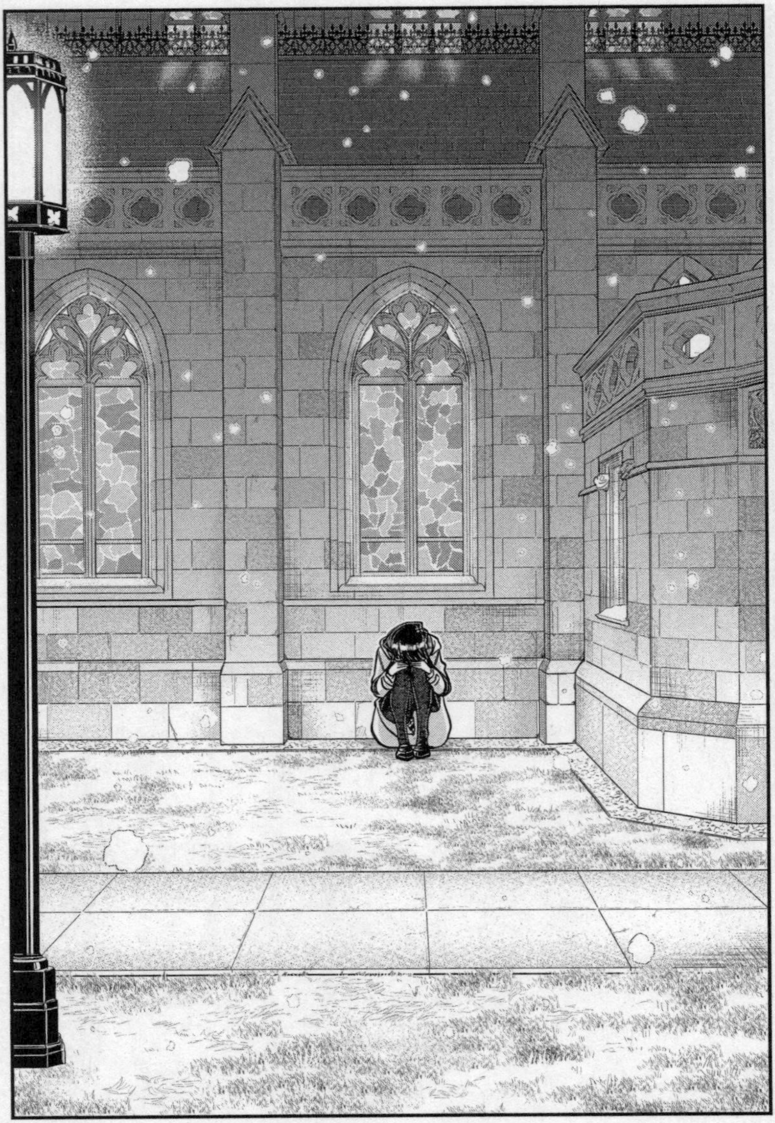

Communication 293 — The End

Komi Can't Communicate

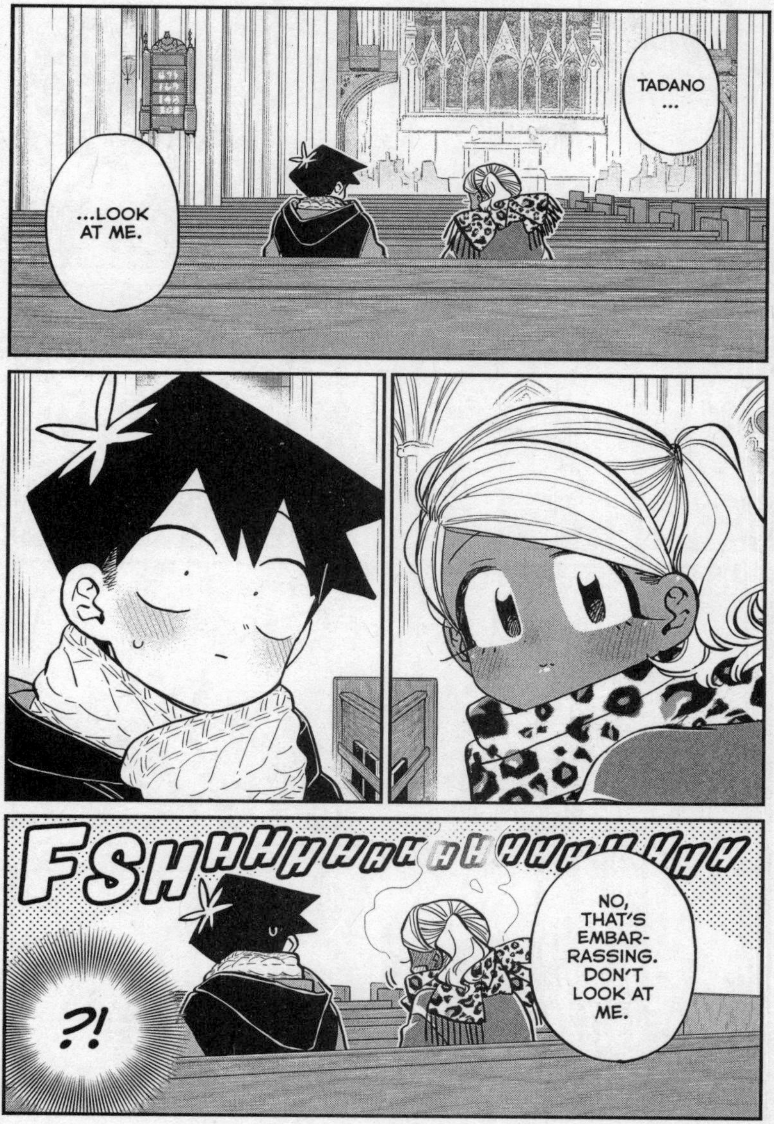
TADANO …
…LOOK AT ME.
NO, THAT'S EMBARRASSING. DON'T LOOK AT ME.
FSHHHHHHHHHHHHHHHHH
?!

Communication 294: I'm Sorry Too

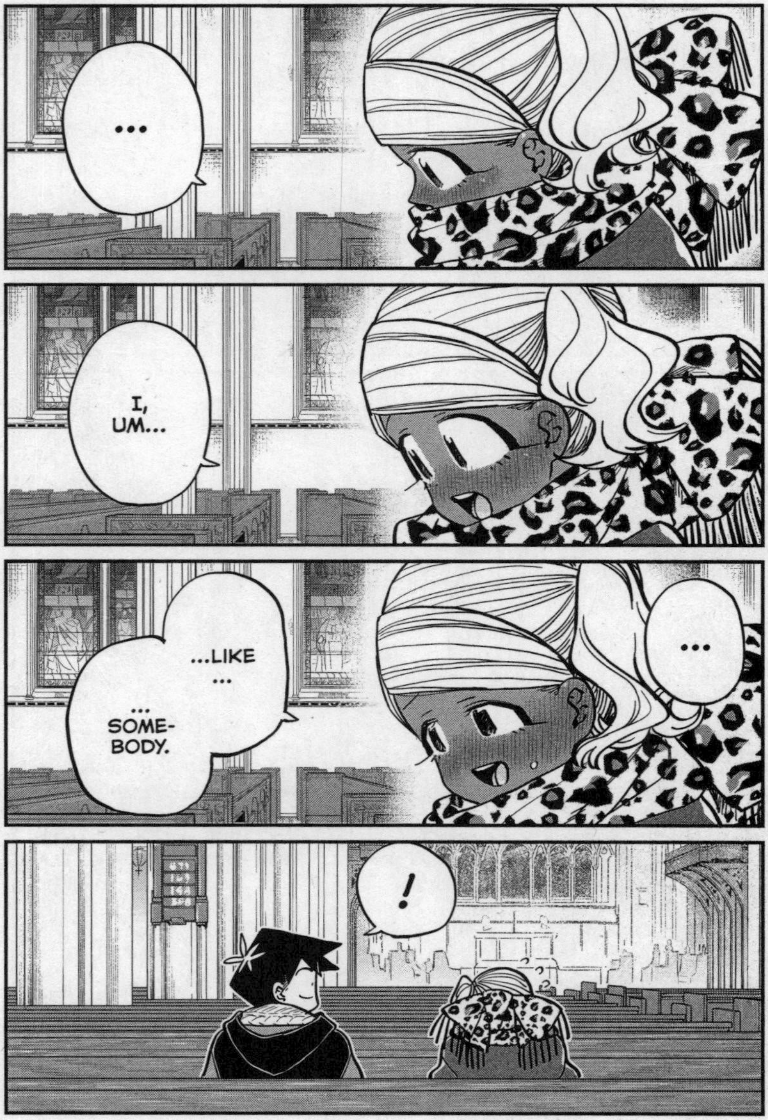
...
I, UM...
...
...LIKE ... ... SOME-BODY.
!

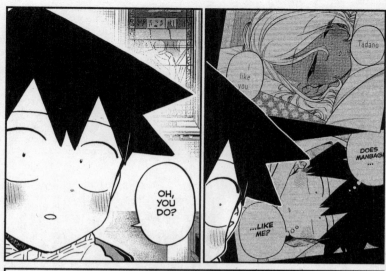

Tadano
I like you.
DOES MANBAG ...
...LIKE ME?
OH, YOU DO?
BUT HE'S CLOSE WITH ANOTHER GIRL...
...AND THEY'RE GOOD TOGETHER.
I ALMOST KINDA ...
... SHIP THEM.
SHIP ?!
W- what do you mean?

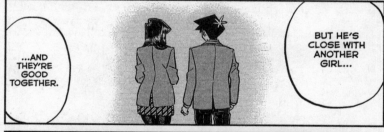

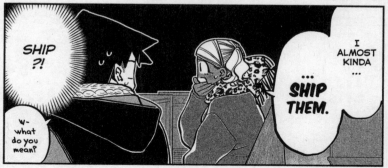

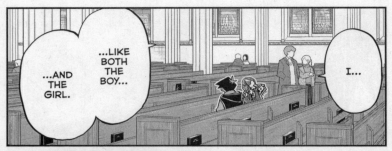

I...
...LIKE BOTH THE BOY...
...AND THE GIRL.
SO WOULD IT BE IT RIGHT FOR ME TO COME BETWEEN THEM?
AFTER ALL, I WISH THE BEST FOR THEM.
BUT I HAVE FEELINGS FOR THE BOY.

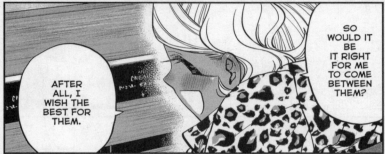

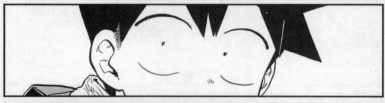

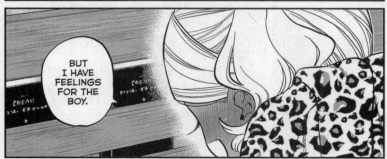

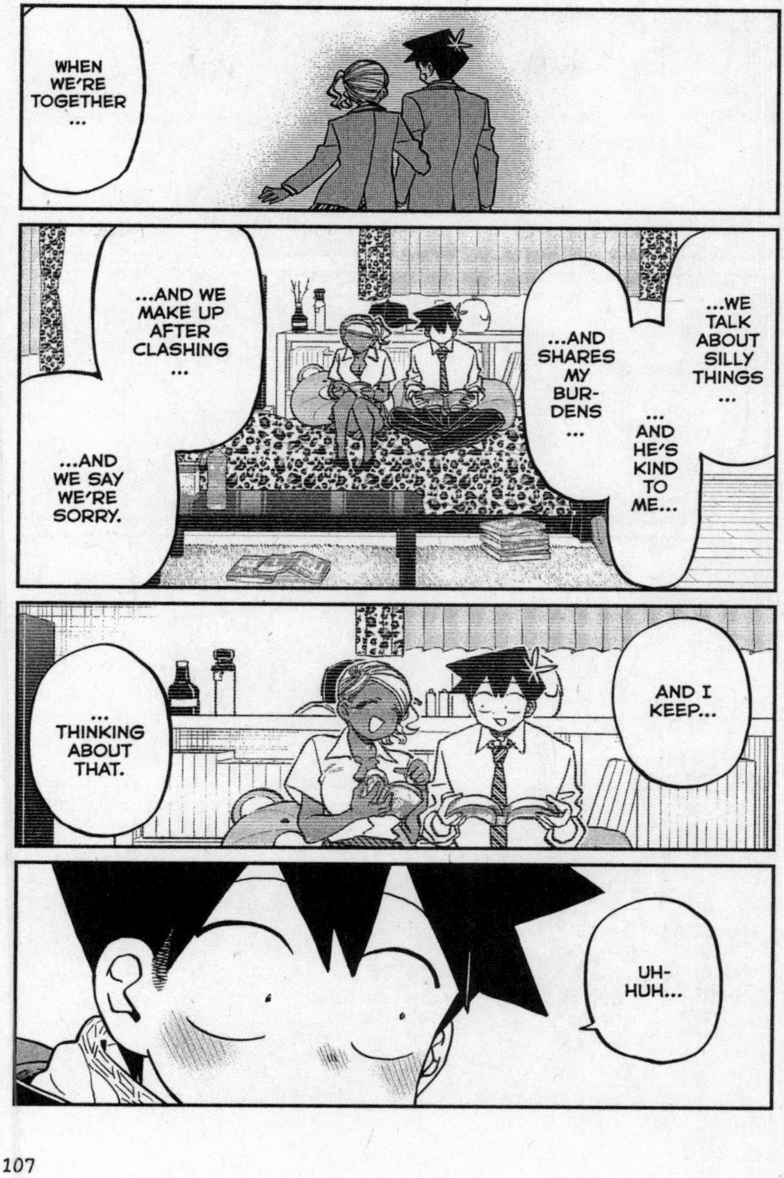
WHEN WE'RE TOGETHER ...
...WE TALK ABOUT SILLY THINGS ...
... AND HE'S KIND TO ME...
...AND SHARES MY BUR- DENS ...
...AND WE MAKE UP AFTER CLASHING ...
...AND WE SAY WE'RE SORRY.
AND I KEEP...
... THINKING ABOUT THAT.
UH- HUH...

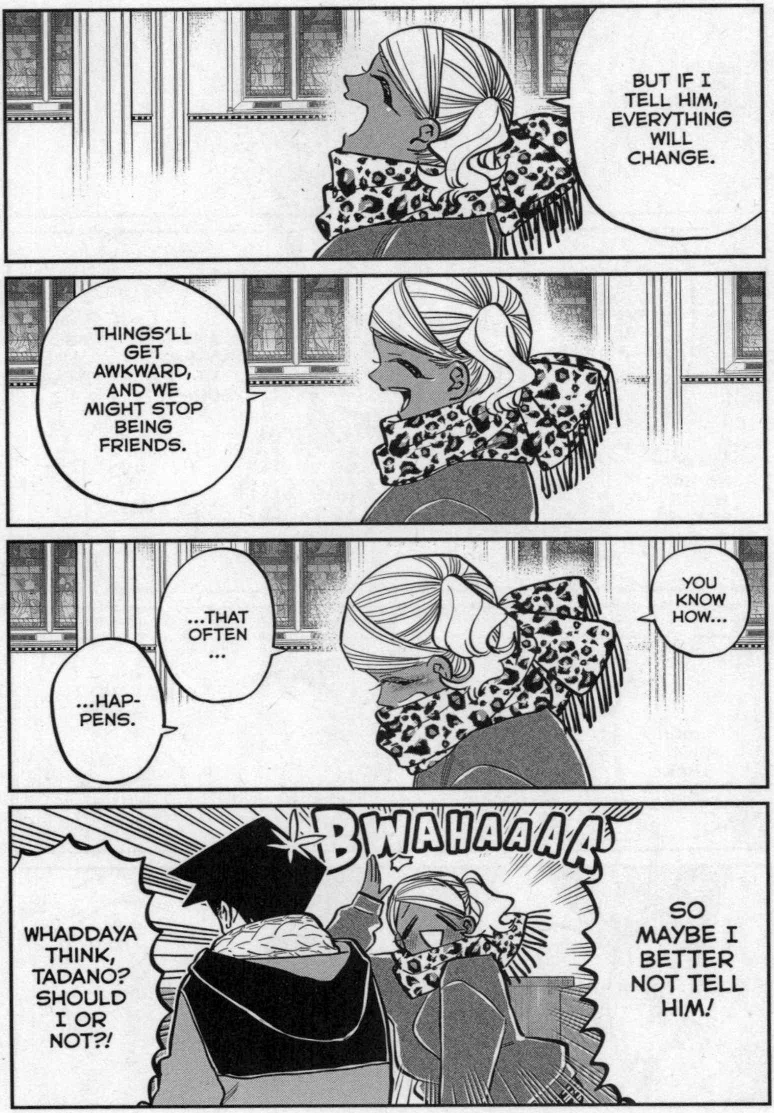
BUT IF I TELL HIM, EVERYTHING WILL CHANGE.
THINGS'LL GET AWKWARD, AND WE MIGHT STOP BEING FRIENDS.
YOU KNOW HOW...
...THAT OFTEN ...
...HAP-PENS.
BWAHAAAAA
SO MAYBE I BETTER NOT TELL HIM!
WHADDAYA THINK, TADANO? SHOULD I OR NOT?!

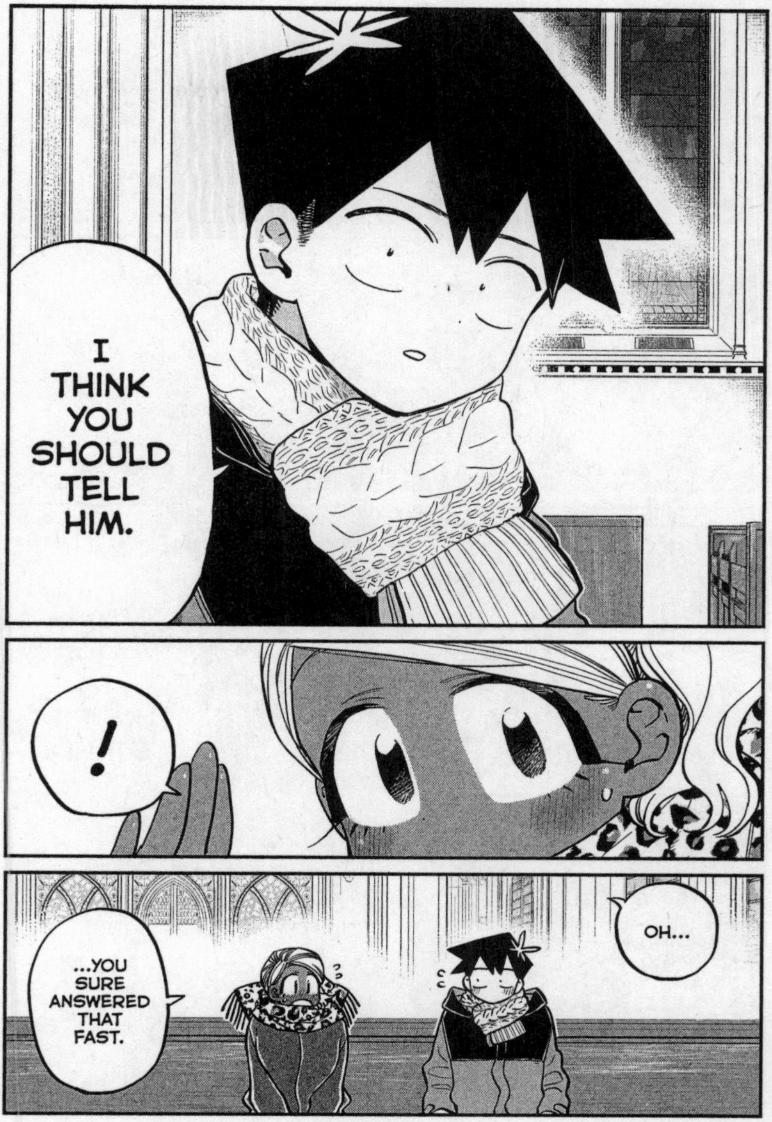
I THINK YOU SHOULD TELL HIM.
!
OH...
...YOU SURE ANSWERED THAT FAST.

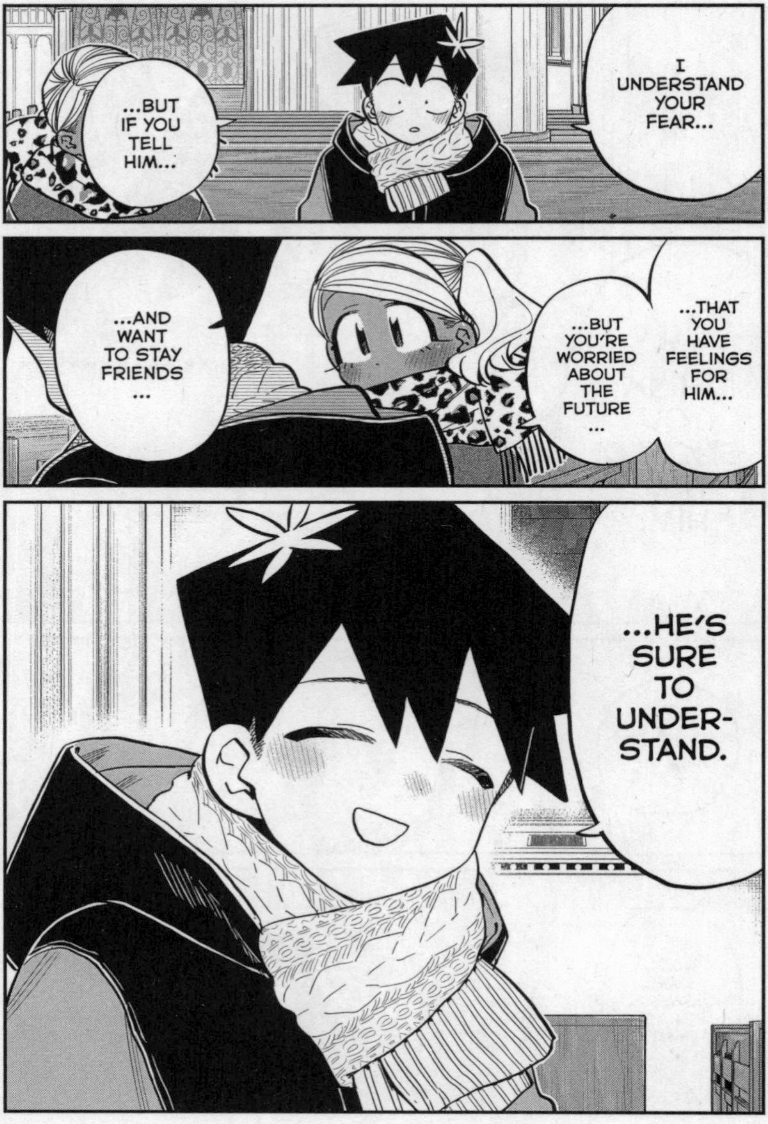
I UNDERSTAND YOUR FEAR...
...BUT IF YOU TELL HIM...
...THAT YOU HAVE FEELINGS FOR HIM...
...BUT YOU'RE WORRIED ABOUT THE FUTURE ...
...AND WANT TO STAY FRIENDS ...
...HE'S SURE TO UNDER-STAND.

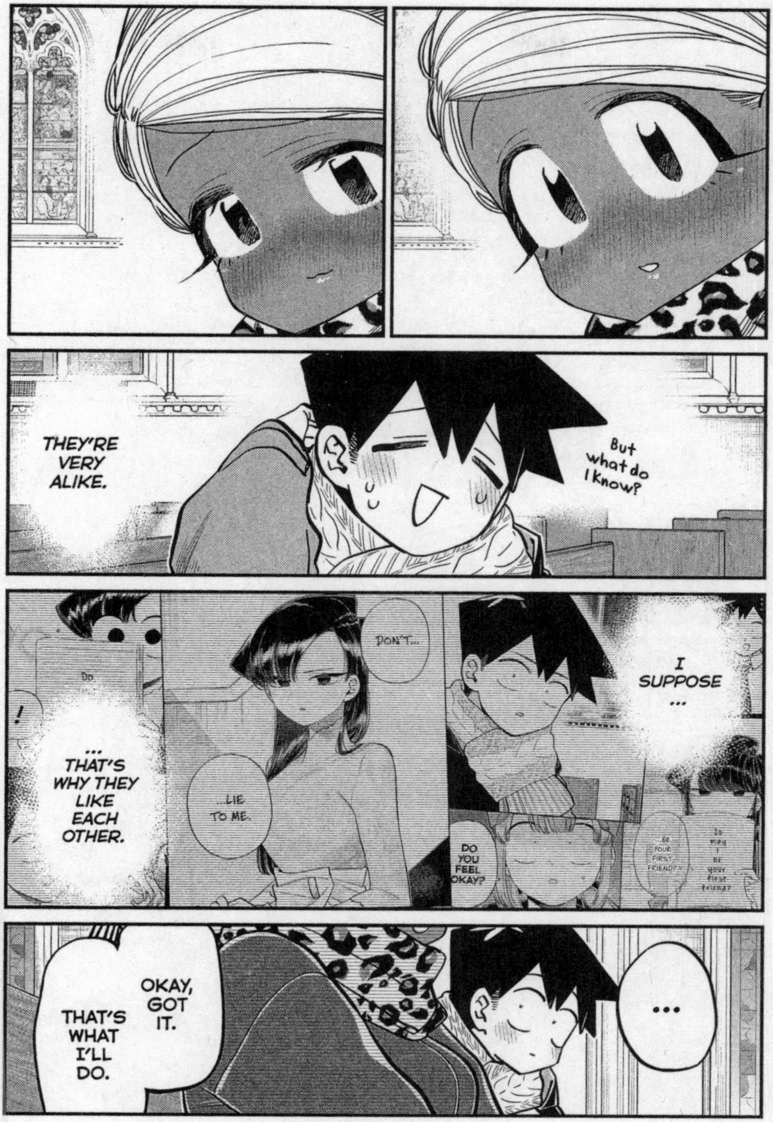
But what do I know?
THEY'RE VERY ALIKE.
I SUPPOSE ...
So may I be your first friend?
...BE YOUR FIRST FRIEND?
DO YOU FEEL OKAY?
DON'T...
...LIE TO ME.
DO
!
... THAT'S WHY THEY LIKE EACH OTHER.
...
OKAY, GOT IT.
THAT'S WHAT I'LL DO.

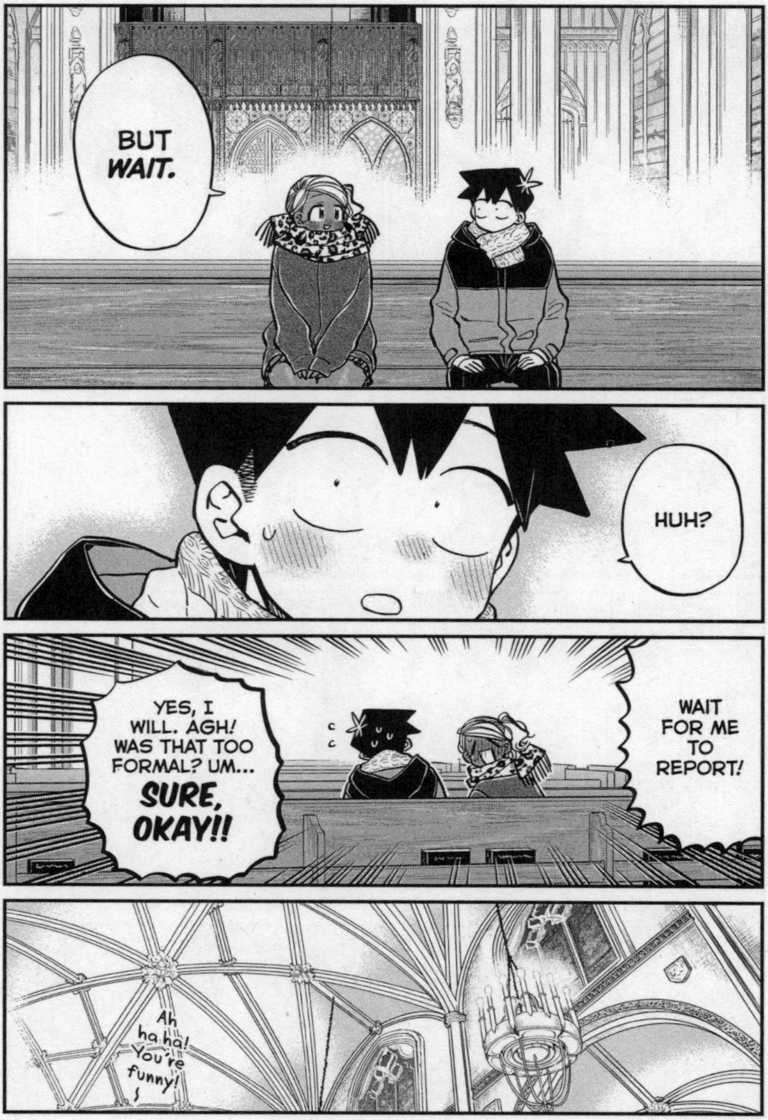
BUT WAIT.
HUH?
WAIT FOR ME TO REPORT!
YES, I WILL. AGH! WAS THAT TOO FORMAL? UM... SURE, OKAY!!
Ah ha ha! You're funny!

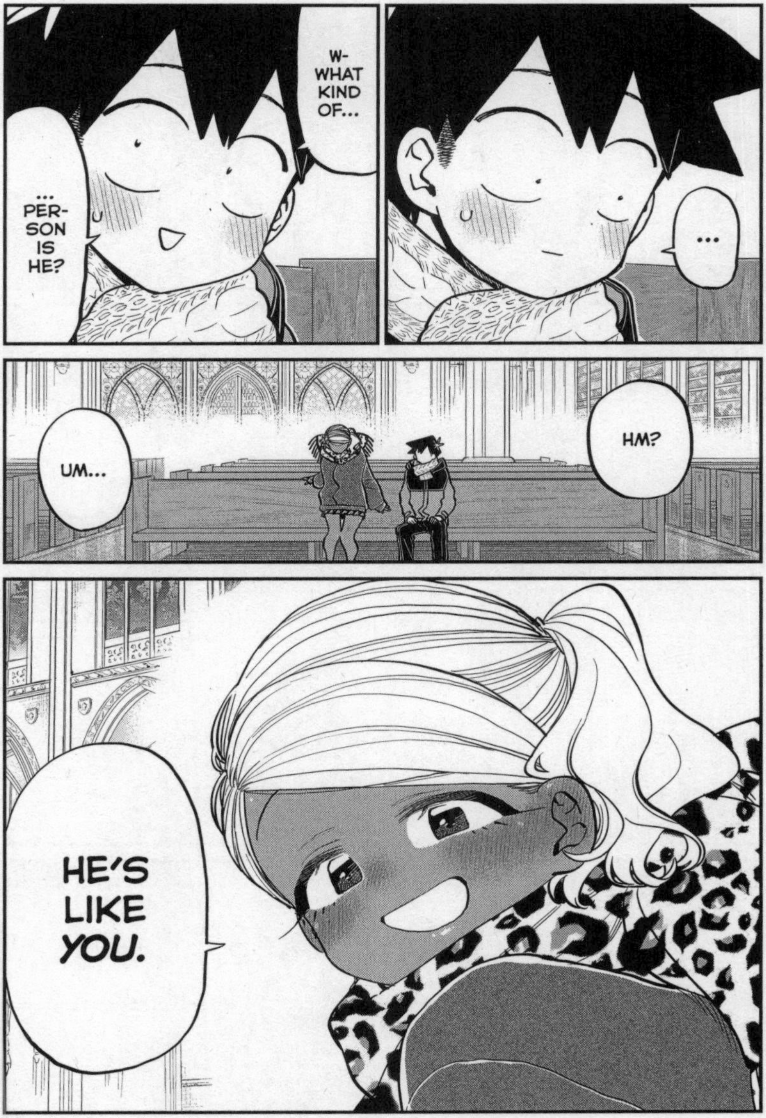
...
W-WHAT KIND OF...
...PER-SON IS HE?
HM?
UM...
HE'S LIKE YOU.

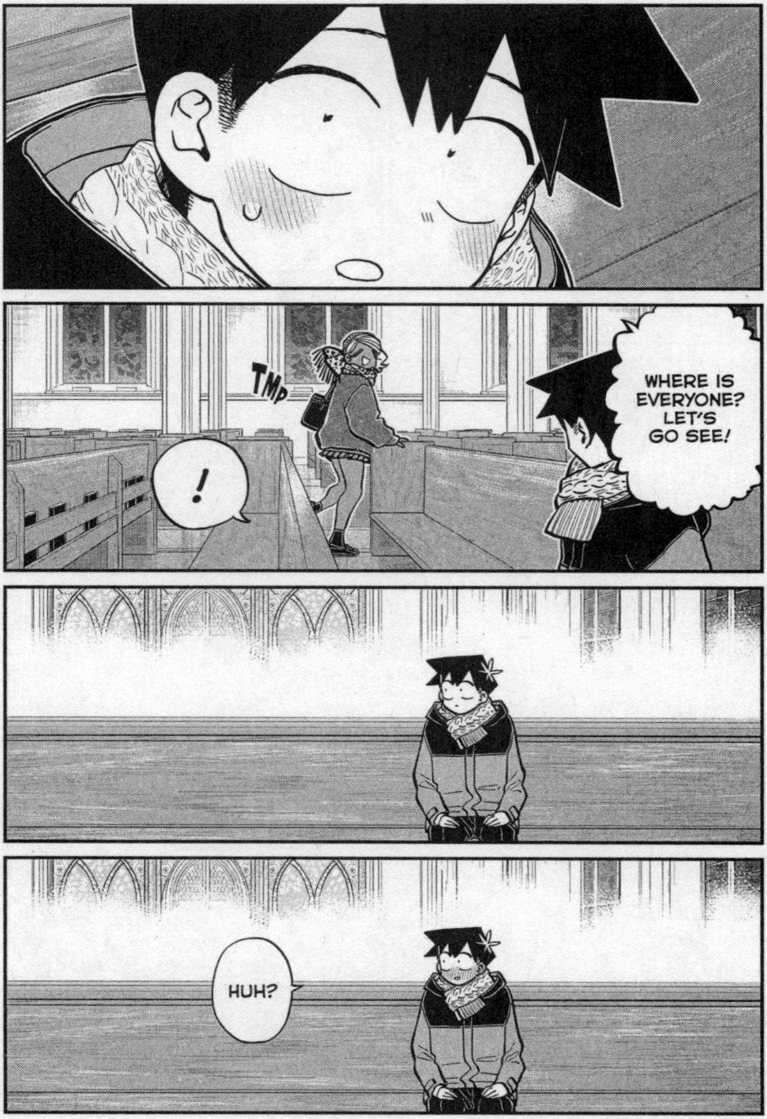
WHERE IS EVERYONE? LET'S GO SEE!
TMP
!
HUH?

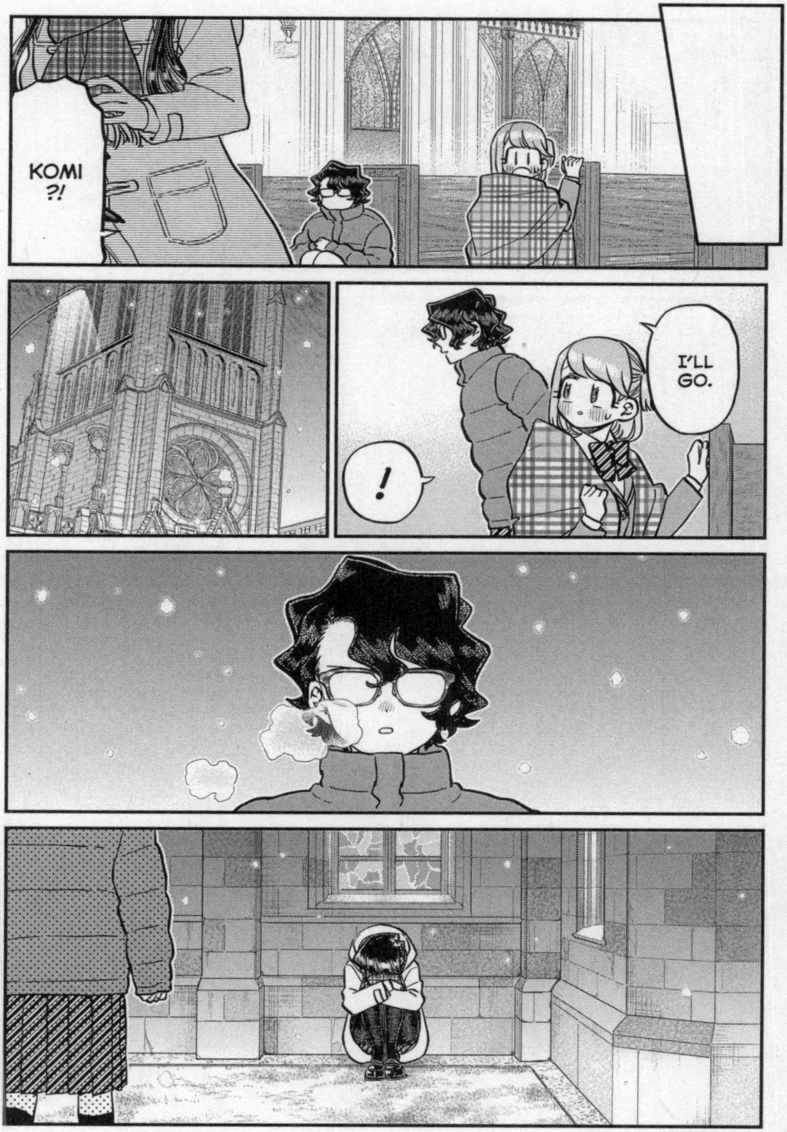
KOMI ?!
I'LL GO.
!

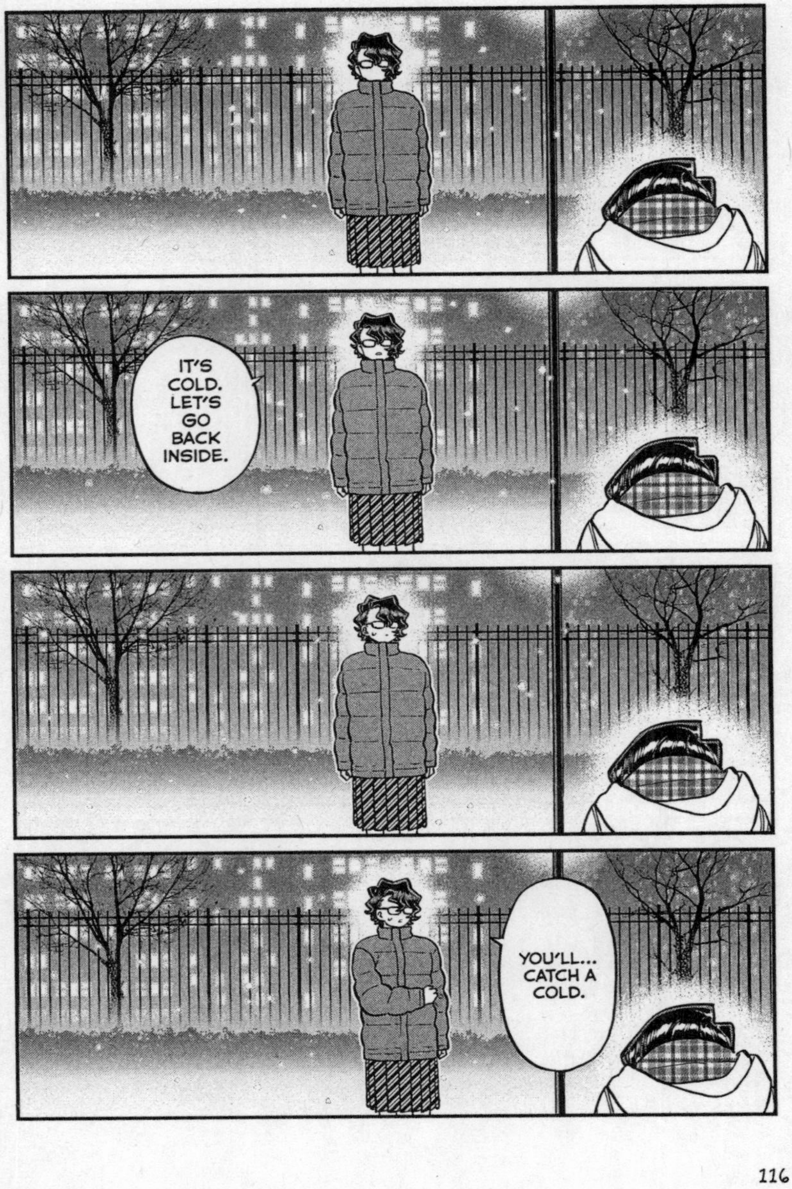
IT'S COLD. LET'S GO BACK INSIDE.
YOU'LL... CATCH A COLD.

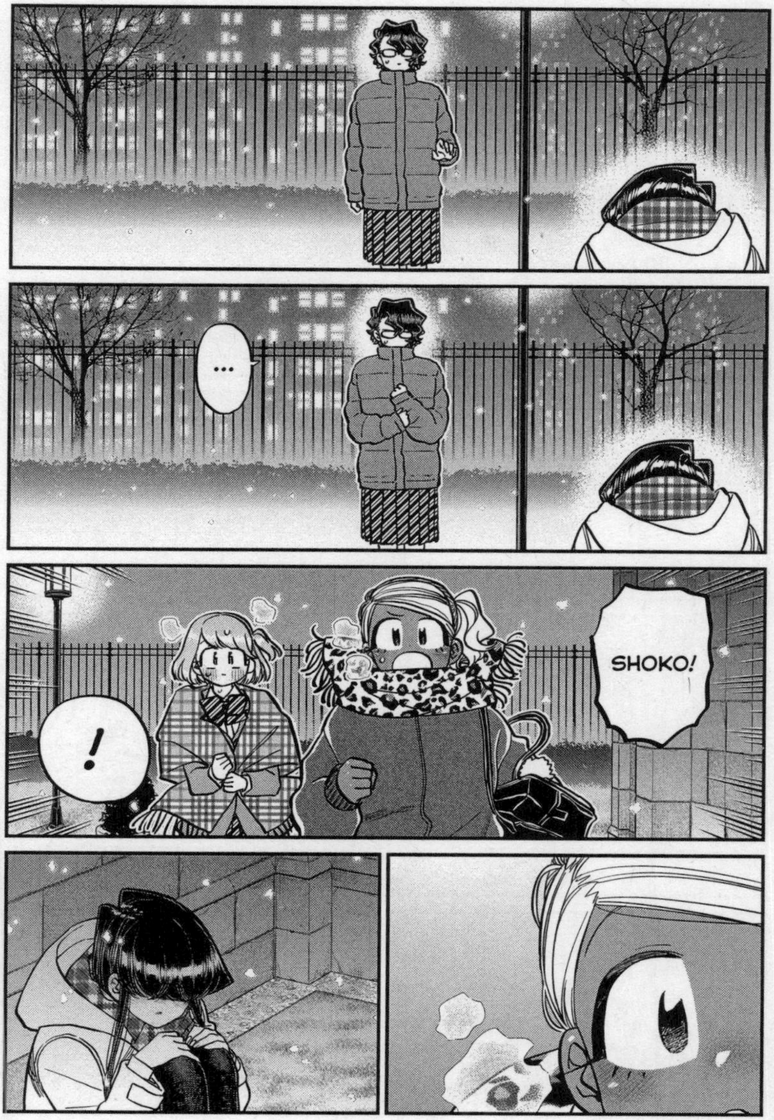
...
SHOKO!
!

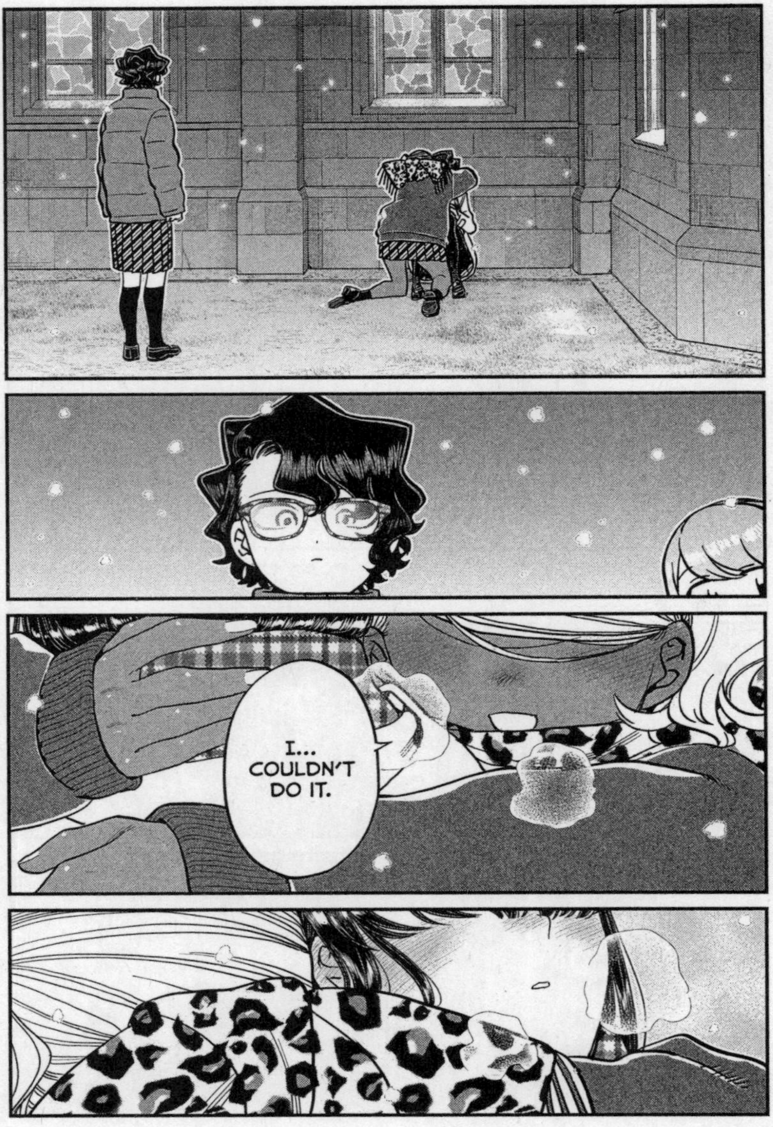
I... COULDN'T DO IT.

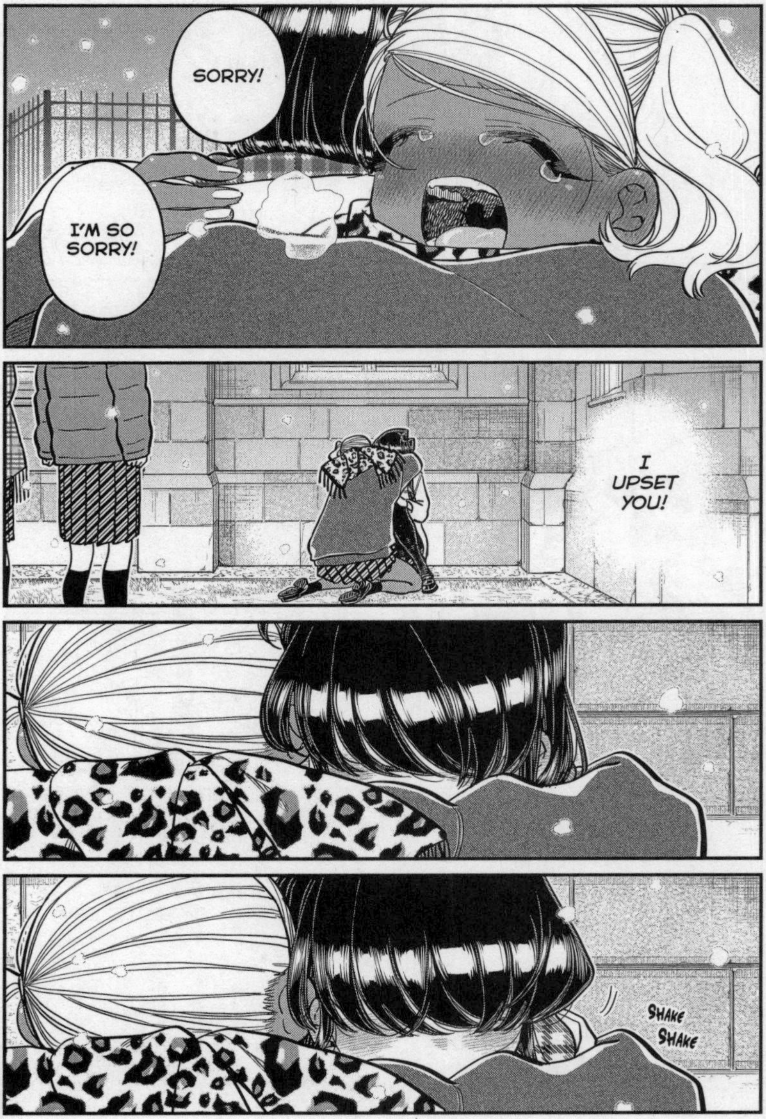
SORRY!
I'M SO SORRY!
I UPSET YOU!
SHAKE SHAKE

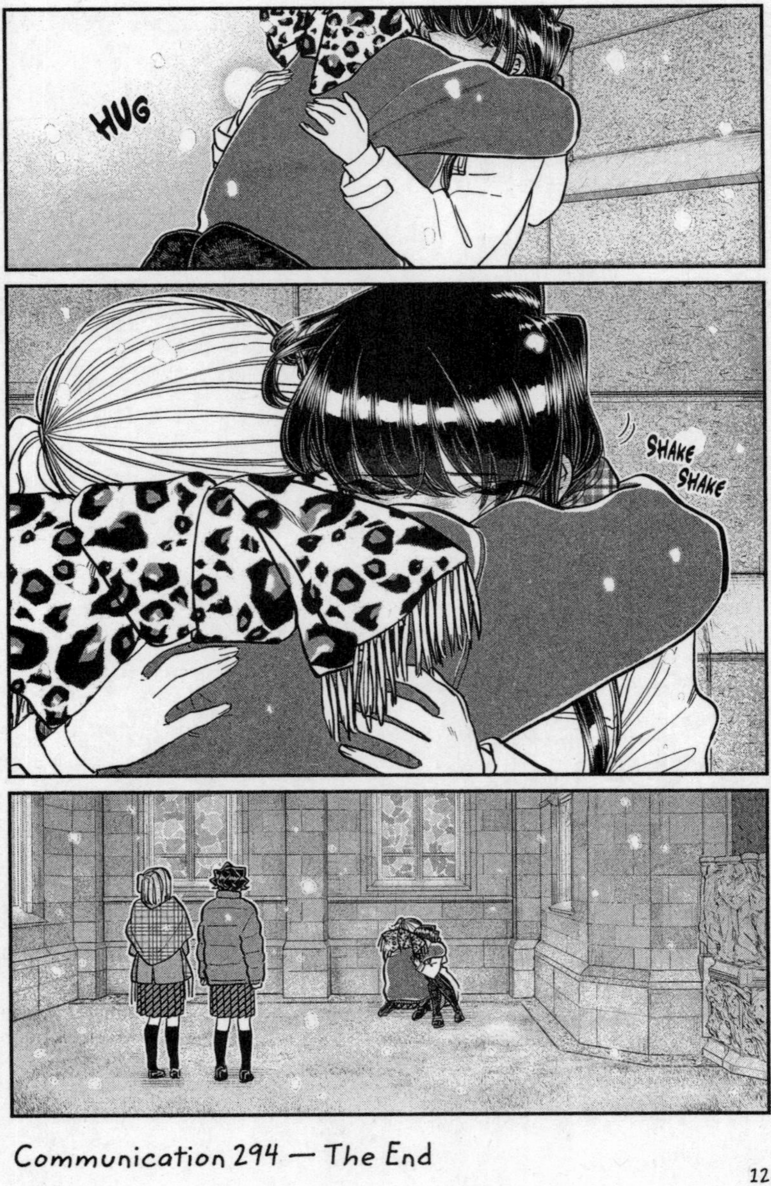
HUG
SHAKE SHAKE

Communication 294 — The End

Komi Can't Communicate

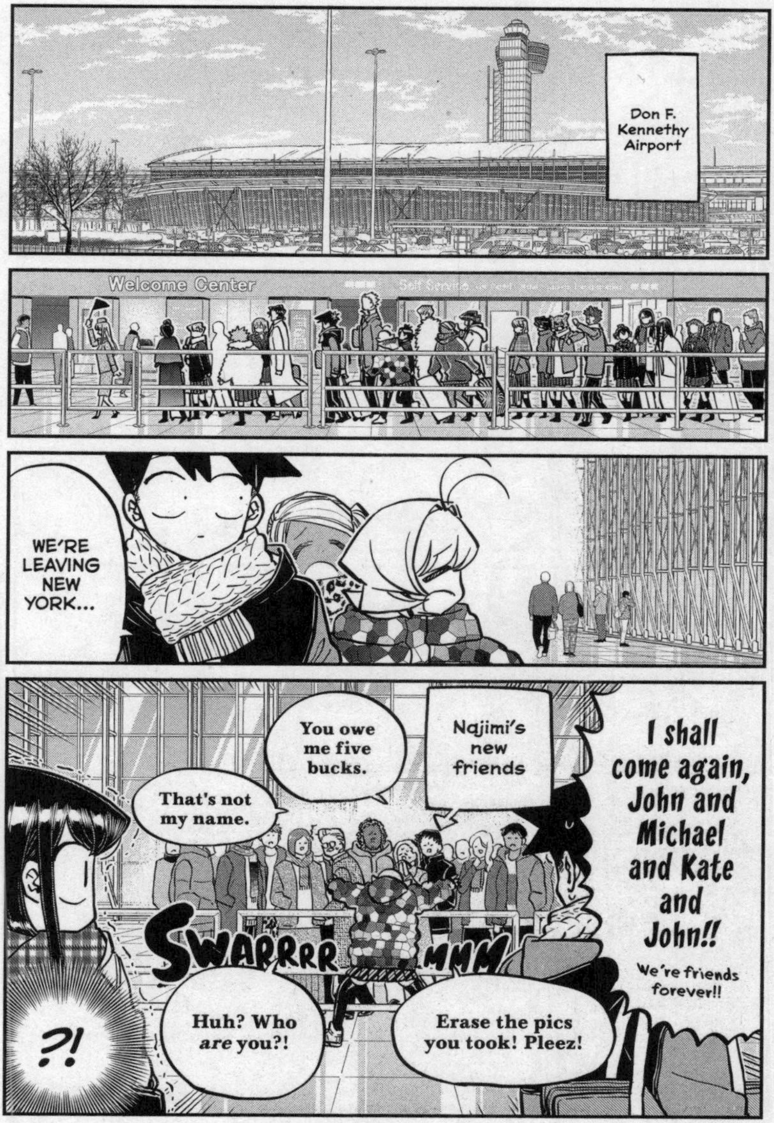
Don F. Kennethy Airport
Welcome Center
WE'RE LEAVING NEW YORK...
I shall come again, John and Michael and Kate and John!!
We're friends forever!!
Najimi's new friends
You owe me five bucks.
That's not my name.
SWARRRR MMM
Erase the pics you took! Pleez!
Huh? Who *are* you?!
?!

Communication 295: Returning Home

I gotta use the bath-room!

!

SPROING

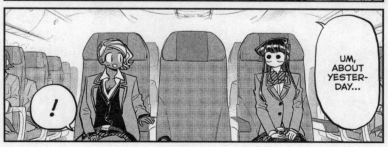

!

UM, ABOUT YESTER-DAY...

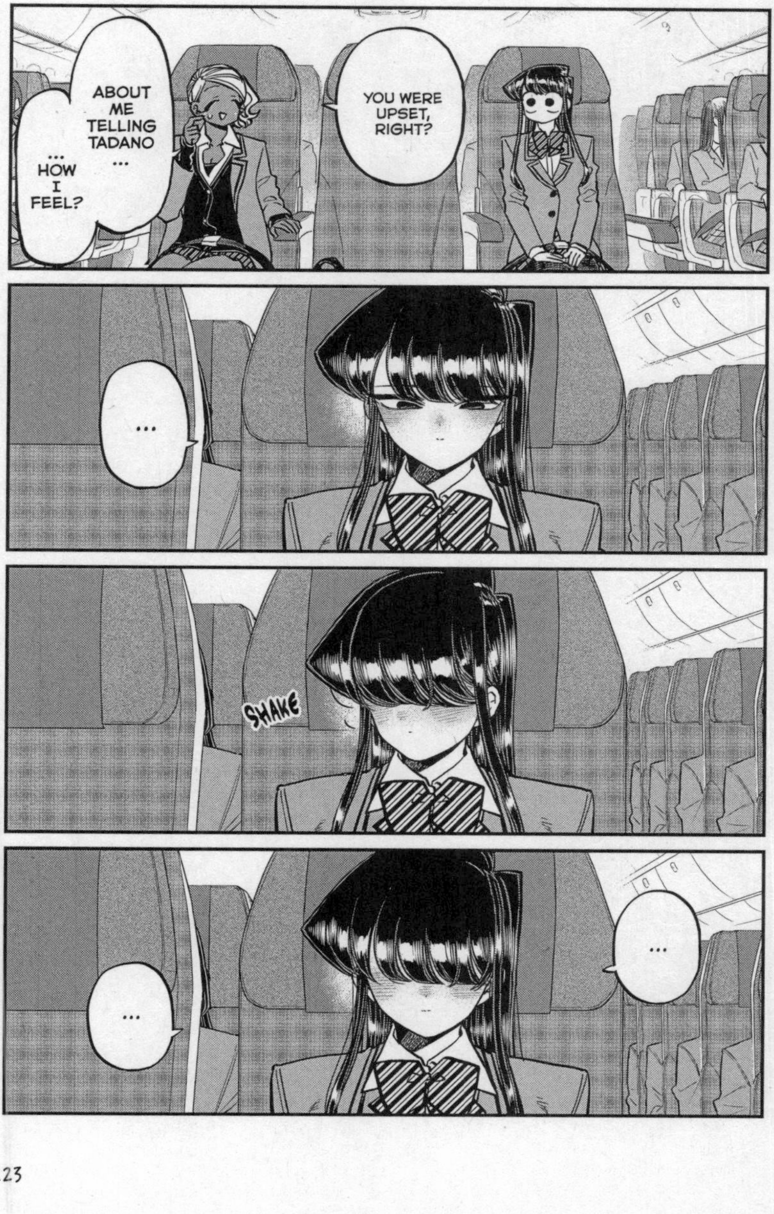
YOU WERE UPSET, RIGHT?
ABOUT ME TELLING TADANO ... ... HOW I FEEL?
...
SHAKE
...
...

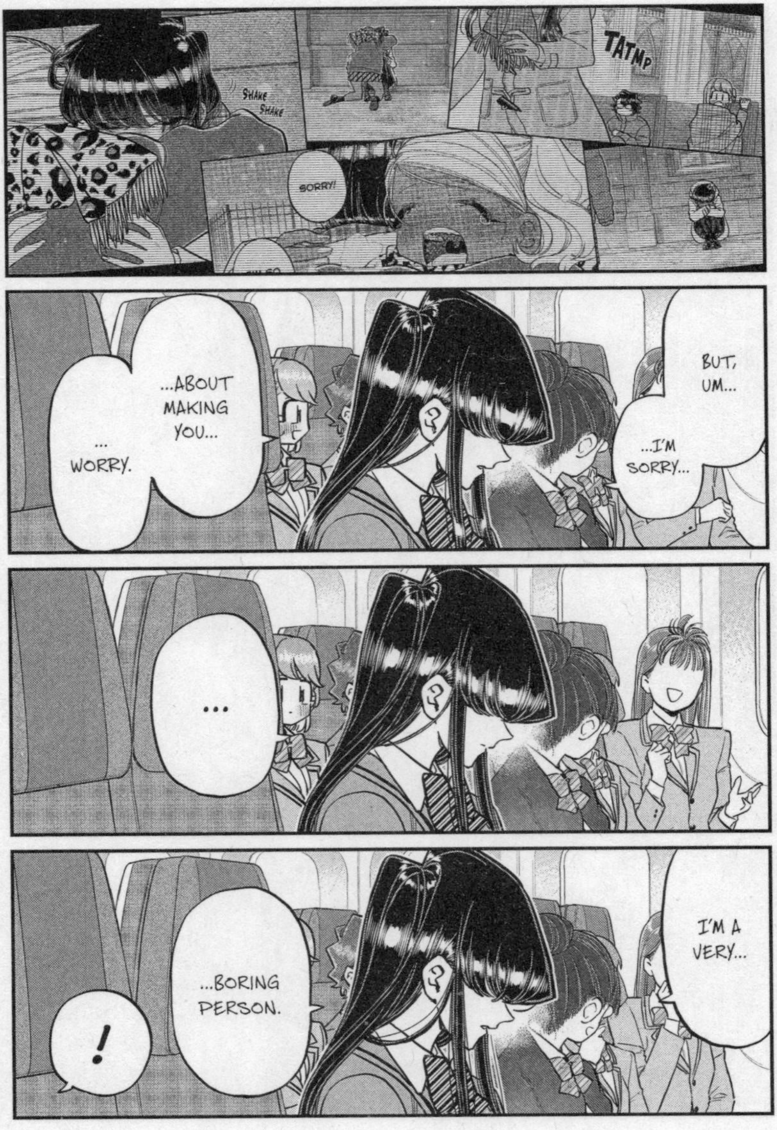
TATMP
SORRY!
SHAKE SHAKE
BUT, UM... ...I'M SORRY...
...ABOUT MAKING YOU...
... WORRY.
...
I'M A VERY...
...BORING PERSON.
!

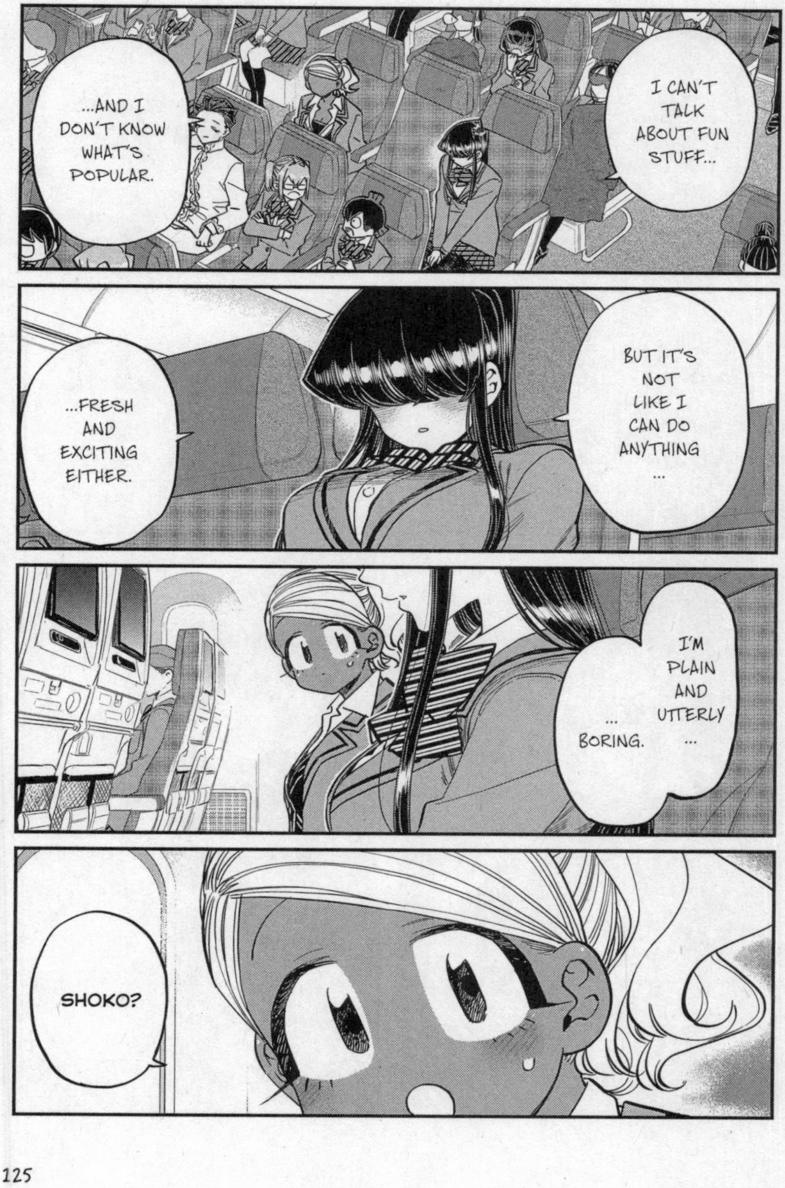
I CAN'T TALK ABOUT FUN STUFF...
...AND I DON'T KNOW WHAT'S POPULAR.
BUT IT'S NOT LIKE I CAN DO ANYTHING ...
...FRESH AND EXCITING EITHER.
I'M PLAIN AND UTTERLY ... ... BORING.
SHOKO?

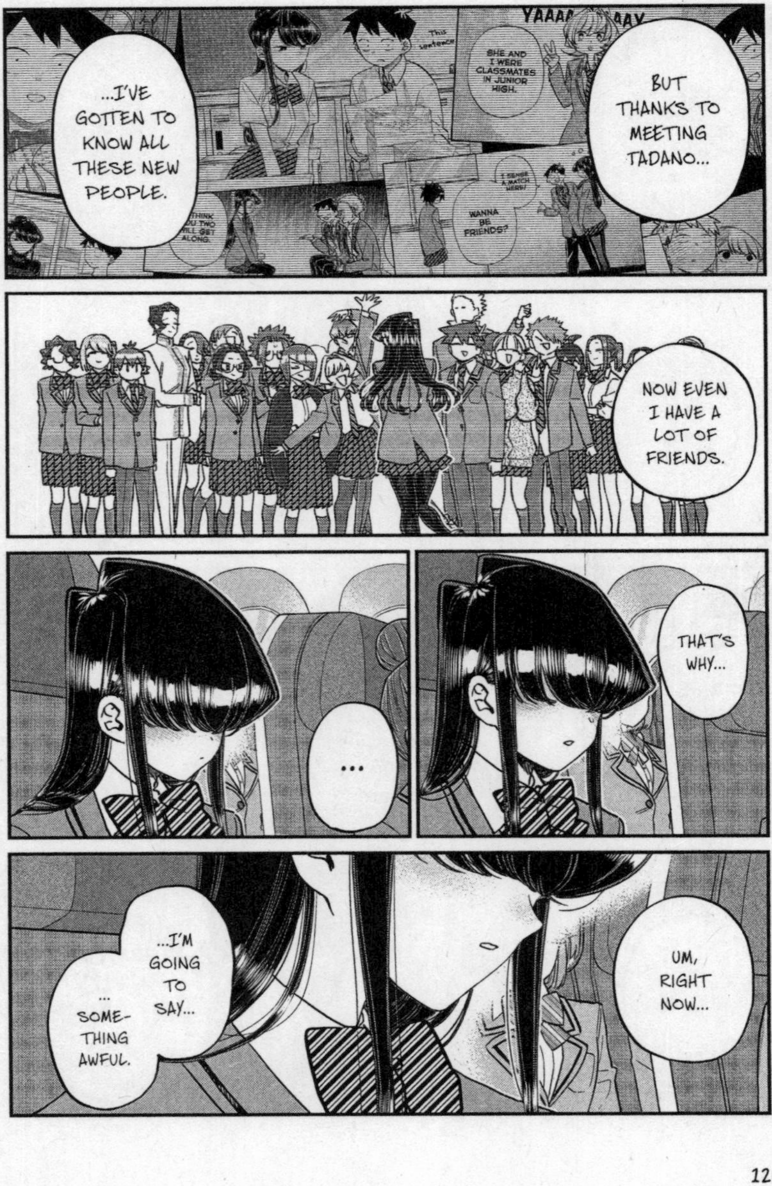
BUT THANKS TO MEETING TADANO...
SHE AND I WERE CLASSMATES IN JUNIOR HIGH.
I SENSE A MATCH HERE!
WANNA BE FRIENDS?
This sentence
...I'VE GOTTEN TO KNOW ALL THESE NEW PEOPLE.
NOW EVEN I HAVE A LOT OF FRIENDS.
THAT'S WHY...
...
UM, RIGHT NOW...
...I'M GOING TO SAY...
... SOME-THING AWFUL.

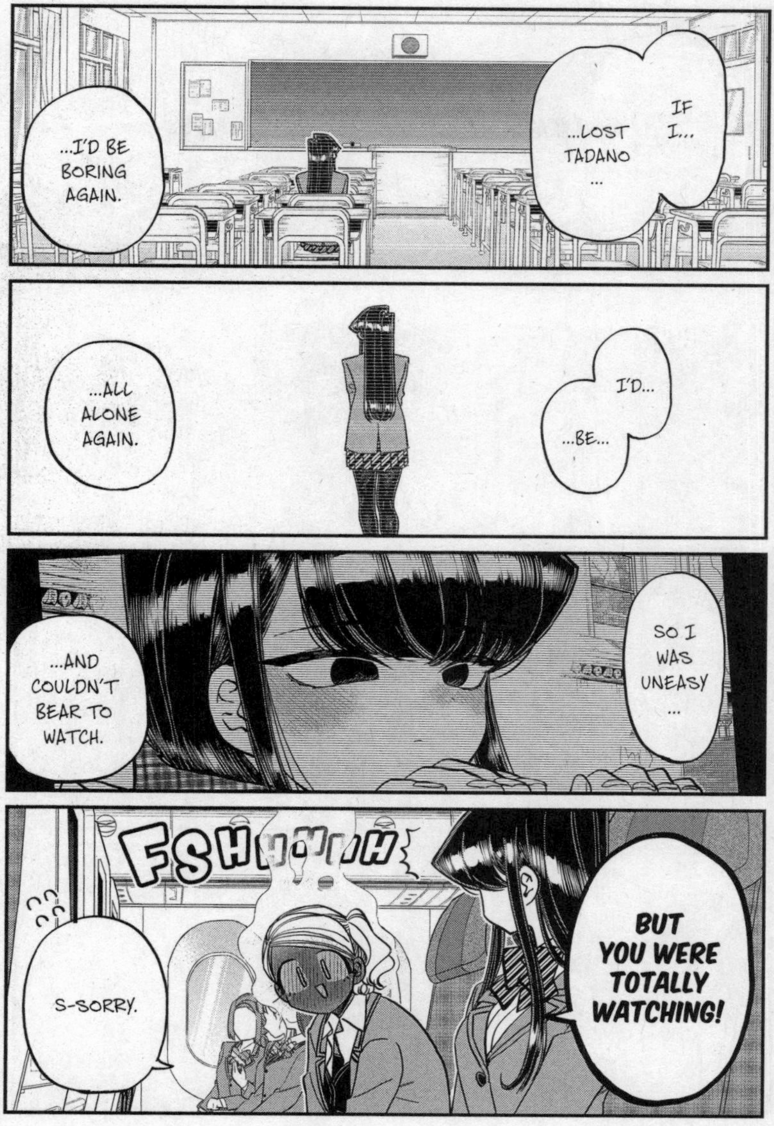
IF I...
...LOST TADANO ...
...I'D BE BORING AGAIN.
I'D...
...BE...
...ALL ALONE AGAIN.
SO I WAS UNEASY ...
...AND COULDN'T BEAR TO WATCH.
BUT YOU WERE TOTALLY WATCHING!
FSHHHHHH
S-SORRY.

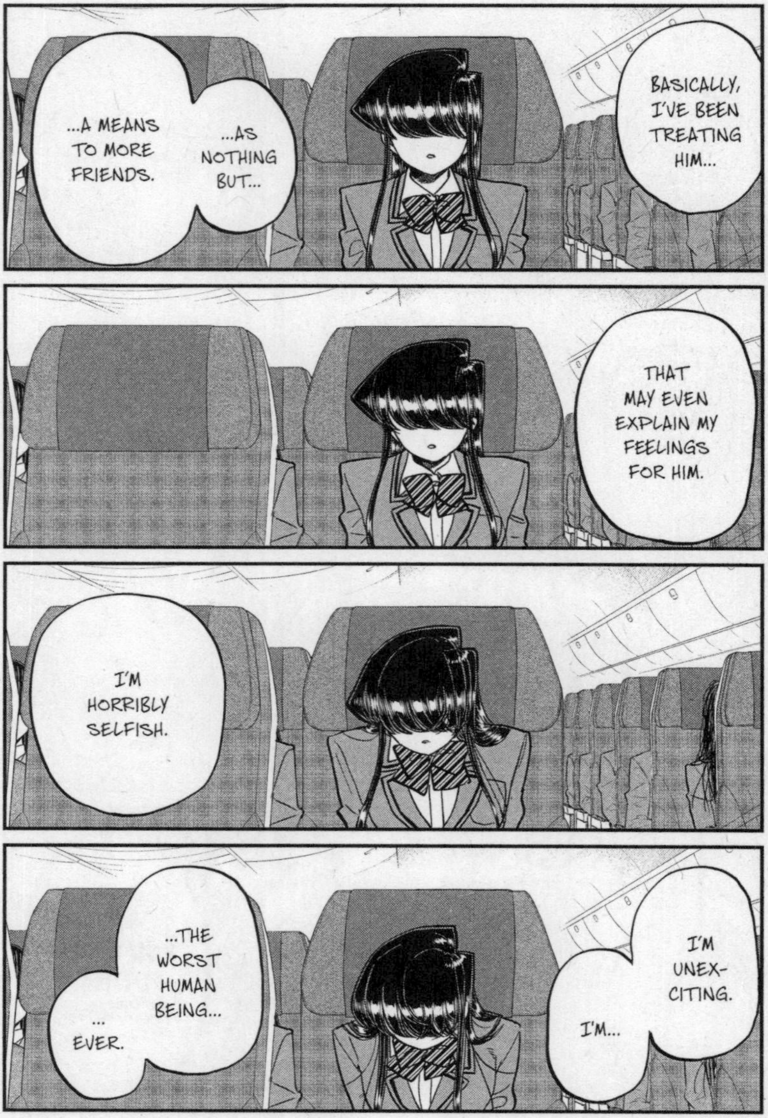
BASICALLY, I'VE BEEN TREATING HIM...
...AS NOTHING BUT...
...A MEANS TO MORE FRIENDS.
THAT MAY EVEN EXPLAIN MY FEELINGS FOR HIM.
I'M HORRIBLY SELFISH.
I'M UNEXCITING.
I'M...
...THE WORST HUMAN BEING...
...EVER.

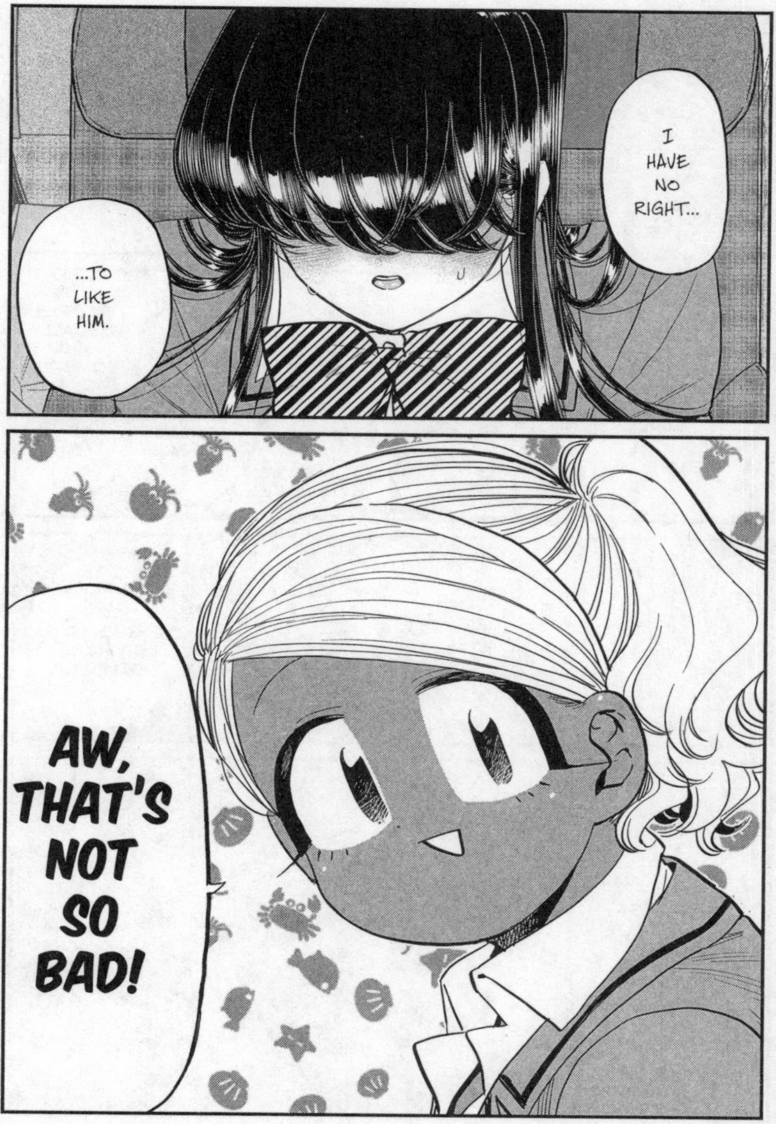
I HAVE NO RIGHT...
...TO LIKE HIM.
AW, THAT'S NOT SO BAD!

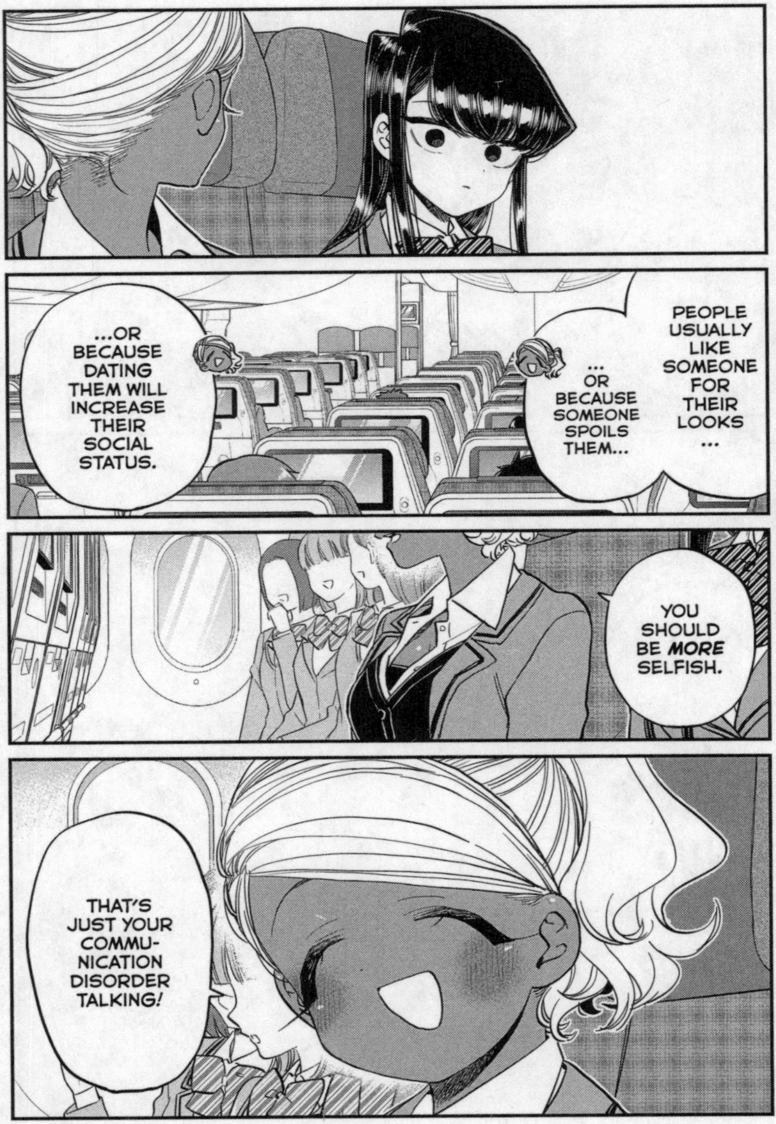
PEOPLE USUALLY LIKE SOMEONE FOR THEIR LOOKS ...
... OR BECAUSE SOMEONE SPOILS THEM...
...OR BECAUSE DATING THEM WILL INCREASE THEIR SOCIAL STATUS.
YOU SHOULD BE *MORE* SELFISH.
THAT'S JUST YOUR COMMU-NICATION DISORDER TALKING!

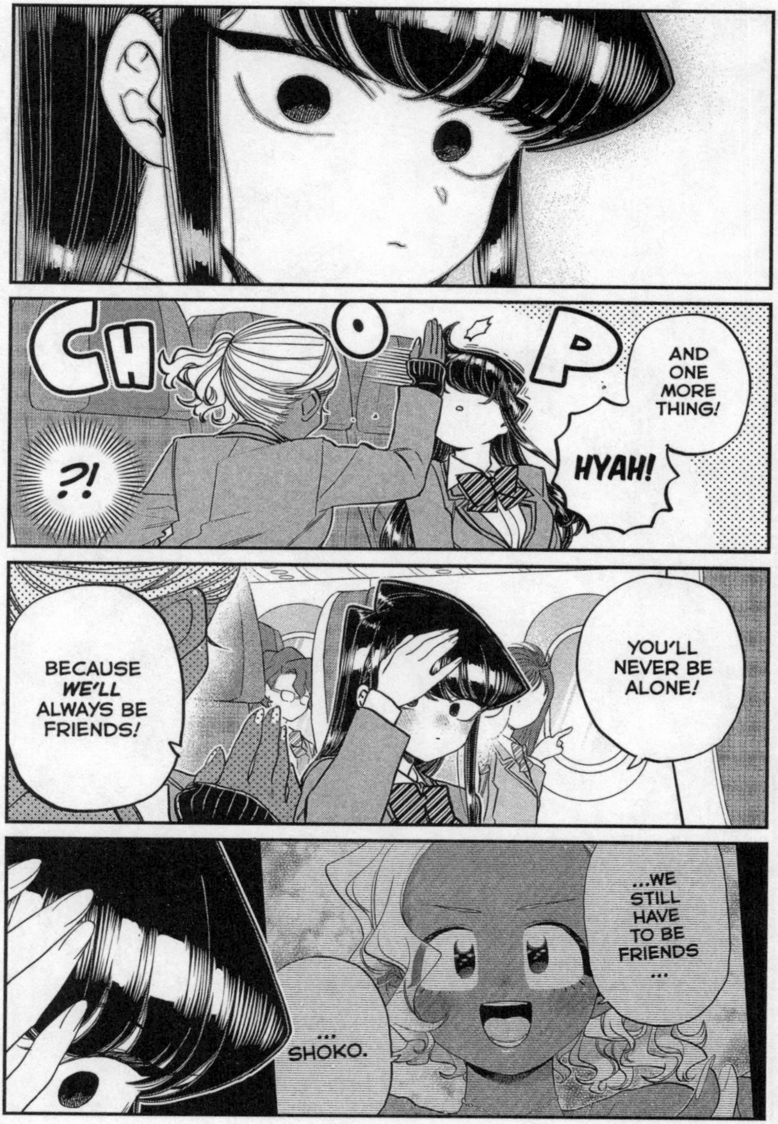
AND ONE MORE THING!
HYAH!
CHOP
?!
YOU'LL NEVER BE ALONE!
BECAUSE *WE'LL* ALWAYS BE FRIENDS!
...WE STILL HAVE TO BE FRIENDS ...
... SHOKO.

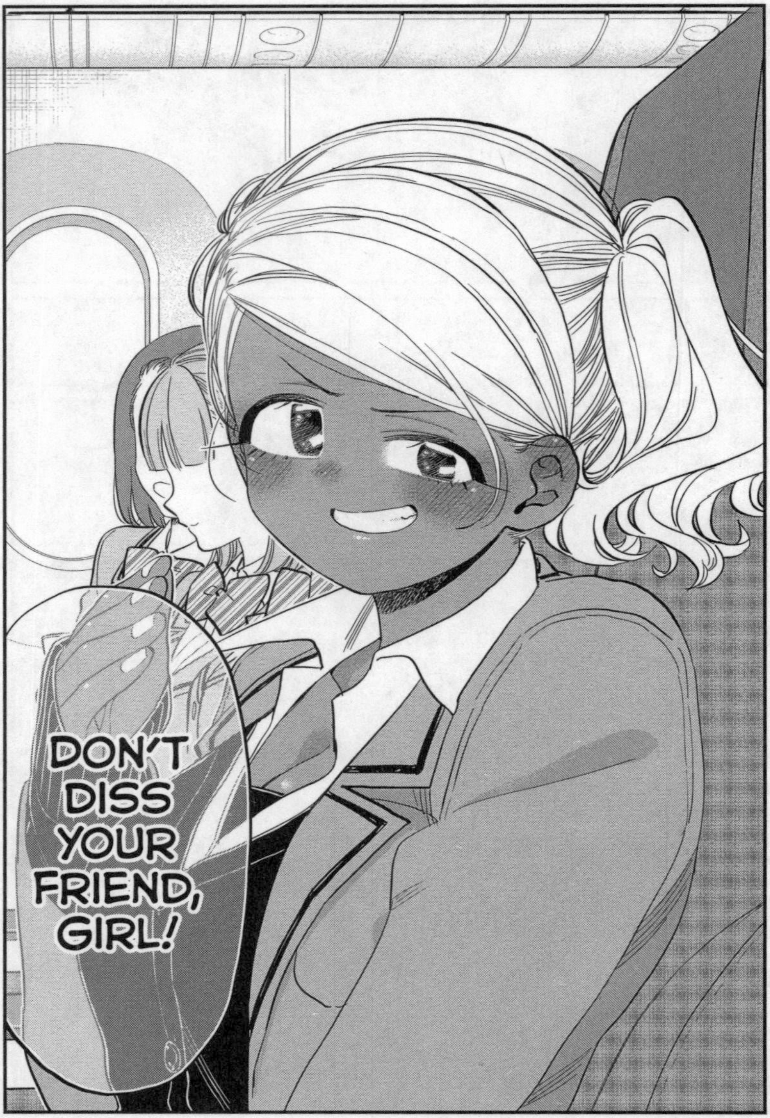
DON'T DISS YOUR FRIEND, GIRL!

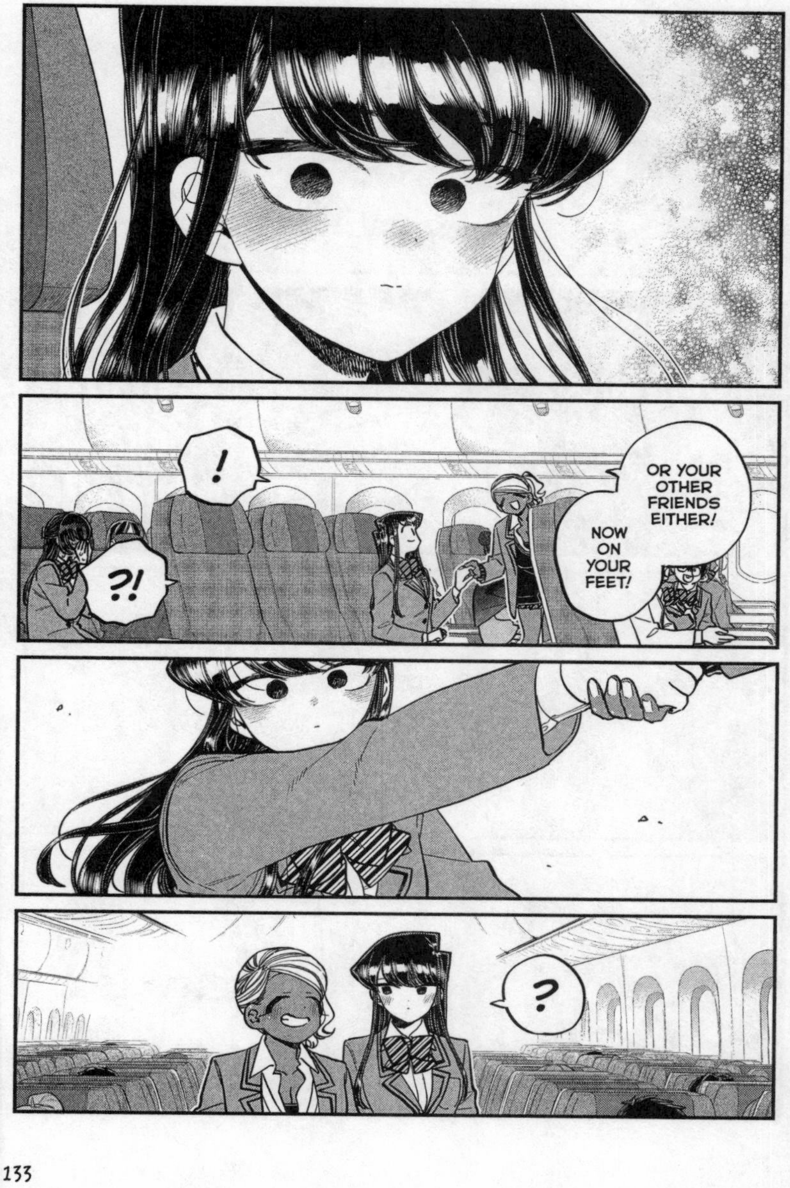
OR YOUR OTHER FRIENDS EITHER!
NOW ON YOUR FEET!
!
?!
?

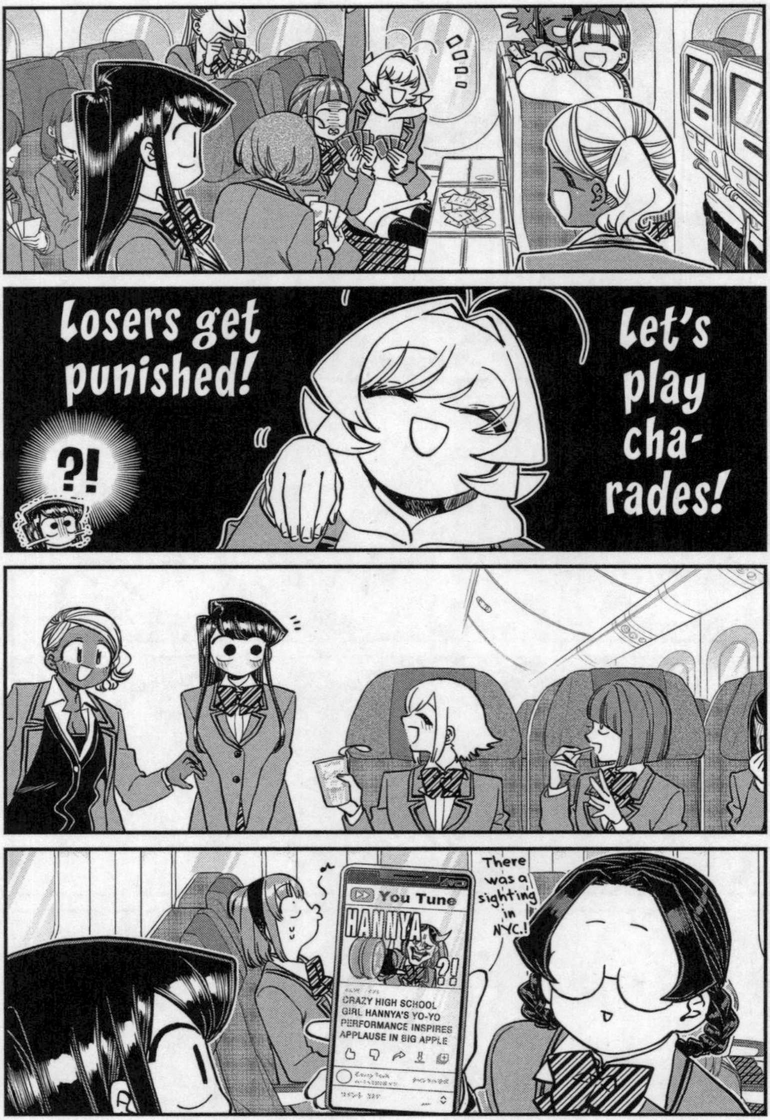
Let's play charades!
Losers get punished!
?!
There was a sighting in NYC!
You Tune
HANNYA
?!
CRAZY HIGH SCHOOL GIRL HANNYA'S YO-YO PERFORMANCE INSPIRES APPLAUSE IN BIG APPLE

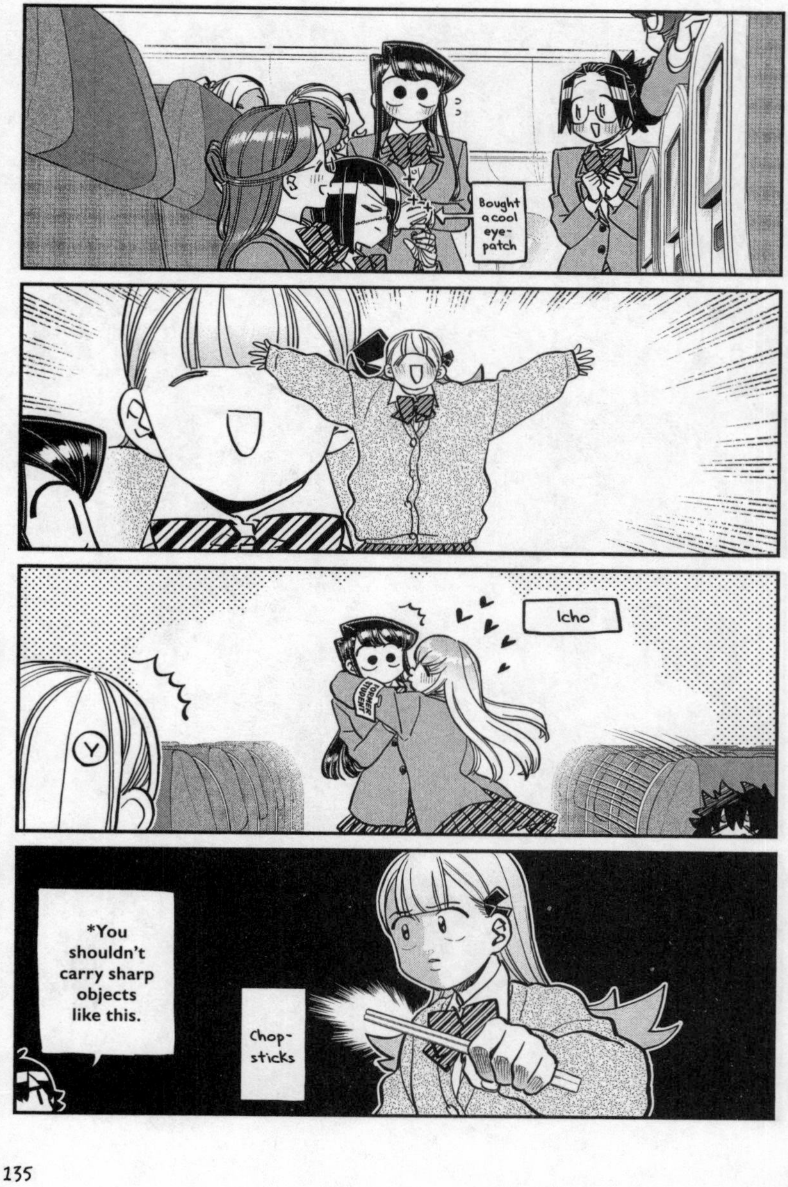
Bought a cool eye-patch
Icho
*You shouldn't carry sharp objects like this.
Chop-sticks

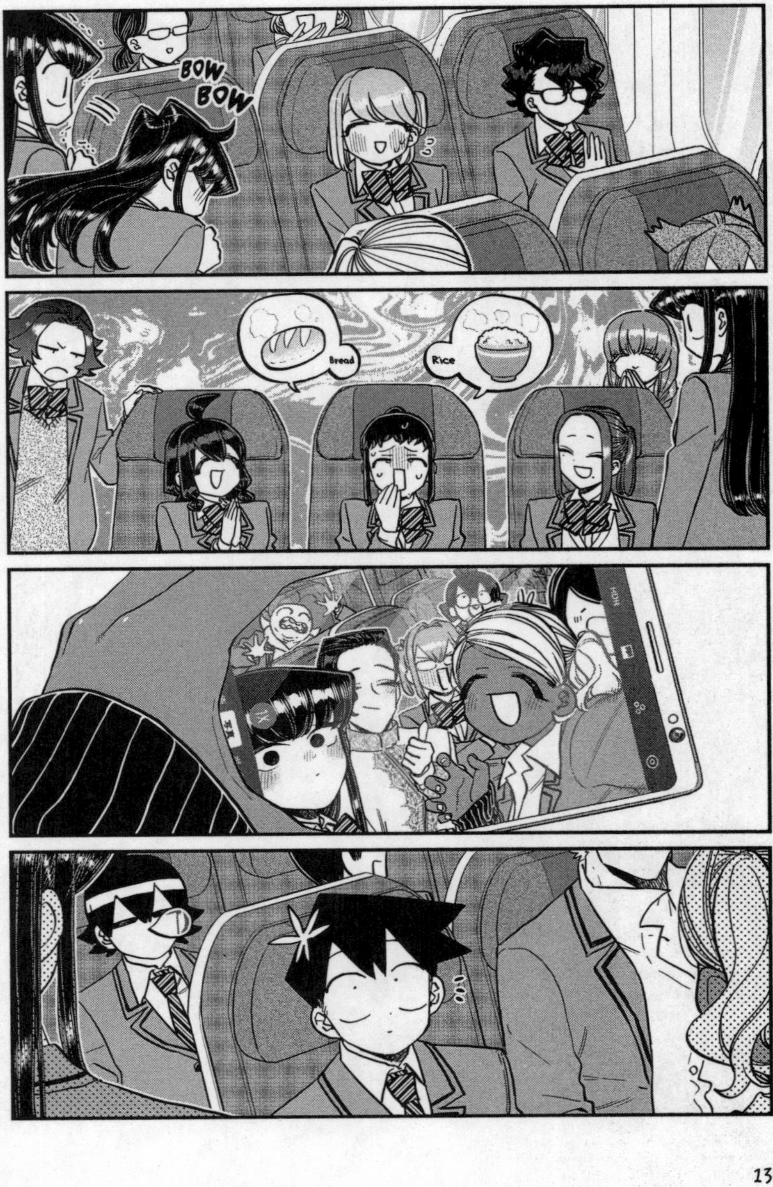
BOW
BOW
Rice
Bread

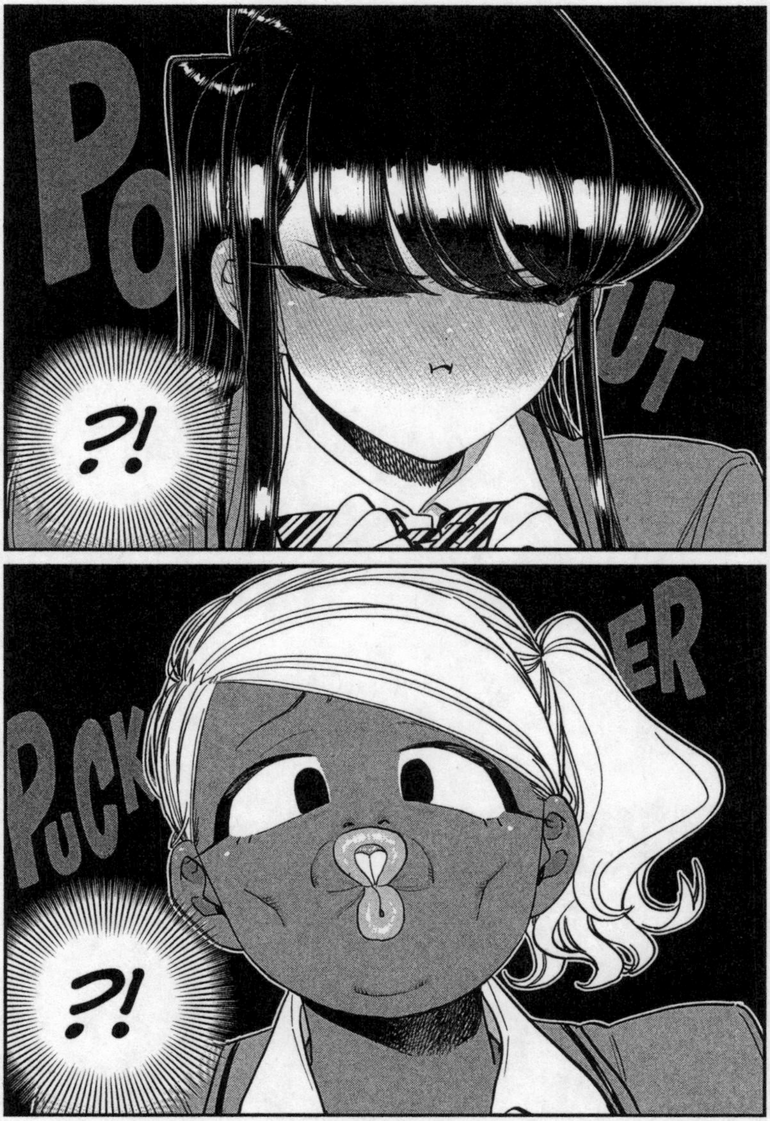
POUT
?!
PUCKER
?!

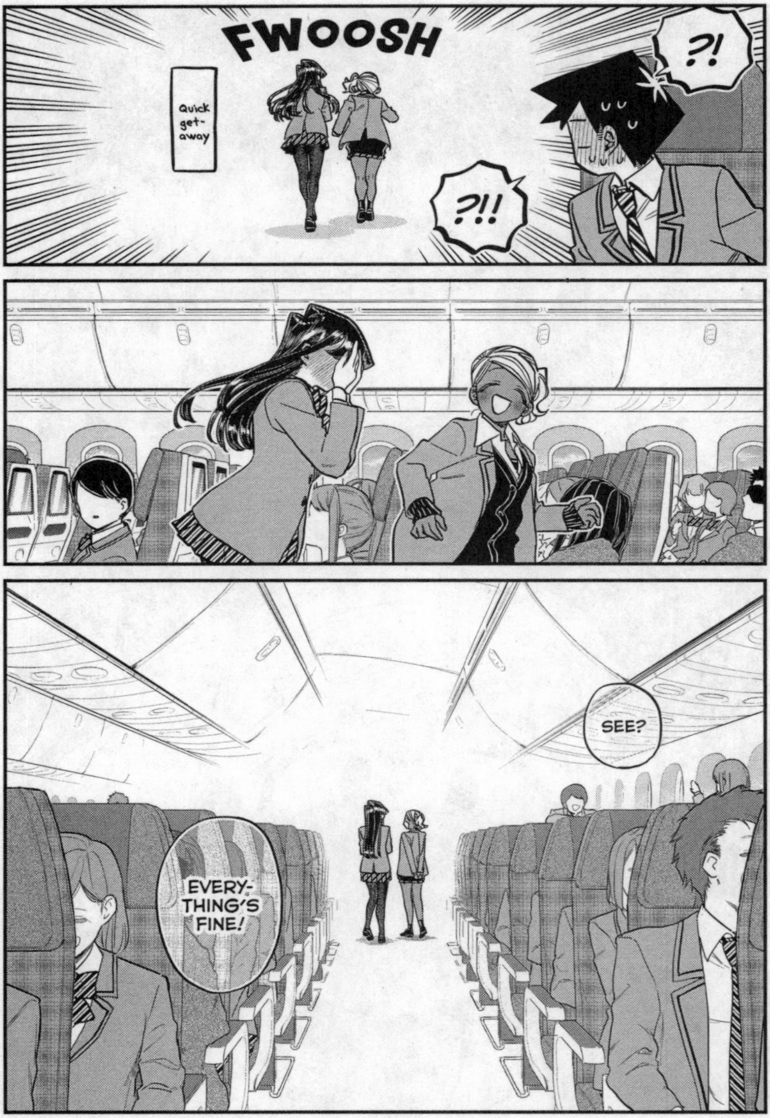
?!
FWOOSH
?!!
Quick get-away
SEE?
EVERY-THING'S FINE!

Communication 295 — The End

Totoi Interrupts a Serious Mood

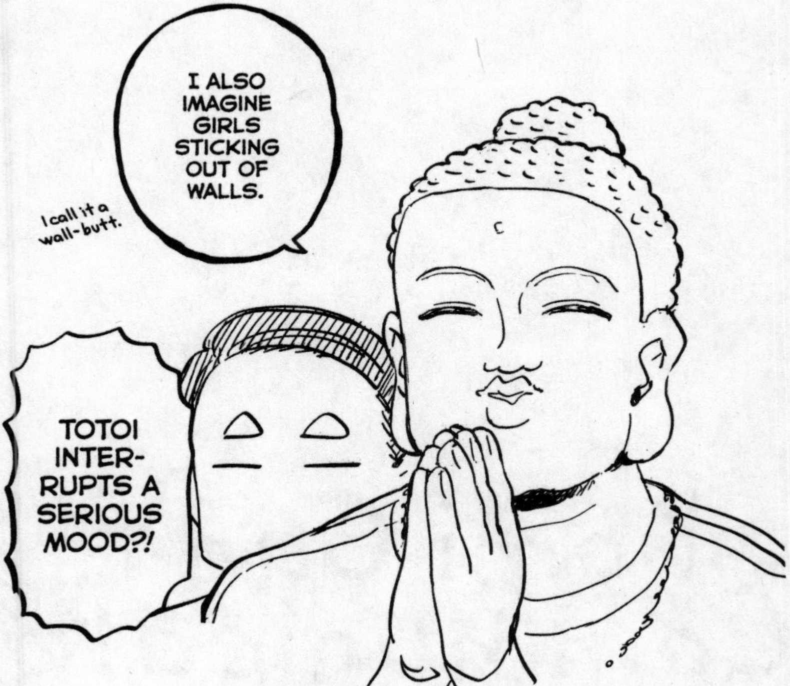
I ALSO IMAGINE GIRLS STICKING OUT OF WALLS.
I call it a wall-butt.
TOTOI INTER-RUPTS A SERIOUS MOOD?!

Komi Can't
Communicate

Komi Can't Communicate

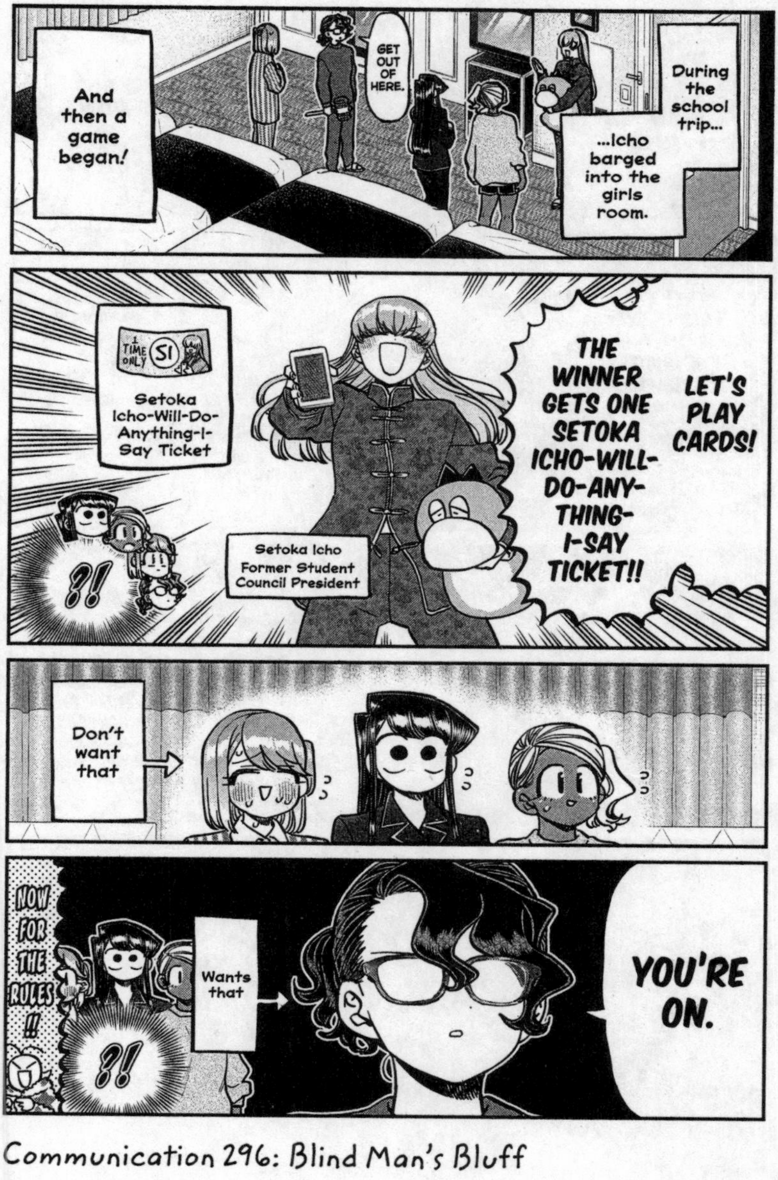
During the school trip...
...Icho barged into the girls room.
GET OUT OF HERE.
And then a game began!
LET'S PLAY CARDS!
THE WINNER GETS ONE SETOKA ICHO-WILL-DO-ANYTHING-I-SAY TICKET!!
Setoka Icho Former Student Council President
1 TIME ONLY SI
Setoka Icho-Will-Do-Anything-I-Say Ticket
?!
Don't want that
YOU'RE ON.
Wants that
?!
NOW FOR THE RULES!!

Communication 296: Blind Man's Bluff

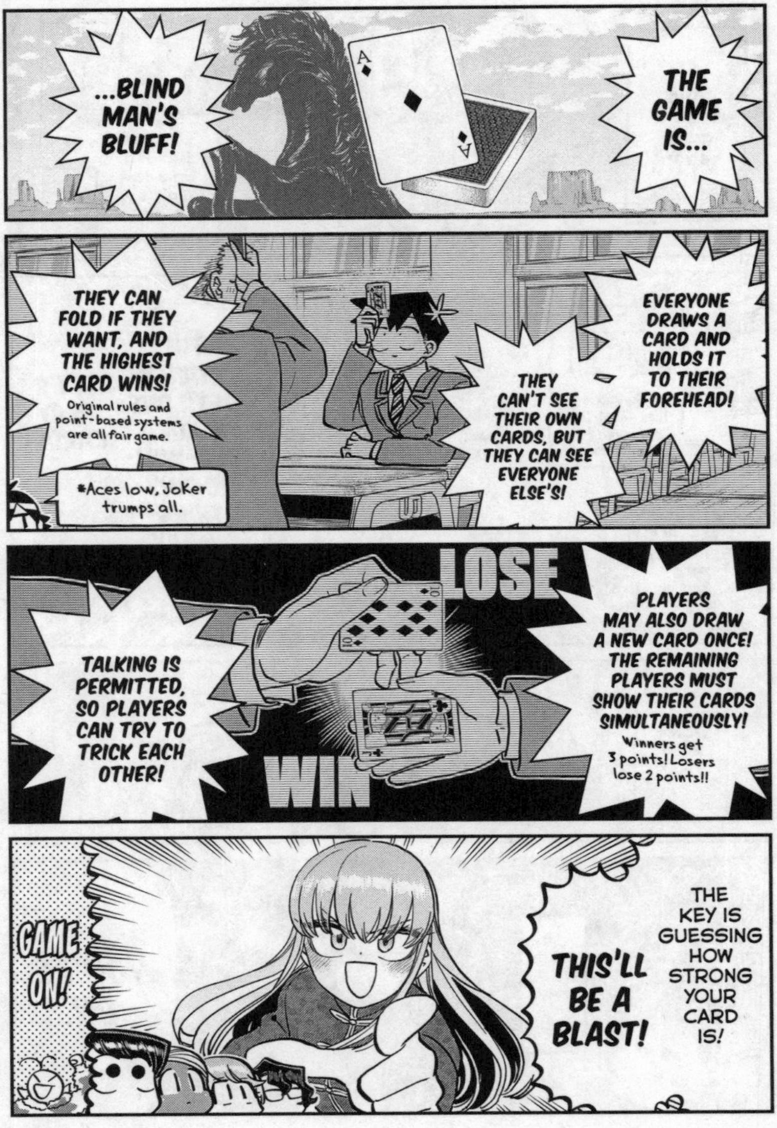
THE GAME IS...
...BLIND MAN'S BLUFF!
EVERYONE DRAWS A CARD AND HOLDS IT TO THEIR FOREHEAD!
THEY CAN'T SEE THEIR OWN CARDS, BUT THEY CAN SEE EVERYONE ELSE'S!
THEY CAN FOLD IF THEY WANT, AND THE HIGHEST CARD WINS!
Original rules and point-based systems are all fair game.
*Aces low, Joker trumps all.
LOSE
PLAYERS MAY ALSO DRAW A NEW CARD ONCE! THE REMAINING PLAYERS MUST SHOW THEIR CARDS SIMULTANEOUSLY!
Winners get 3 points! Losers lose 2 points!!
TALKING IS PERMITTED, SO PLAYERS CAN TRY TO TRICK EACH OTHER!
WIN
THE KEY IS GUESSING HOW STRONG YOUR CARD IS!
THIS'LL BE A BLAST!
GAME ON!

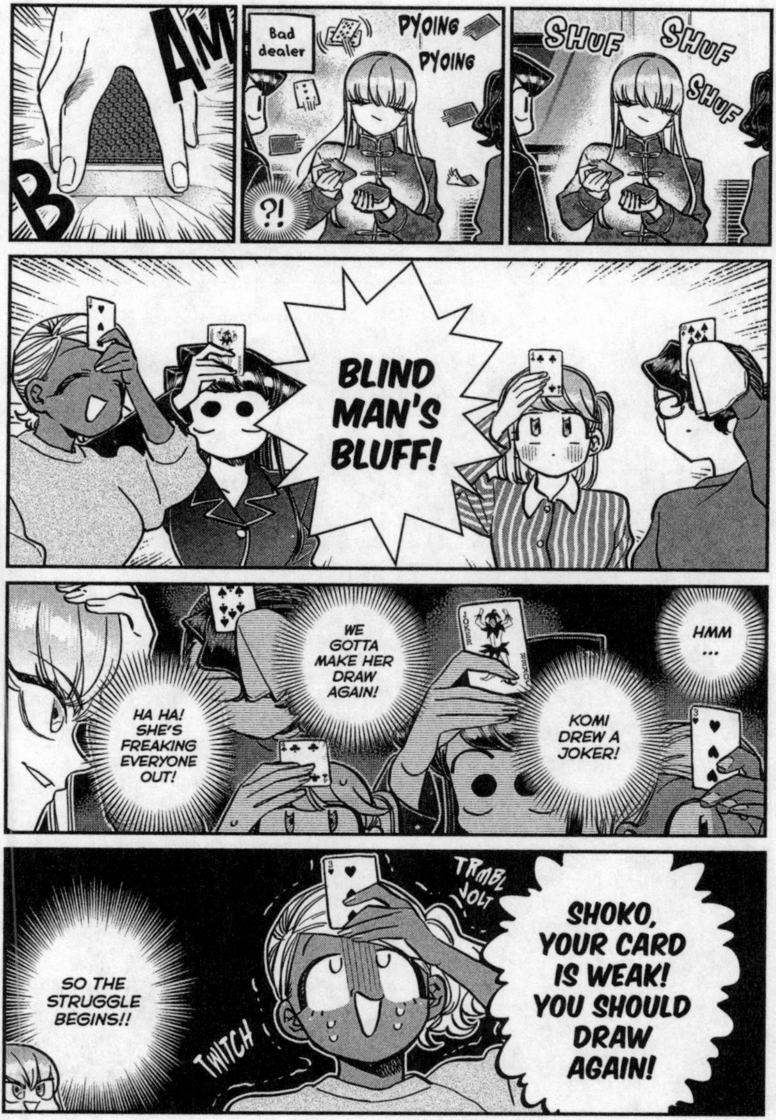
SHUF
SHUF
SHUF
PYOING
PYOING
Bad dealer
?!
BAM
BLIND MAN'S BLUFF!
HMM ...
WE GOTTA MAKE HER DRAW AGAIN!
KOMI DREW A JOKER!
HA HA! SHE'S FREAKING EVERYONE OUT!
TRMBL
JOLT
SHOKO, YOUR CARD IS WEAK! YOU SHOULD DRAW AGAIN!
TWITCH
SO THE STRUGGLE BEGINS!!

*Read vertically.

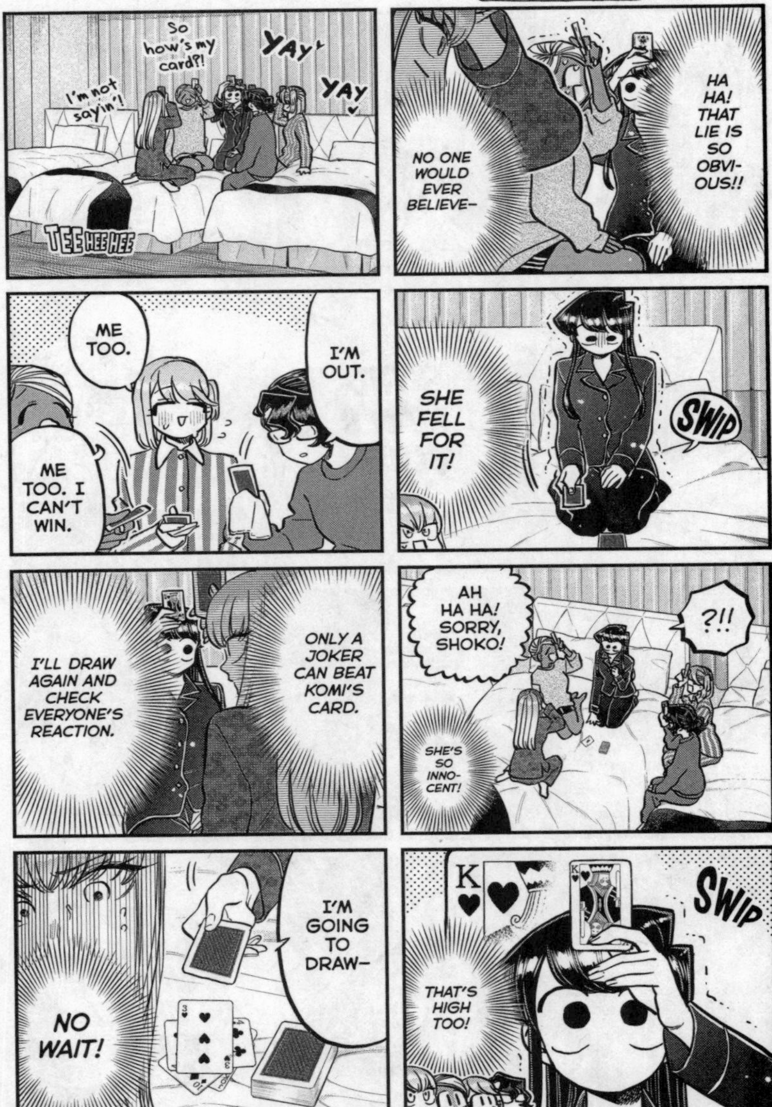
HA HA! THAT LIE IS SO OBVIOUS!!
NO ONE WOULD EVER BELIEVE—
SWIP
SHE FELL FOR IT!
?!!
AH HA HA! SORRY, SHOKO!
SHE'S SO INNOCENT!
SWIP
K
THAT'S HIGH TOO!
YAY
YAY
So how's my card?!
I'm not sayin'!
TEE HEE HEE
I'M OUT.
ME TOO.
ME TOO. I CAN'T WIN.
ONLY A JOKER CAN BEAT KOMI'S CARD.
I'LL DRAW AGAIN AND CHECK EVERYONE'S REACTION.
I'M GOING TO DRAW—
NO WAIT!

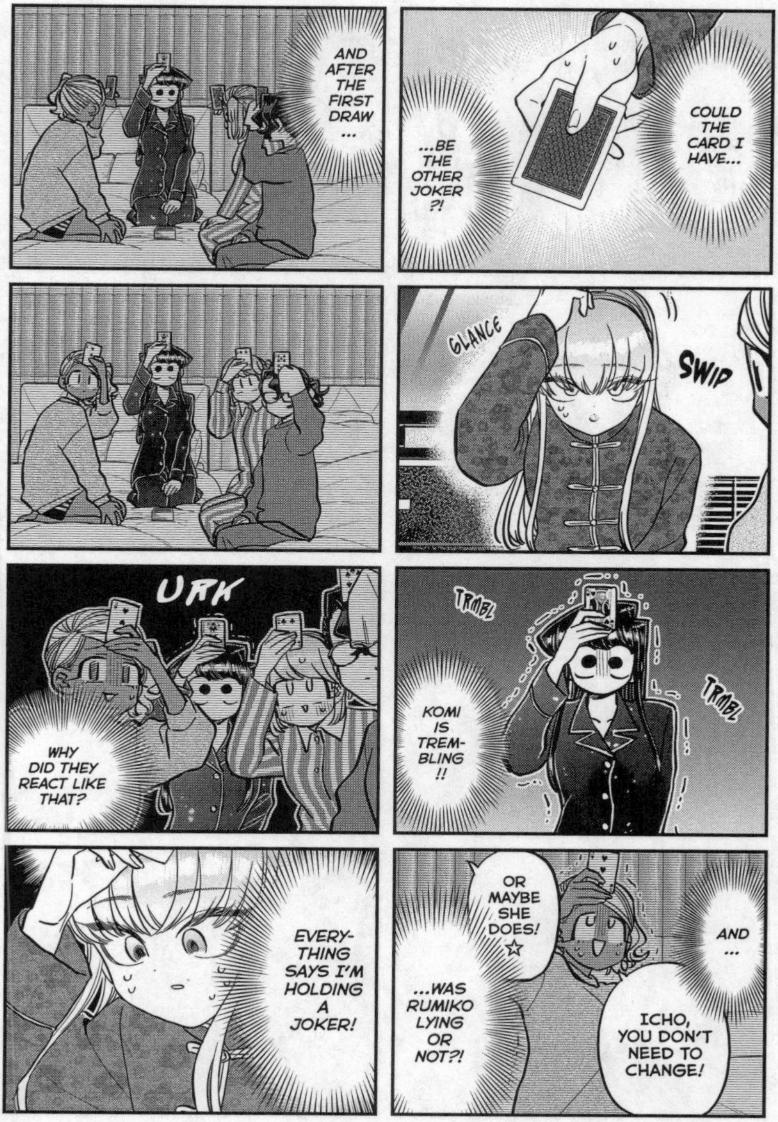
COULD THE CARD I HAVE...
...BE THE OTHER JOKER?!
AND AFTER THE FIRST DRAW...
SWIP
GLANCE
TRMBL
TRMBL
KOMI IS TREMBLING!!
URK
WHY DID THEY REACT LIKE THAT?
AND...
ICHO, YOU DON'T NEED TO CHANGE!
OR MAYBE SHE DOES! ☆
...WAS RUMIKO LYING OR NOT?!
EVERYTHING SAYS I'M HOLDING A JOKER!

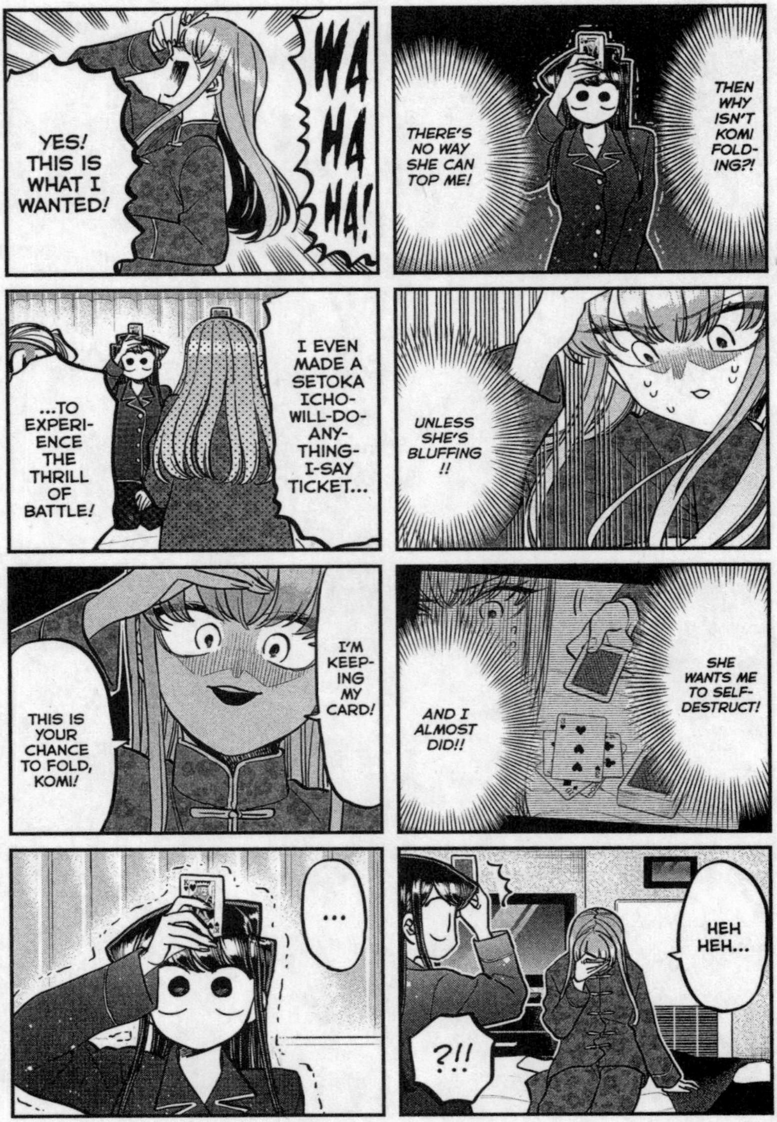
THEN WHY ISN'T KOMI FOLDING?!
THERE'S NO WAY SHE CAN TOP ME!
WAHAHA!
YES! THIS IS WHAT I WANTED!
UNLESS SHE'S BLUFFING!!
I EVEN MADE A SETOKA ICHO-WILL-DO-ANYTHING-I-SAY TICKET...
...TO EXPERIENCE THE THRILL OF BATTLE!
SHE WANTS ME TO SELF-DESTRUCT!
AND I ALMOST DID!!
I'M KEEPING MY CARD!
THIS IS YOUR CHANCE TO FOLD, KOMI!
HEH HEH...
?!!
...

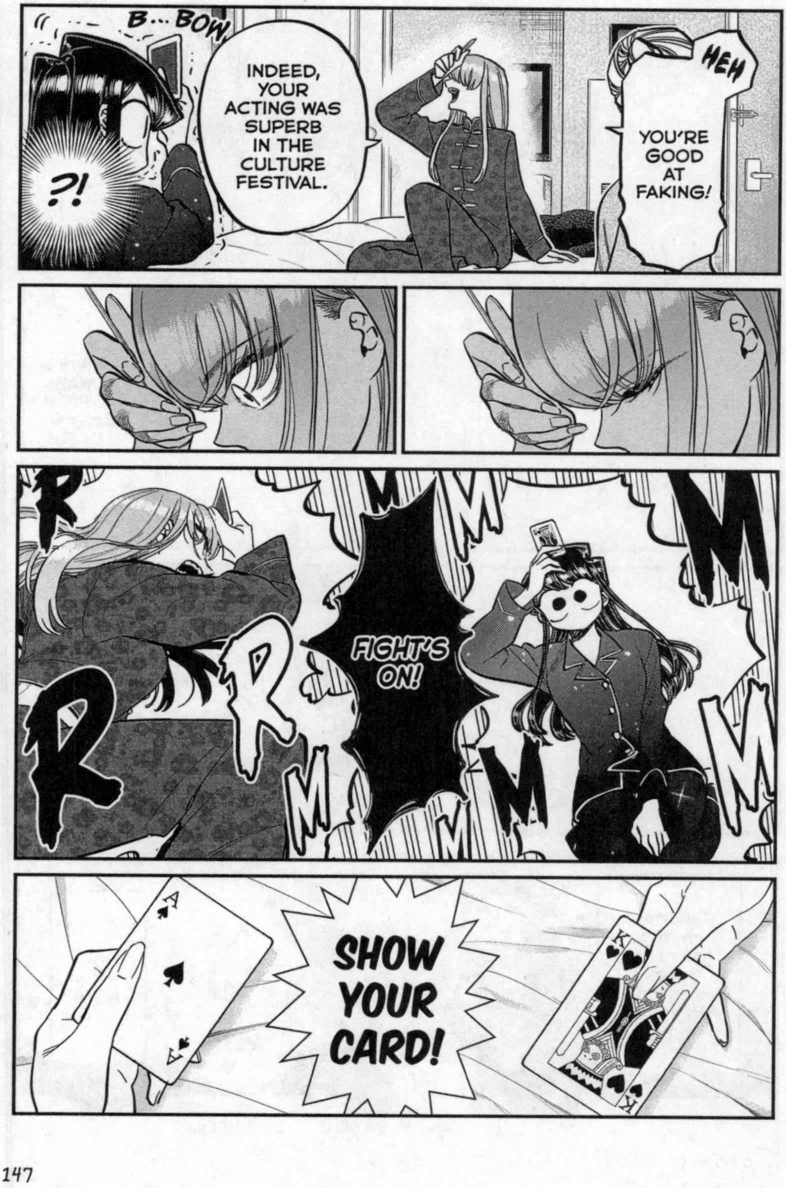
HEH
YOU'RE GOOD AT FAKING!
INDEED, YOUR ACTING WAS SUPERB IN THE CULTURE FESTIVAL.
B... BOW
?!
FIGHT'S ON!
SHOW YOUR CARD!

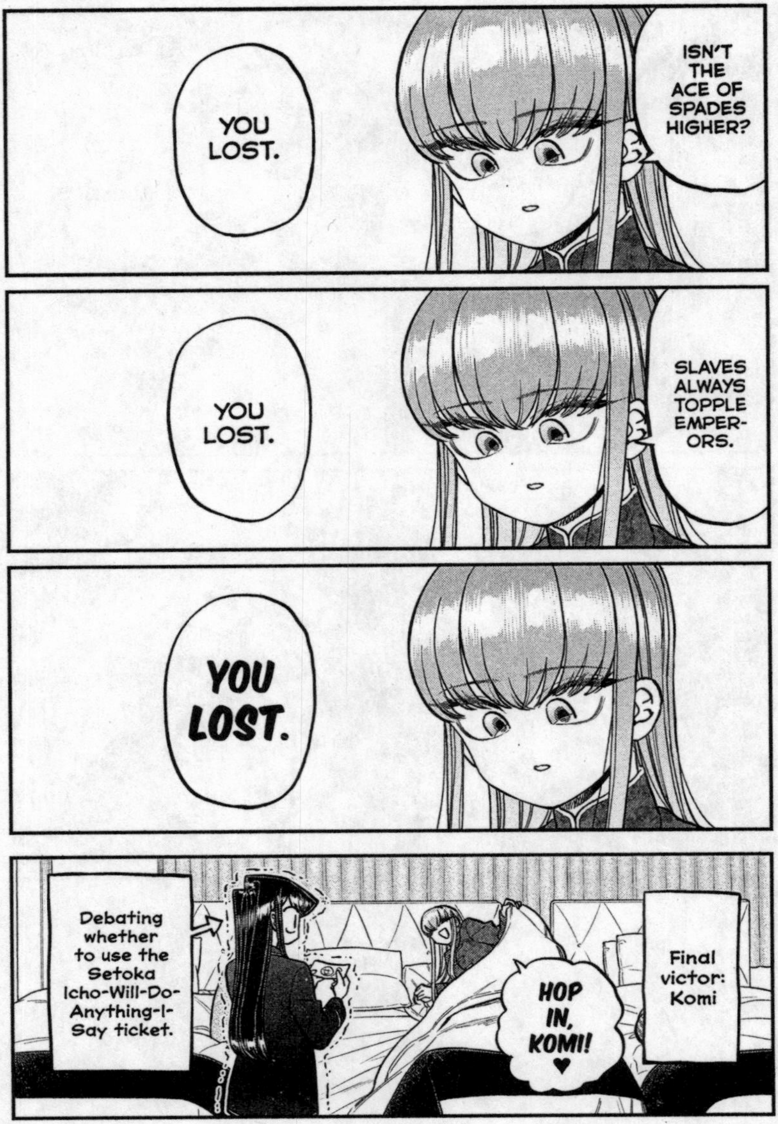
ISN'T THE ACE OF SPADES HIGHER?
YOU LOST.
SLAVES ALWAYS TOPPLE EMPER-ORS.
YOU LOST.
YOU LOST.
Final victor: Komi
HOP IN, KOMI! ♥
Debating whether to use the Setoka Icho-Will-Do-Anything-I-Say ticket.

Communication 296 — The End

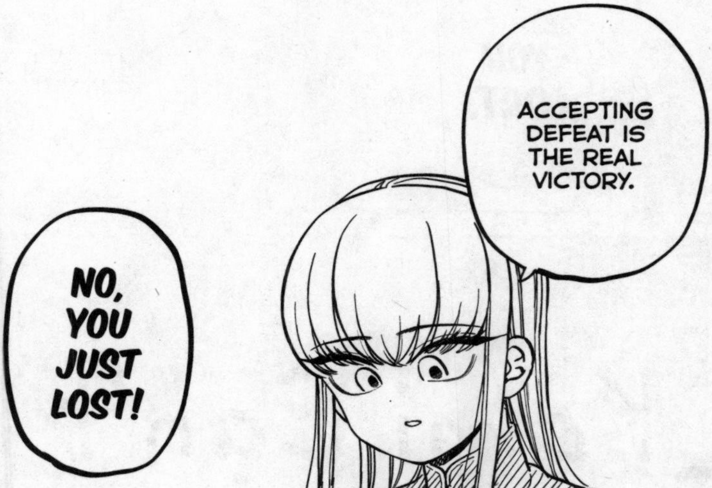
ACCEPTING DEFEAT IS THE REAL VICTORY.
NO, YOU JUST LOST!

Komi Can't
Communicate

Komi Can't Communicate

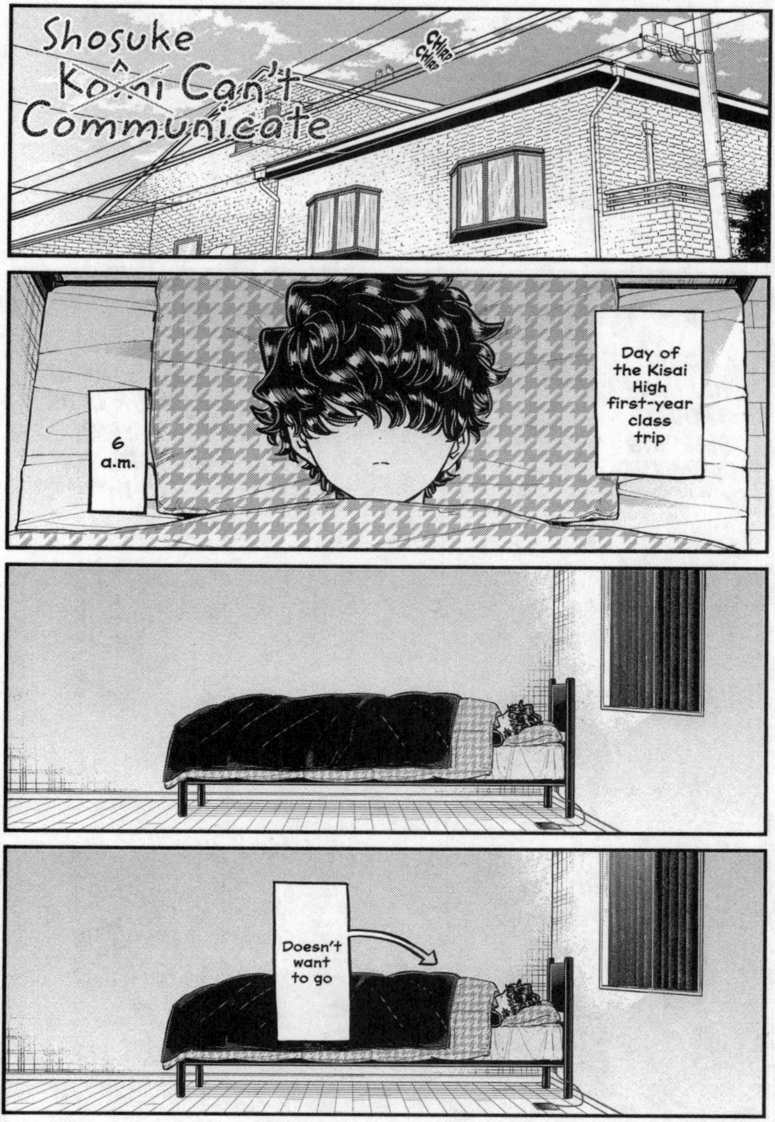
Shosuke
Komi Can't
Communicate
CHIRP CHIRP
Day of the Kisai High first-year class trip
6 a.m.
Doesn't want to go

Communication 297: Class Trip

SIGH...
Already exhausted from imagining three days of group activities
SHO! TODAY IS YOUR CLASS TRIP! ARE YOU UP?!
BAM
DID YOU HAVE TROUBLE SLEEPING FROM THE EXCITEMENT?!

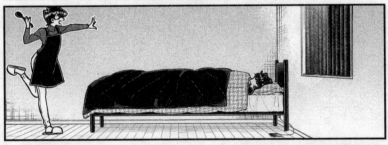

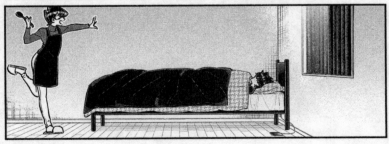

...
KOFF
Fak-ing
?!

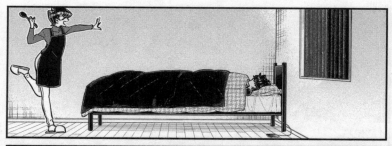

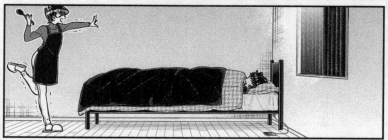

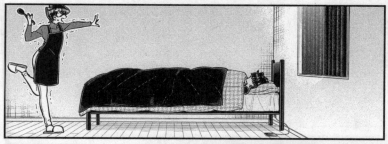

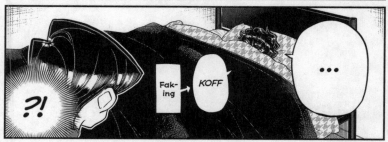

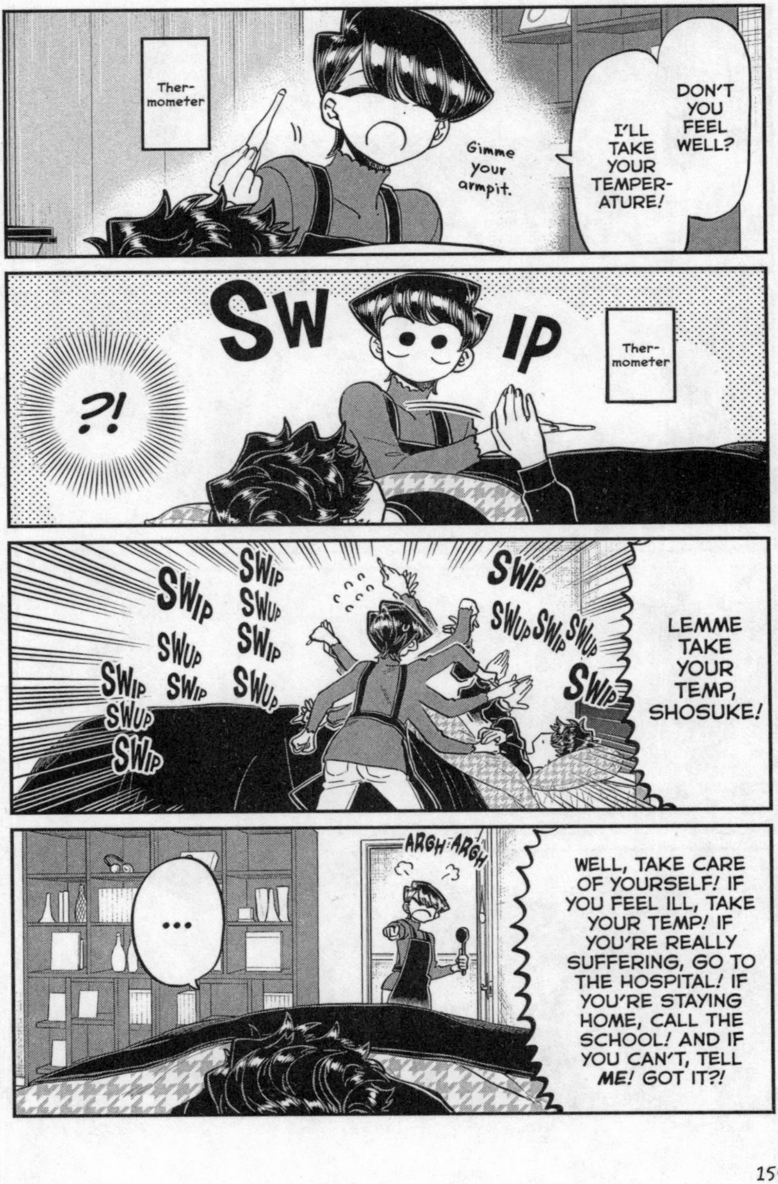
DON'T YOU FEEL WELL? I'LL TAKE YOUR TEMPERATURE!
Gimme your armpit.
Ther-mometer
Ther-mometer
SW IP
?!
LEMME TAKE YOUR TEMP, SHOSUKE!
SWIP
SWUP SWIP SWUP
SWIP
SWIP SWUP SWIP SWUP
SWIP SWUP SWIP
SWIP SWUP SWIP
WELL, TAKE CARE OF YOURSELF! IF YOU FEEL ILL, TAKE YOUR TEMP! IF YOU'RE REALLY SUFFERING, GO TO THE HOSPITAL! IF YOU'RE STAYING HOME, CALL THE SCHOOL! AND IF YOU CAN'T, TELL ME! GOT IT?!
ARGH ARGH
...

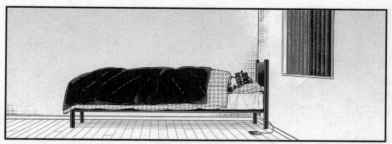

WELCOME HOME! HOW WAS YOUR SCHOOL TRIP?

I'M GLAD TO HEAR IT!

HMPH HMPH

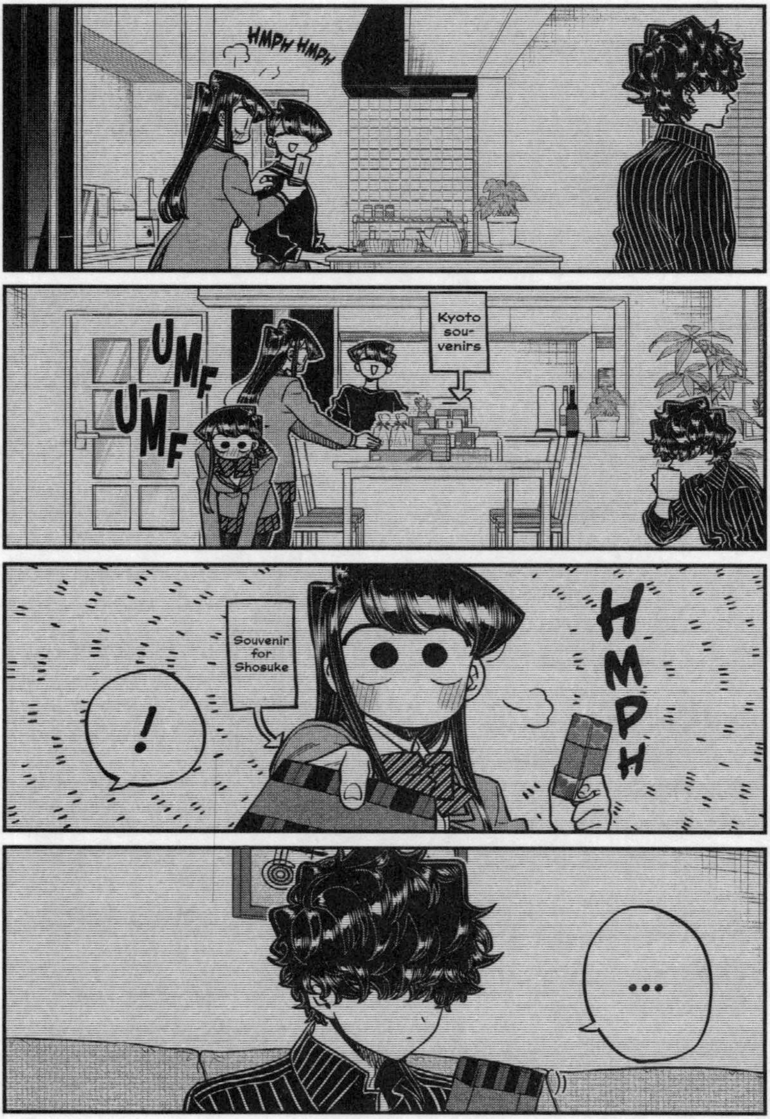
HMPH HMPH
Kyoto sou-venirs
UMF UMF UMF
HMPH
Souvenir for Shosuke
!
...

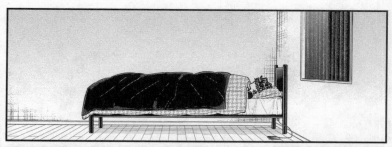

He went back to bed.

FWUF

GULP GULP

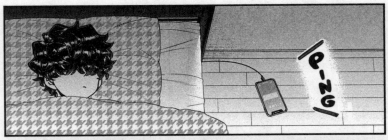

IT'S HITOMI!

tadano-hitomi41@mail.com

HEY! YOU UP?! TODAY IS OUR LONG-AWAITED CLASS TRIP! AND I CAN'T WAIT! I'LL BRING CARDS, SO LET'S PLAY BLIND MAN'S BLUFF! FOR HIGH STAKES!

All from Hitomi

?!

PING PING PING PING

TOSS

He shut it off.

CLIK

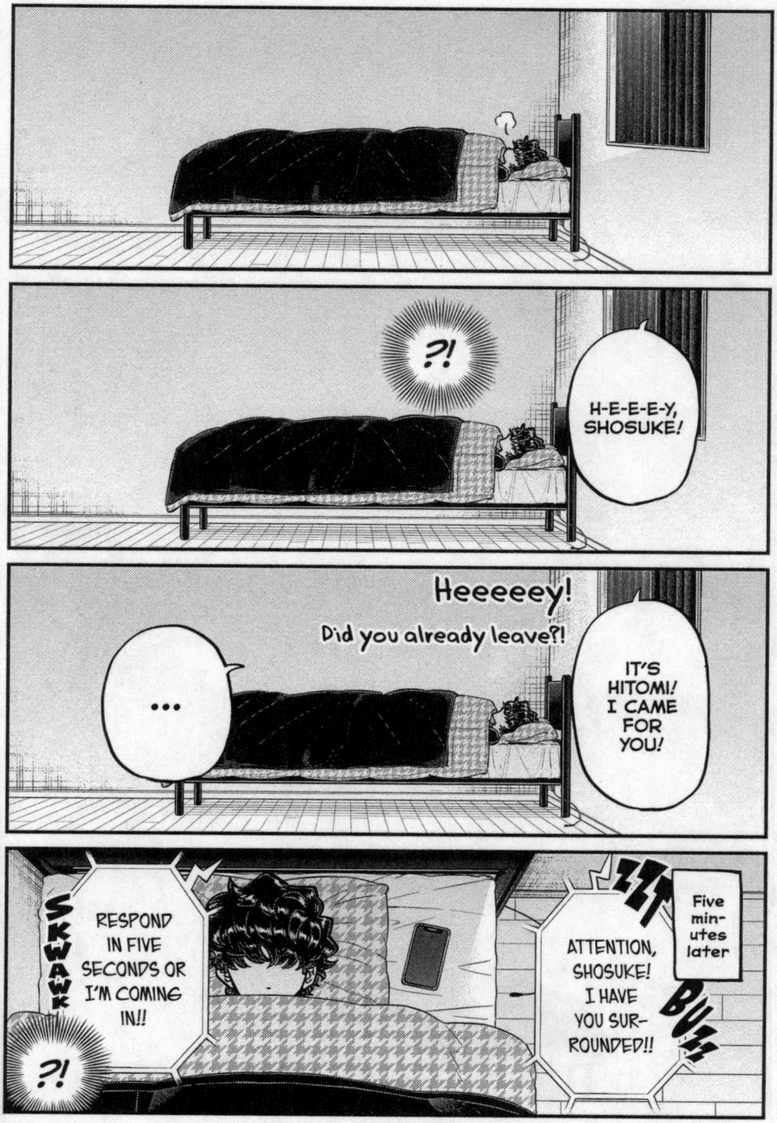
H-E-E-E-Y, SHOSUKE!
?!
Heeeeey!
Did you already leave?!
IT'S HITOMI! I CAME FOR YOU!
...
Five minutes later
ZZT
ATTENTION, SHOSUKE! I HAVE YOU SURROUNDED!!
BUZZ
RESPOND IN FIVE SECONDS OR I'M COMING IN!!
SKWAWK
?!

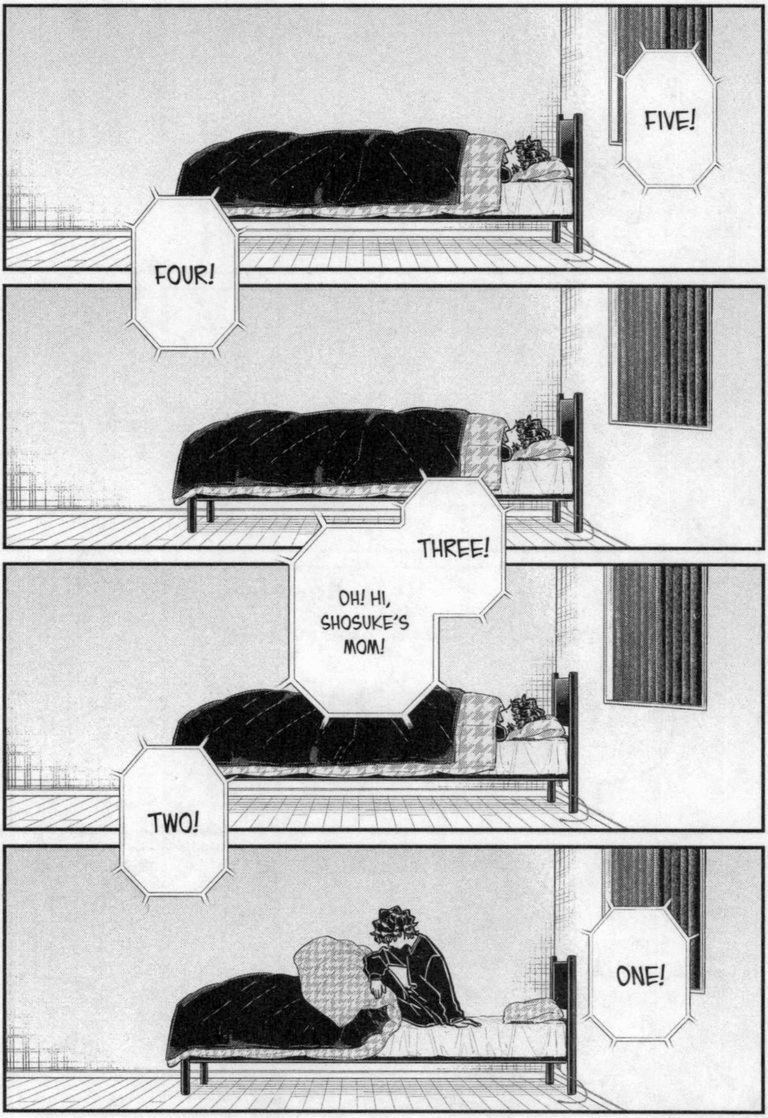
FIVE!
FOUR!
THREE!
OH! HI, SHOSUKE'S MOM!
TWO!
ONE!

Arriving in Okinawa

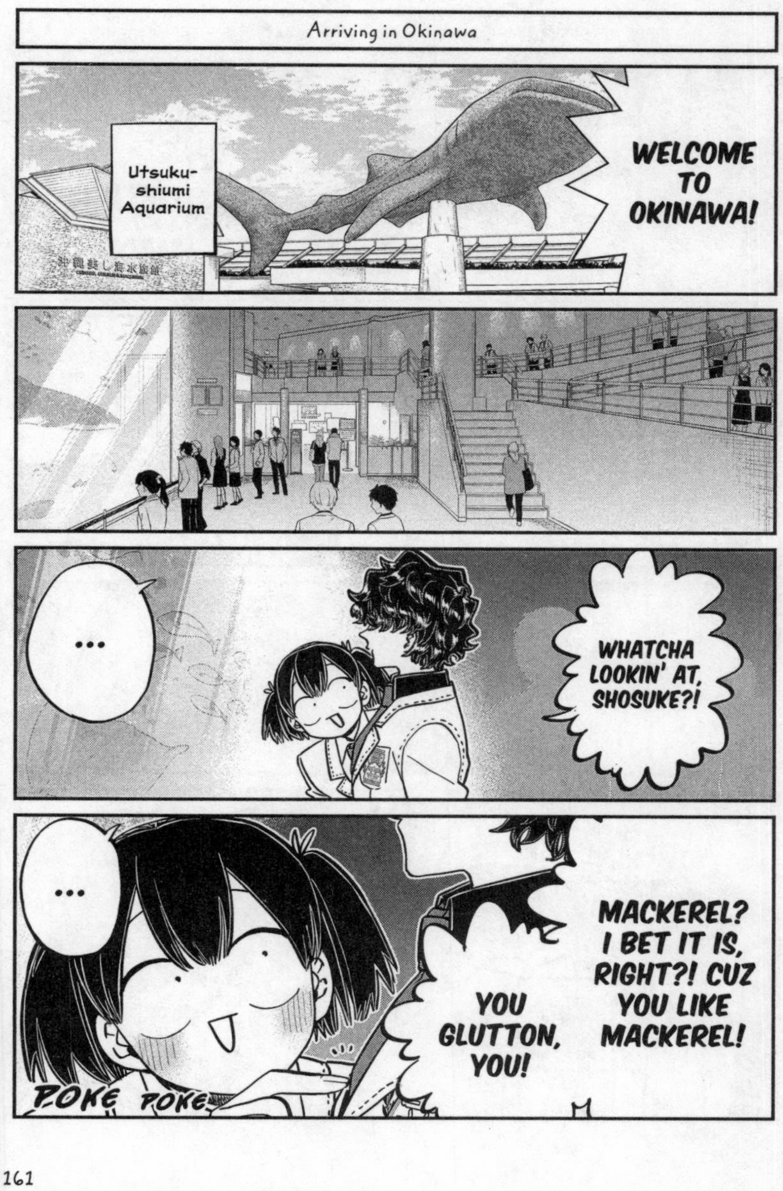

WELCOME TO OKINAWA!
Utsuku-shiumi Aquarium
WHATCHA LOOKIN' AT, SHOSUKE?!
...
MACKEREL? I BET IT IS, RIGHT?! CUZ YOU LIKE MACKEREL!
YOU GLUTTON, YOU!
...
POKE POKE

The Limestone-Cave Incident

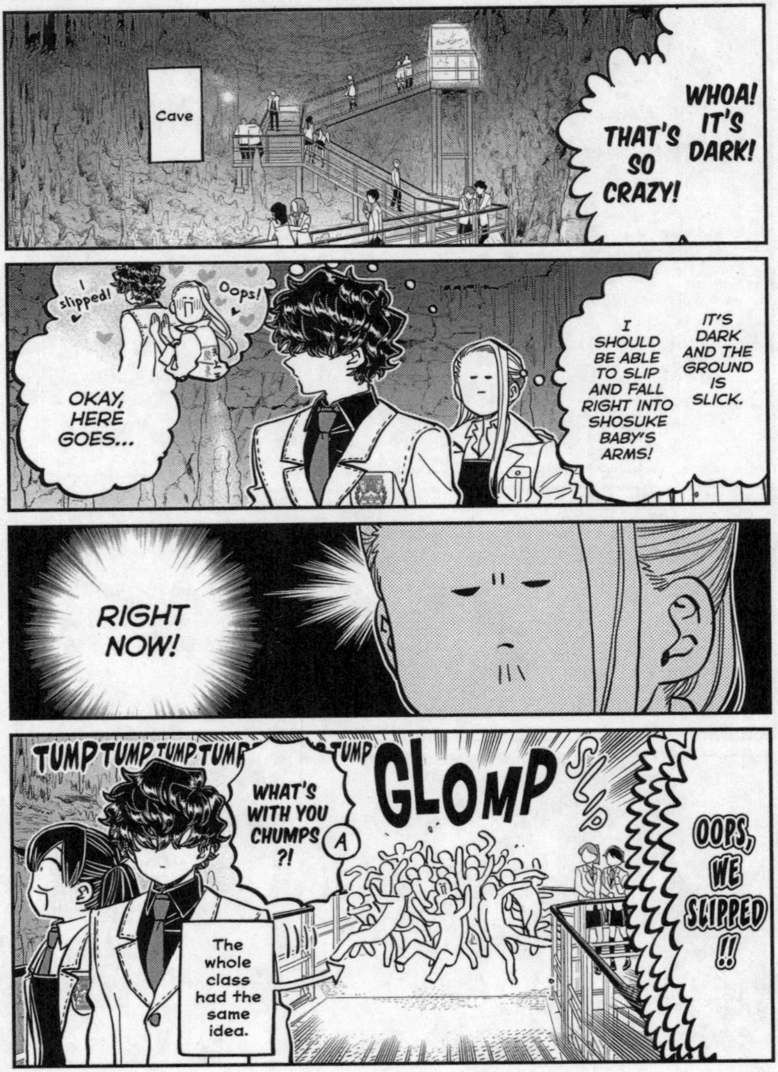
WHOA! IT'S DARK!
THAT'S SO CRAZY!
Cave
IT'S DARK AND THE GROUND IS SLICK.
I SHOULD BE ABLE TO SLIP AND FALL RIGHT INTO SHOSUKE BABY'S ARMS!
Oops!
I slipped!
OKAY, HERE GOES...
RIGHT NOW!
OOPS, WE SLIPPED!!
Slip
GLOMP
TUMP
WHAT'S WITH YOU CHUMPS?!
A
TUMP TUMP TUMP
The whole class had the same idea.

Take a Shower First

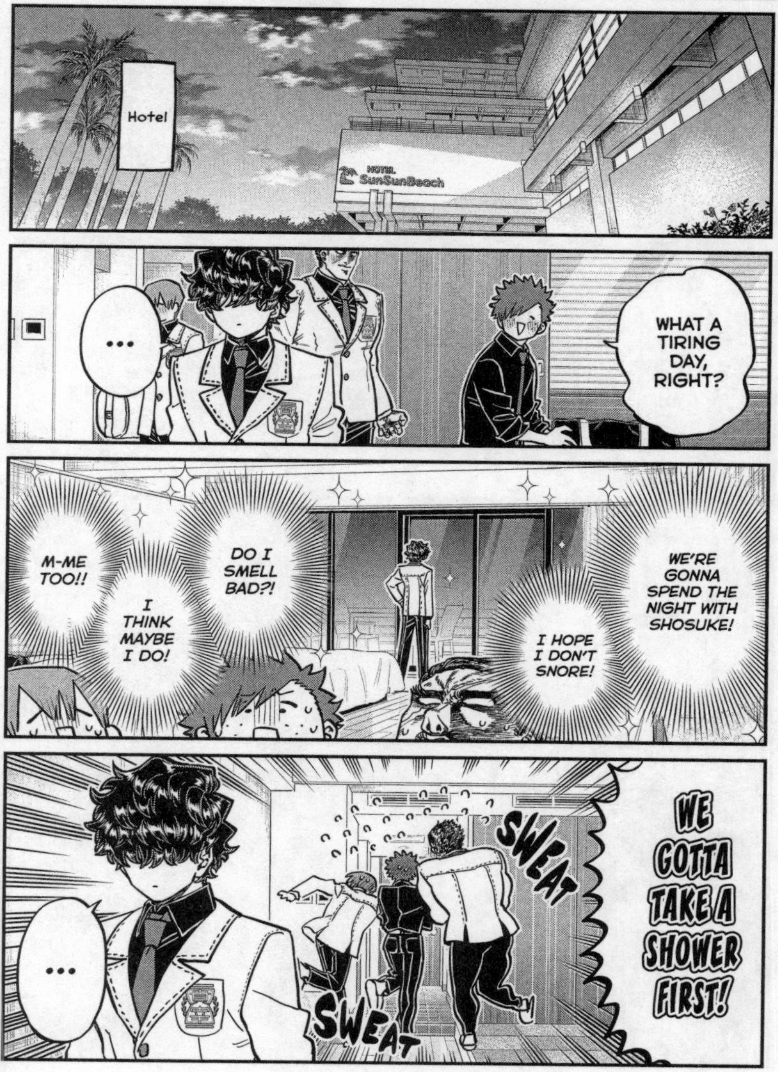
Hotel
HOTEL SunSunBeach
WHAT A TIRING DAY, RIGHT?
...
WE'RE GONNA SPEND THE NIGHT WITH SHOSUKE!
I HOPE I DON'T SNORE!
DO I SMELL BAD?!
I THINK MAYBE I DO!
M-ME TOO!!
WE GOTTA TAKE A SHOWER FIRST!
SWEAT
SWEAT
...

The Ocean at Night

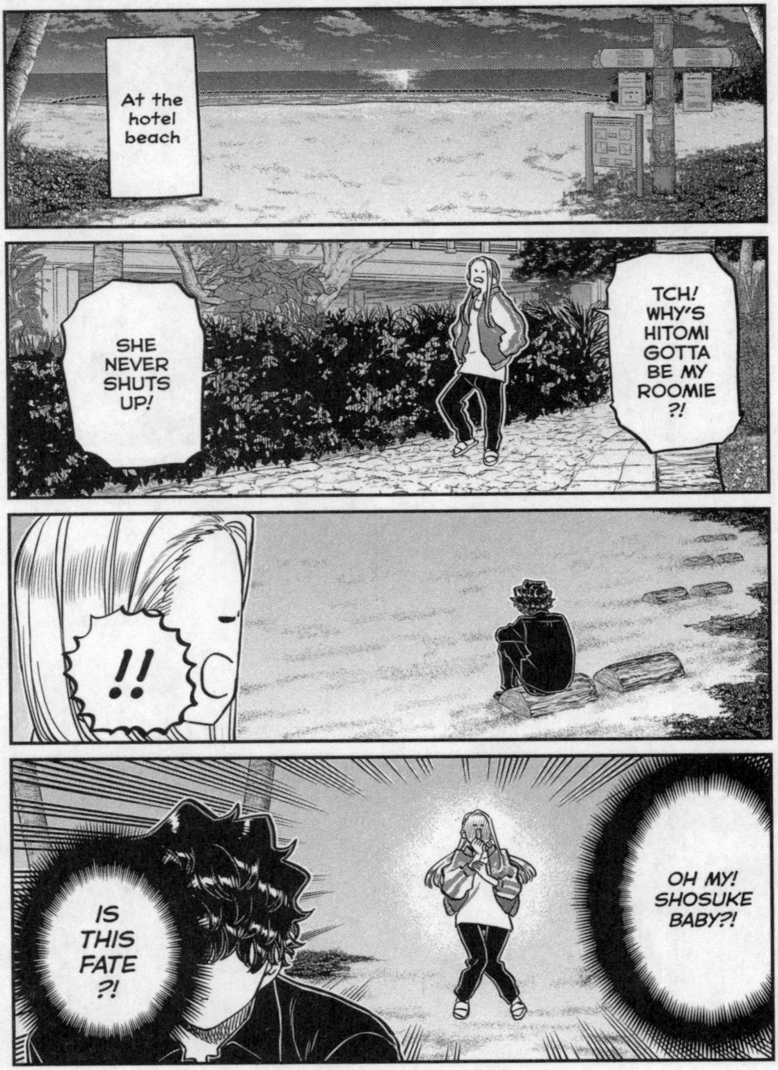
At the hotel beach
TCH! WHY'S HITOMI GOTTA BE MY ROOMIE?!
SHE NEVER SHUTS UP!
!!
OH MY! SHOSUKE BABY?!
IS THIS FATE?!

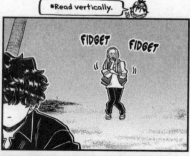

*Read vertically.

FIDGET
FIDGET
JOLT
BE A BRAVE WOMAN
SLAP
UM, MAY I JOIN YOU?
...
FWIP
!!!
I VOWED TO WALK THREE STEPS BEHIND HIM, BUT NOW HE THINKS I'M IMMODEST!
I'M SUCH A DUMB, DUMB, DUMMY!
...
...?
C-CAN I REALLY SIT HERE?
...
PLOP

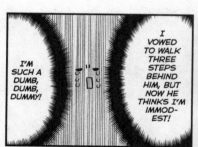

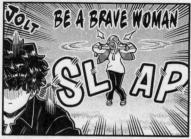

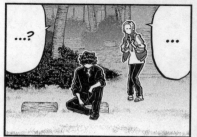

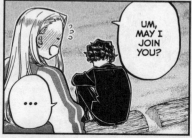

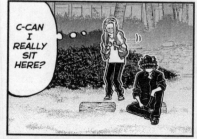

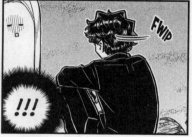

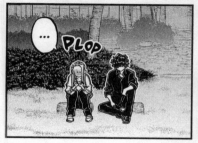

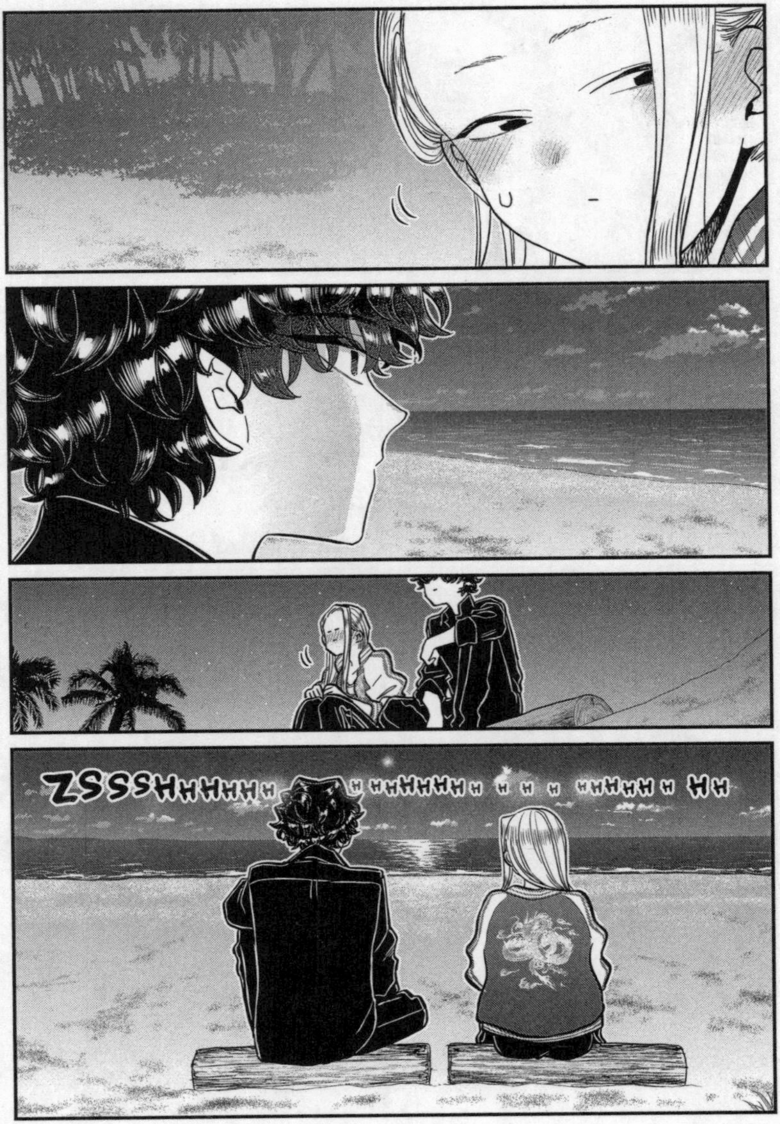
ZSSSHHHHHHH HHHHHHH H H H HHHHHH H HH

School Trip Highlights

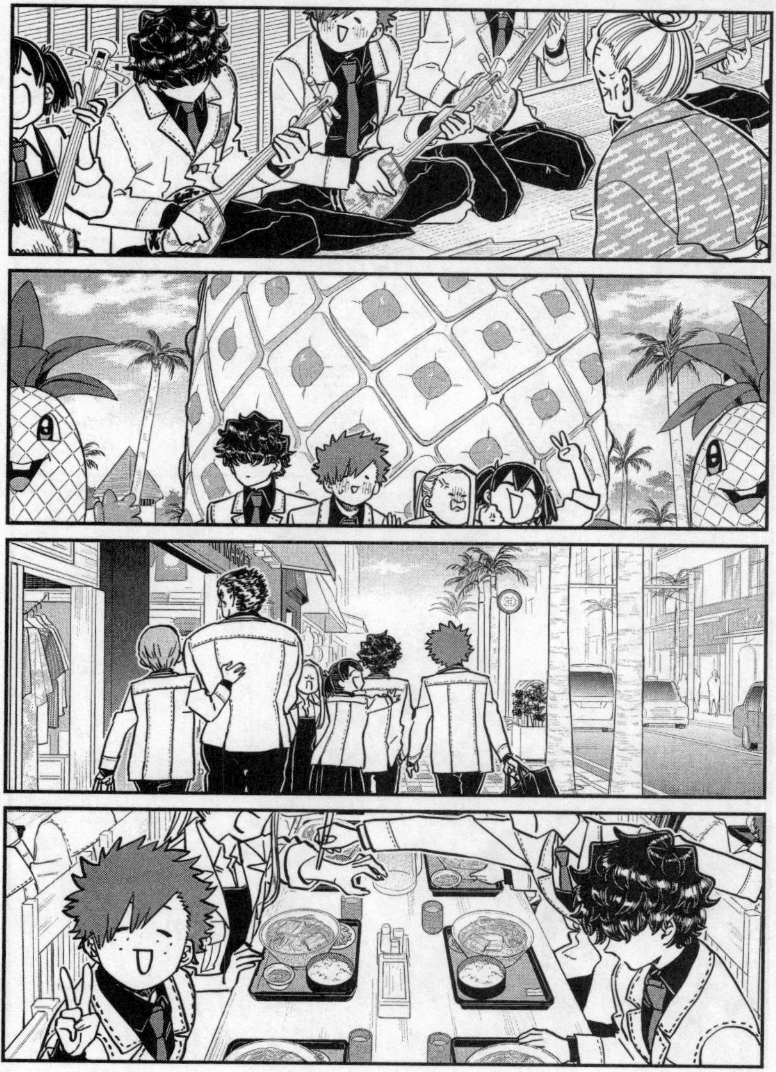

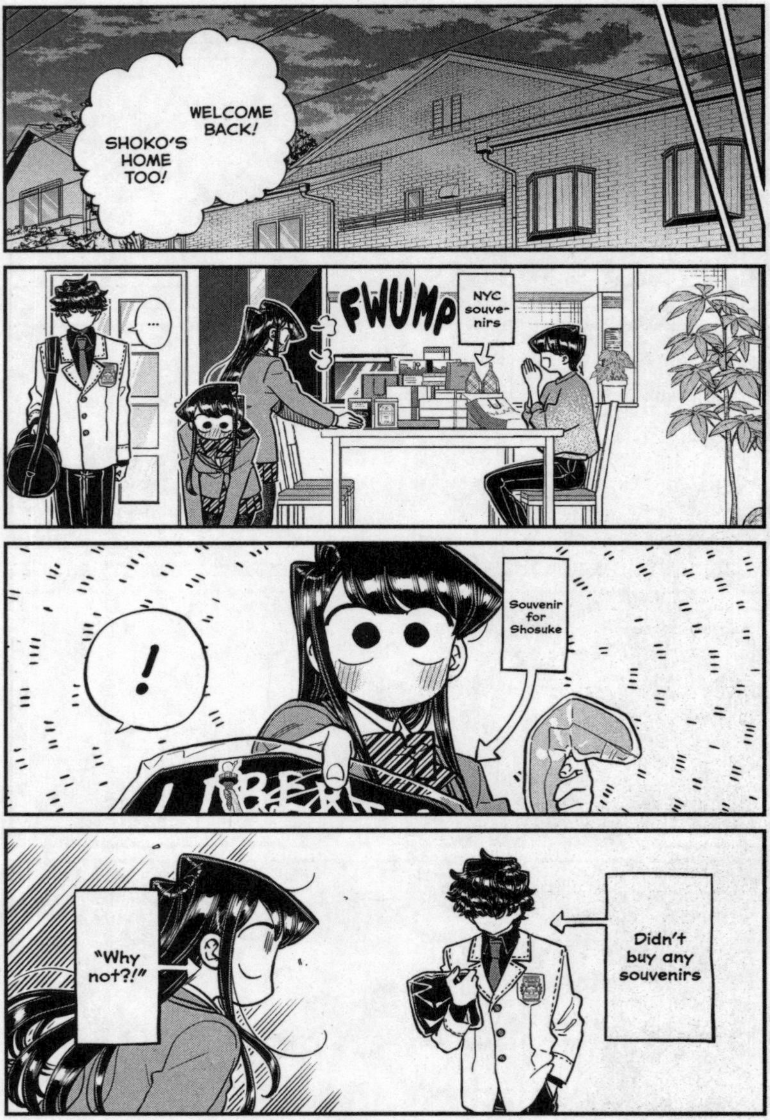
WELCOME BACK!
SHOKO'S HOME TOO!
NYC souvenirs
FWUMP
...
Souvenir for Shosuke
!
Didn't buy any souvenirs
"Why not?!"

Communication 297 — The End

Komi Can't Communicate

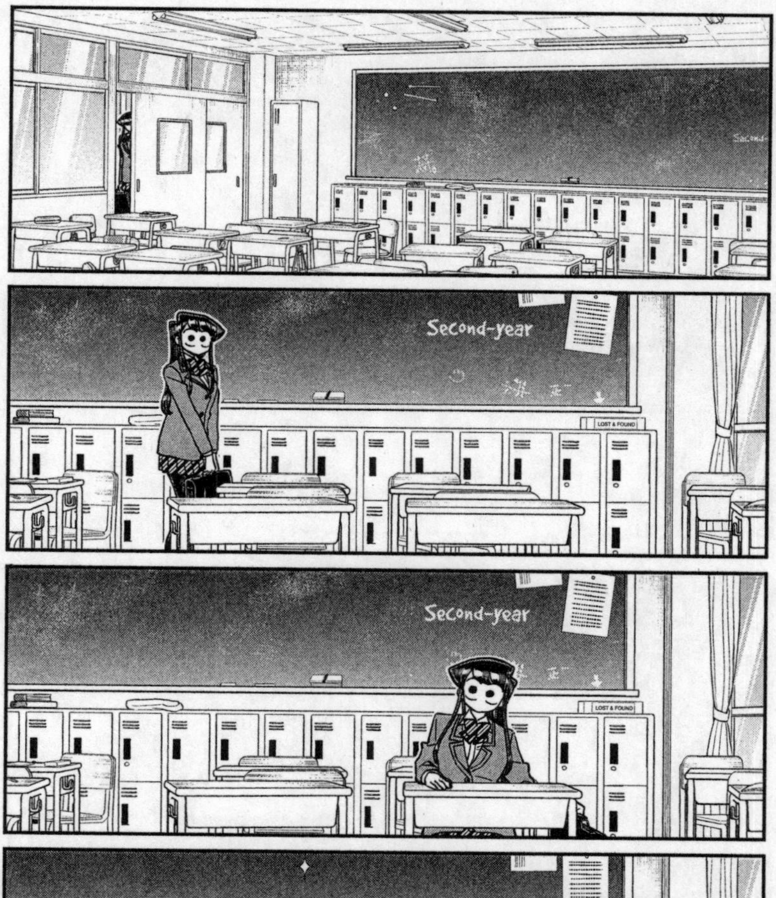
Second-year
LOST & FOUND
Second-year
LOST & FOUND
CLUNK
LOST & FOUND

Communication 298: School

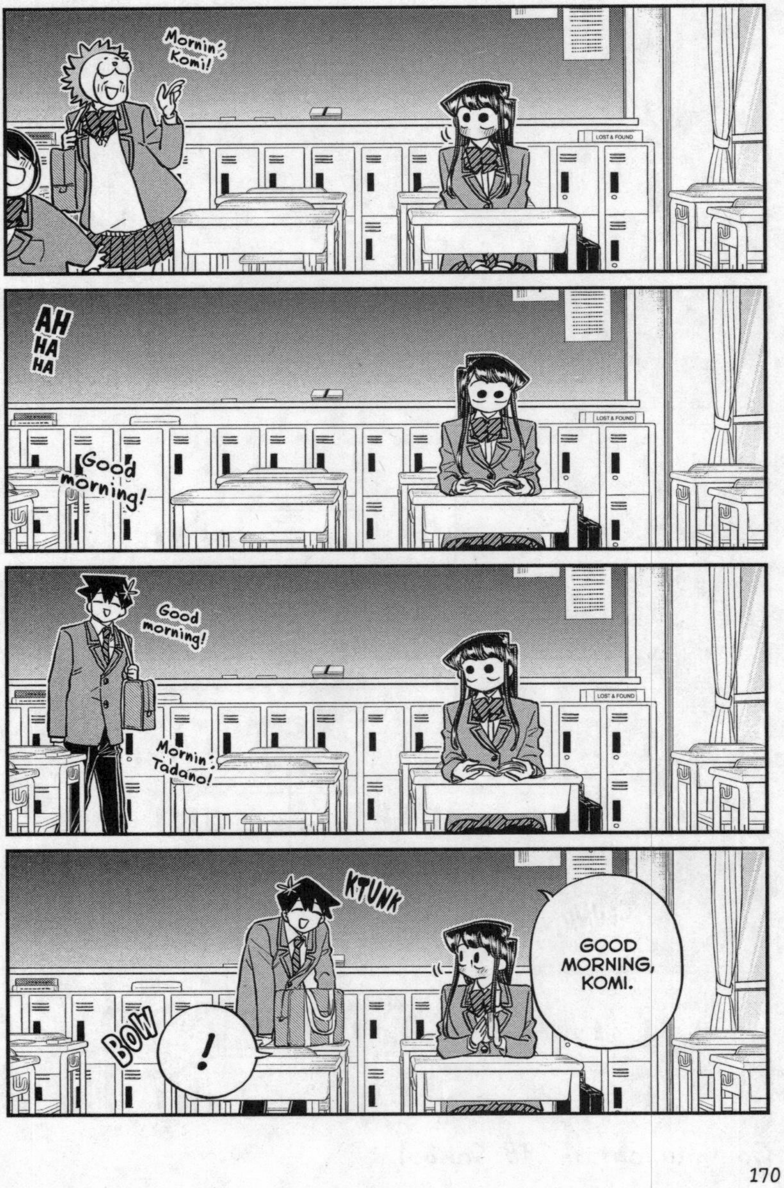
Mornin', Komi!
AH HA HA
Good morning!
Good morning!
Mornin', Tadano!
KTUNK
GOOD MORNING, KOMI.
!
BOW

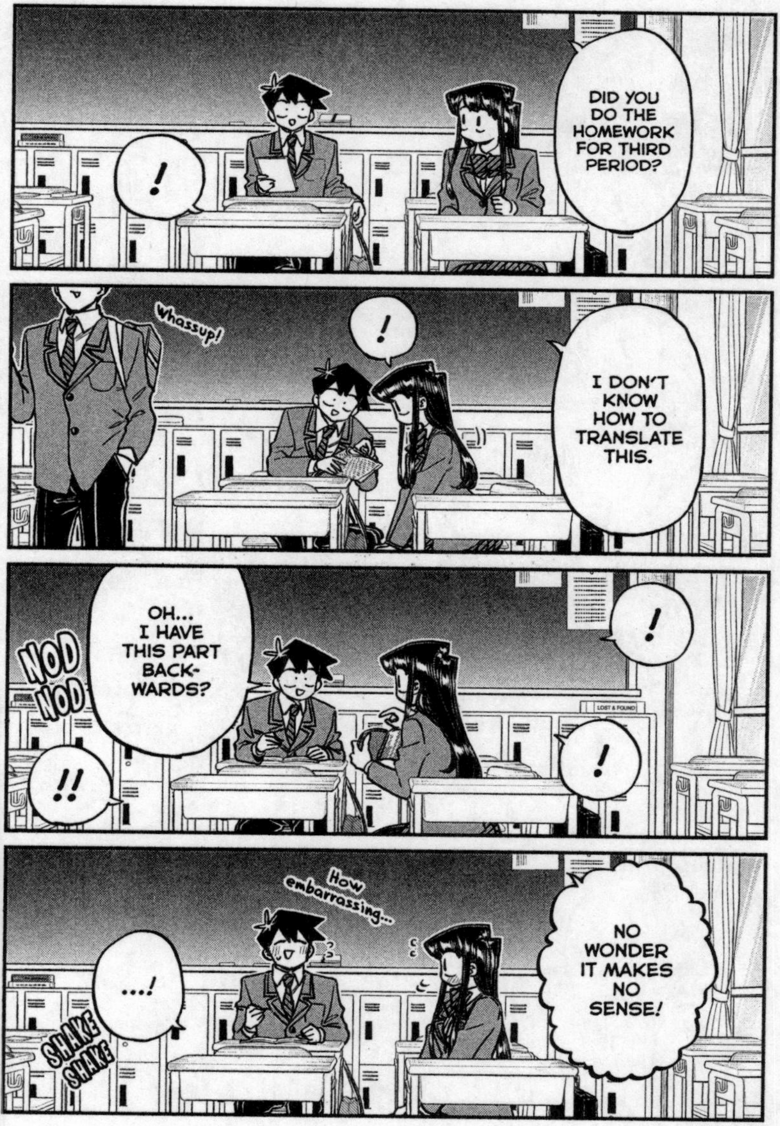
DID YOU DO THE HOMEWORK FOR THIRD PERIOD?
!
I DON'T KNOW HOW TO TRANSLATE THIS.
!
Whassup!
!
!
OH... I HAVE THIS PART BACKWARDS?
NOD NOD
!!
NO WONDER IT MAKES NO SENSE!
How embarrassing...
...!
SHAKE SHAKE

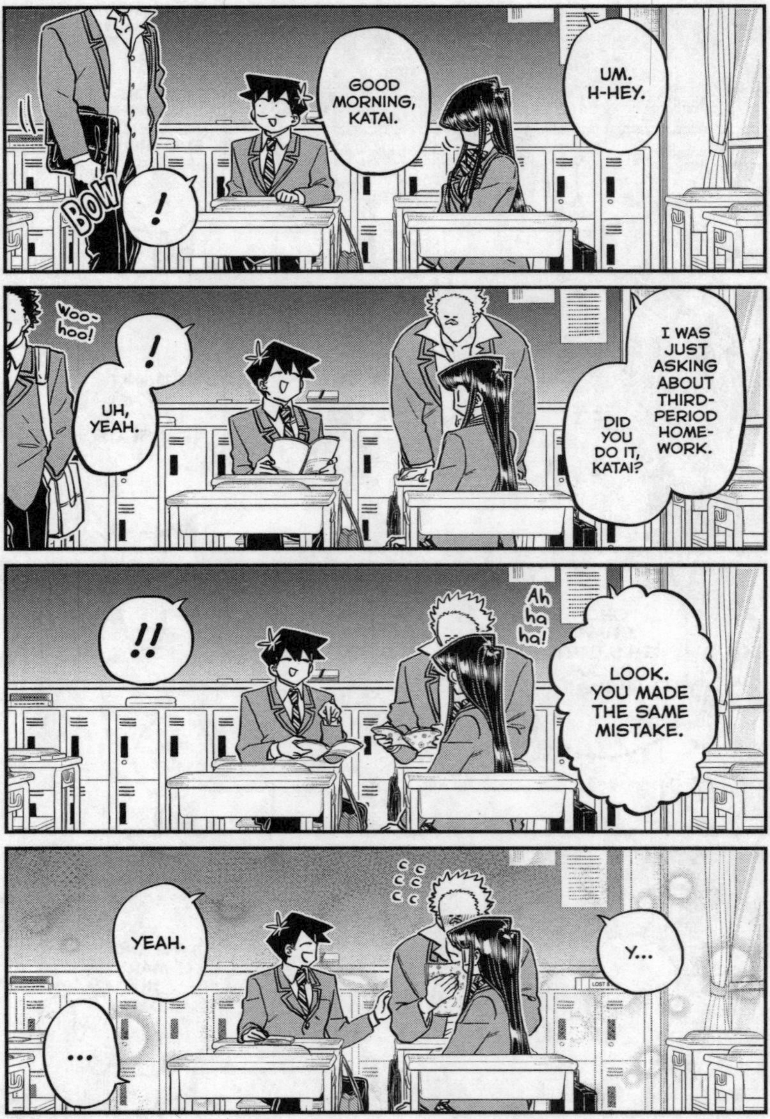
UM. H-HEY.
GOOD MORNING, KATAI.
!
BOW
I WAS JUST ASKING ABOUT THIRD-PERIOD HOMEWORK.
DID YOU DO IT, KATAI?
!
UH, YEAH.
Woo-hoo!
LOOK. YOU MADE THE SAME MISTAKE.
Ah ha ha!
!!
Y...
YEAH.
...

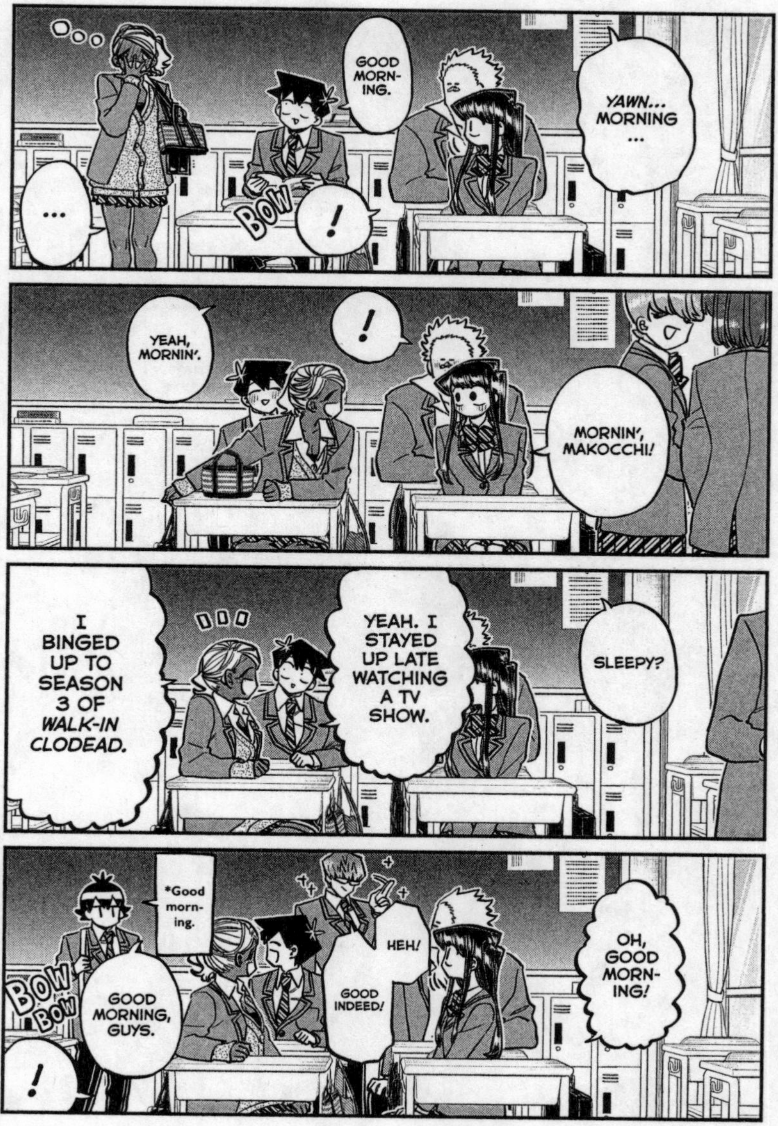
YAWN... MORNING ...
GOOD MORNING.
!
BOW
...
MORNIN', MAKOCCHI!
!
YEAH, MORNIN'.
SLEEPY?
YEAH. I STAYED UP LATE WATCHING A TV SHOW.
I BINGED UP TO SEASON 3 OF *WALK-IN CLODEAD.*
OH, GOOD MORNING!
HEH!
GOOD INDEED!
*Good morning.
GOOD MORNING, GUYS.
BOW BOW
!

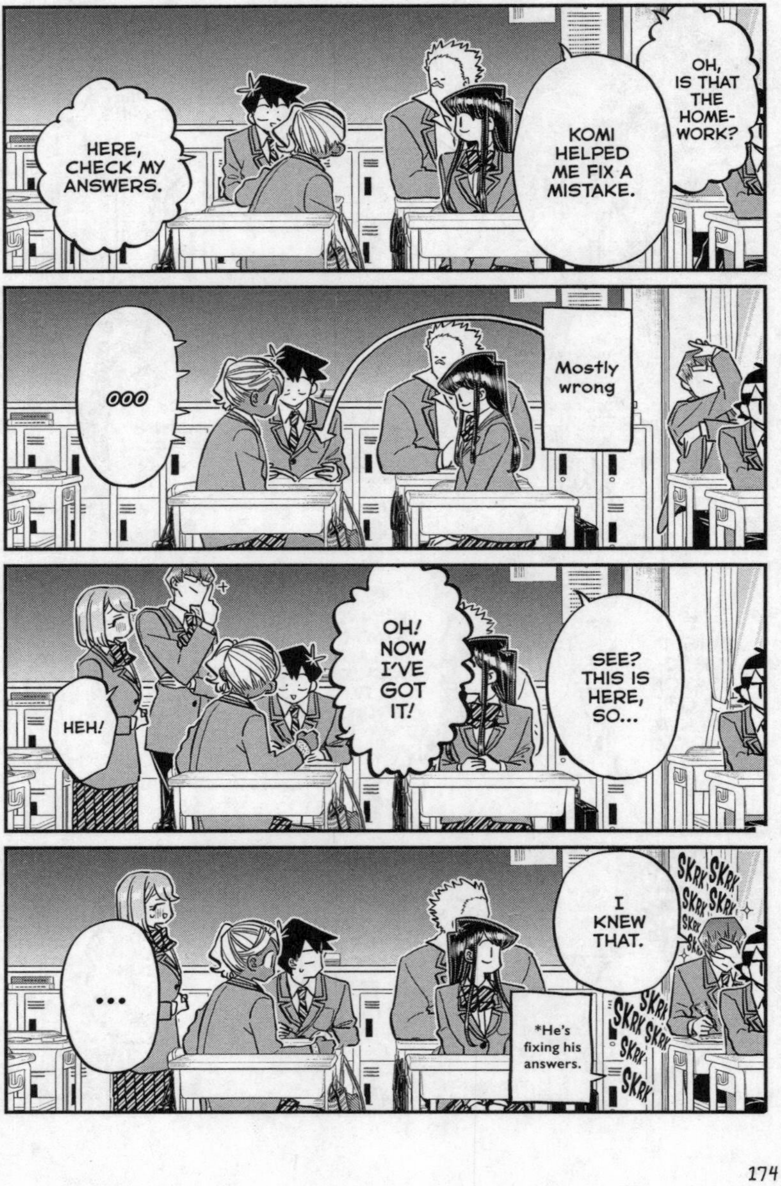
OH, IS THAT THE HOME-WORK?
KOMI HELPED ME FIX A MISTAKE.
HERE, CHECK MY ANSWERS.
Mostly wrong
OOO
SEE? THIS IS HERE, SO...
OH! NOW I'VE GOT IT!
HEH!
SKRK SKRK SKRK SKRK
I KNEW THAT.
SKRK SKRK SKRK SKRK SKRK
*He's fixing his answers.
...

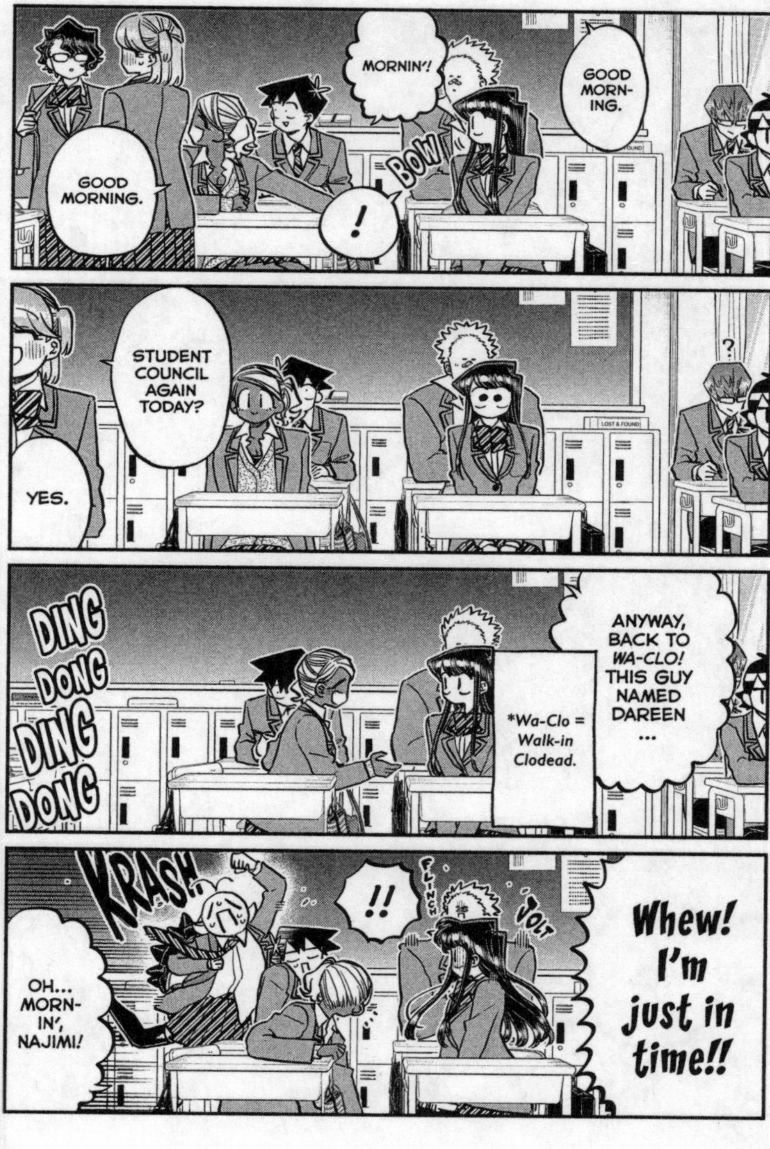
GOOD MORN-ING.
MORNIN'!
BOW
!
GOOD MORNING.
?
STUDENT COUNCIL AGAIN TODAY?
YES.
ANYWAY, BACK TO WA-CLO! THIS GUY NAMED DAREEN ...
*Wa-Clo = Walk-in Clodead.
DING DONG DING DONG
Whew! I'm just in time!!
JOLT
FLINCH
!!
KRASH
OH... MORN-IN', NAJIMI!

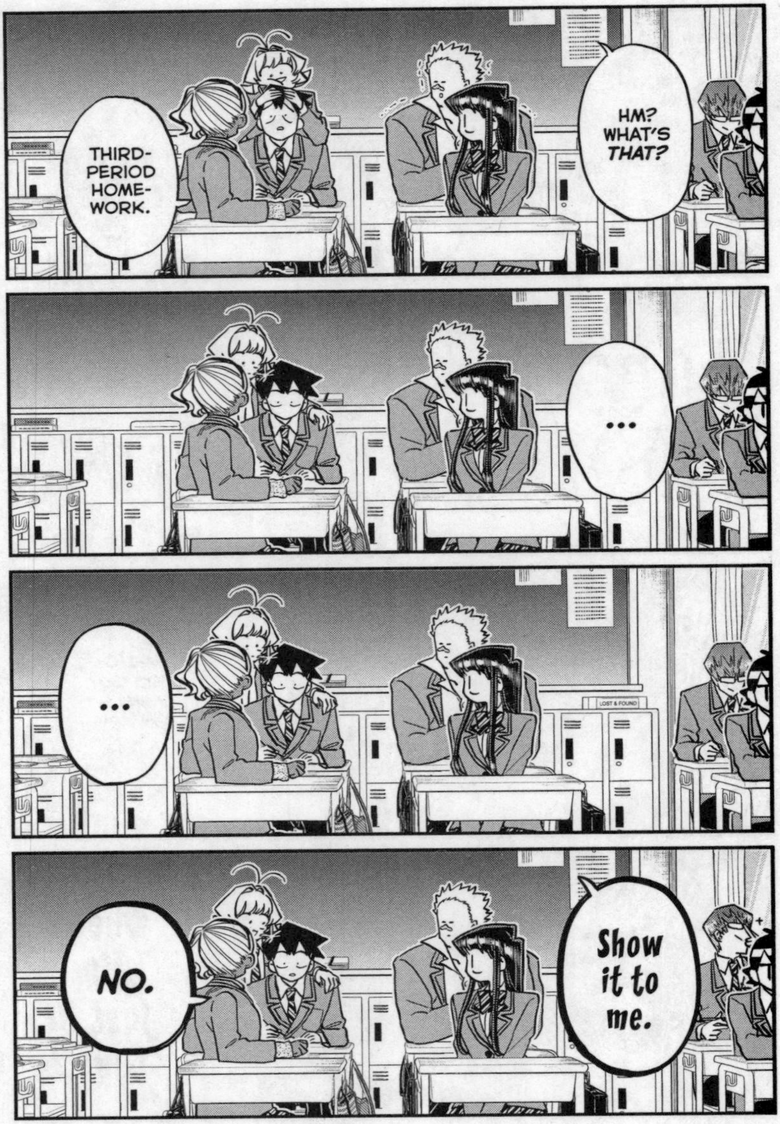
HM? WHAT'S *THAT?*
THIRD-PERIOD HOMEWORK.
...
LOST & FOUND
...
Show it to me.
NO.

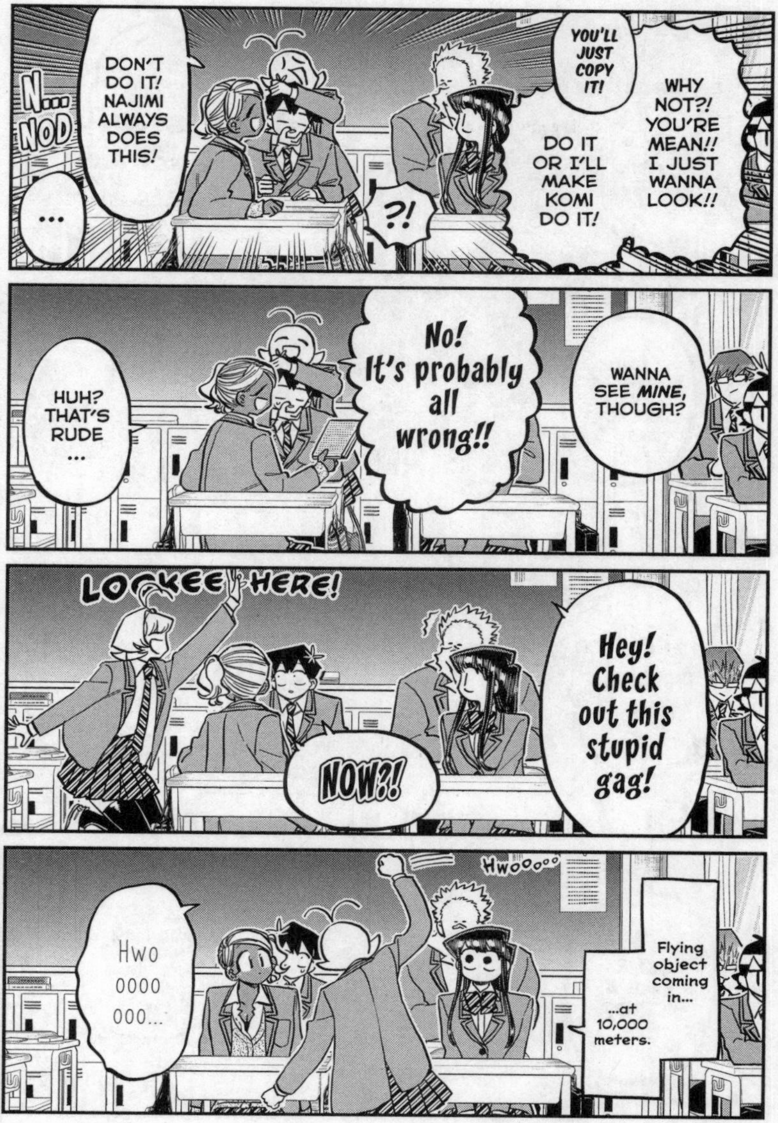
WHY NOT?! YOU'RE MEAN!! I JUST WANNA LOOK!!
YOU'LL JUST COPY IT!
DO IT OR I'LL MAKE KOMI DO IT!
?!
DON'T DO IT! NAJIMI ALWAYS DOES THIS!
N... NOD
...
WANNA SEE MINE, THOUGH?
No! It's probably all wrong!!
HUH? THAT'S RUDE ...
Hey! Check out this stupid gag!
NOW?!
LOOKEE HERE!
HWOOOOO
Flying object coming in...
...at 10,000 meters.
Hwo 0000 000...

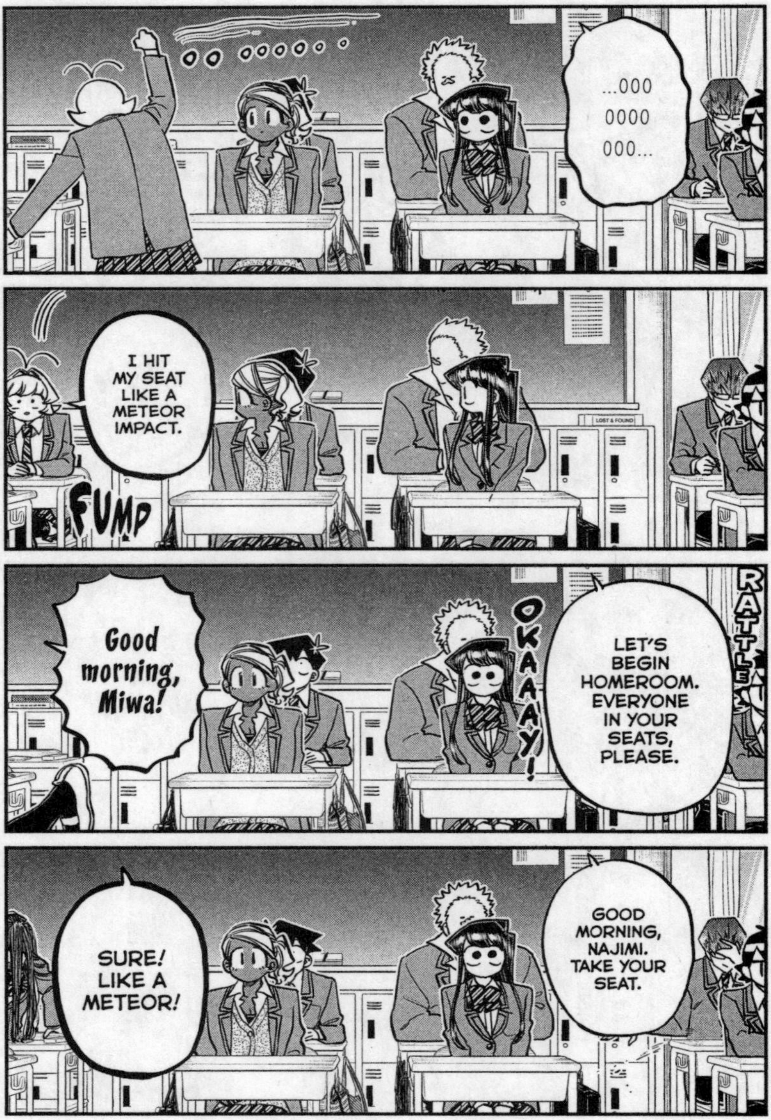
...OOO OOOO OOO...
I HIT MY SEAT LIKE A METEOR IMPACT.
FUMP
RATTLE
LET'S BEGIN HOMEROOM. EVERYONE IN YOUR SEATS, PLEASE.
OKAAAY!
Good morning, Miwa!
GOOD MORNING, NAJIMI. TAKE YOUR SEAT.
SURE! LIKE A METEOR!

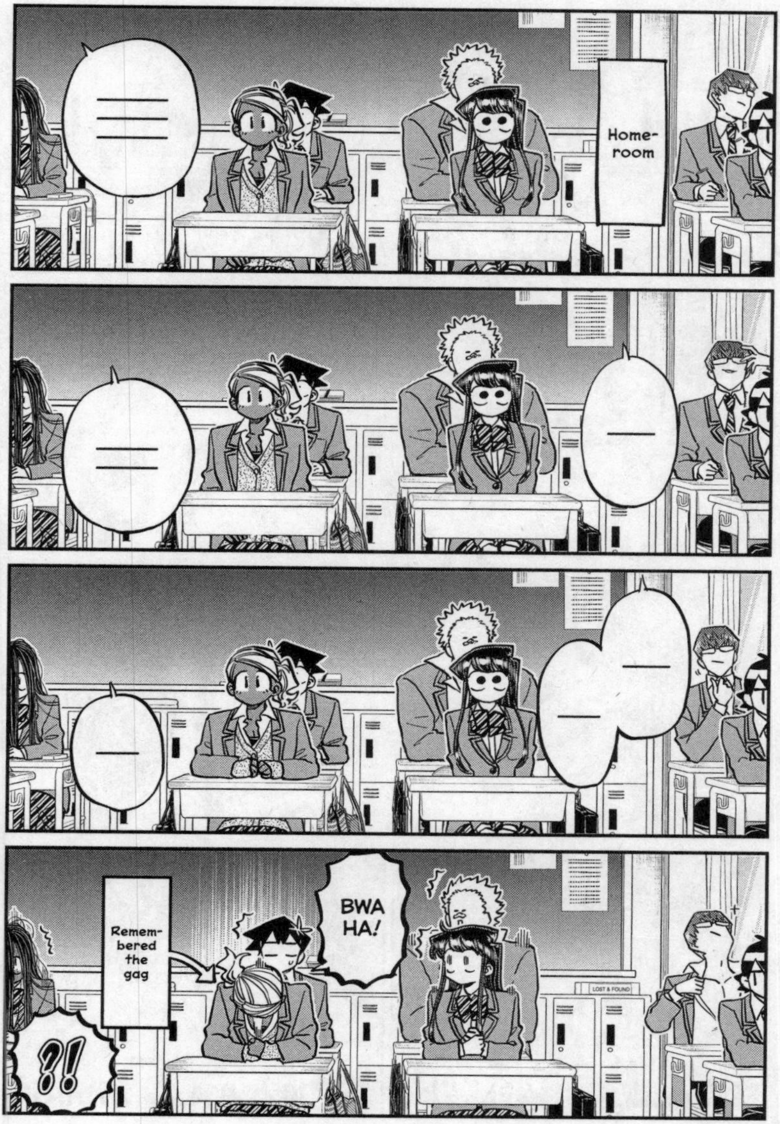
Home-room
BWA HA!
Remembered the gag
?!

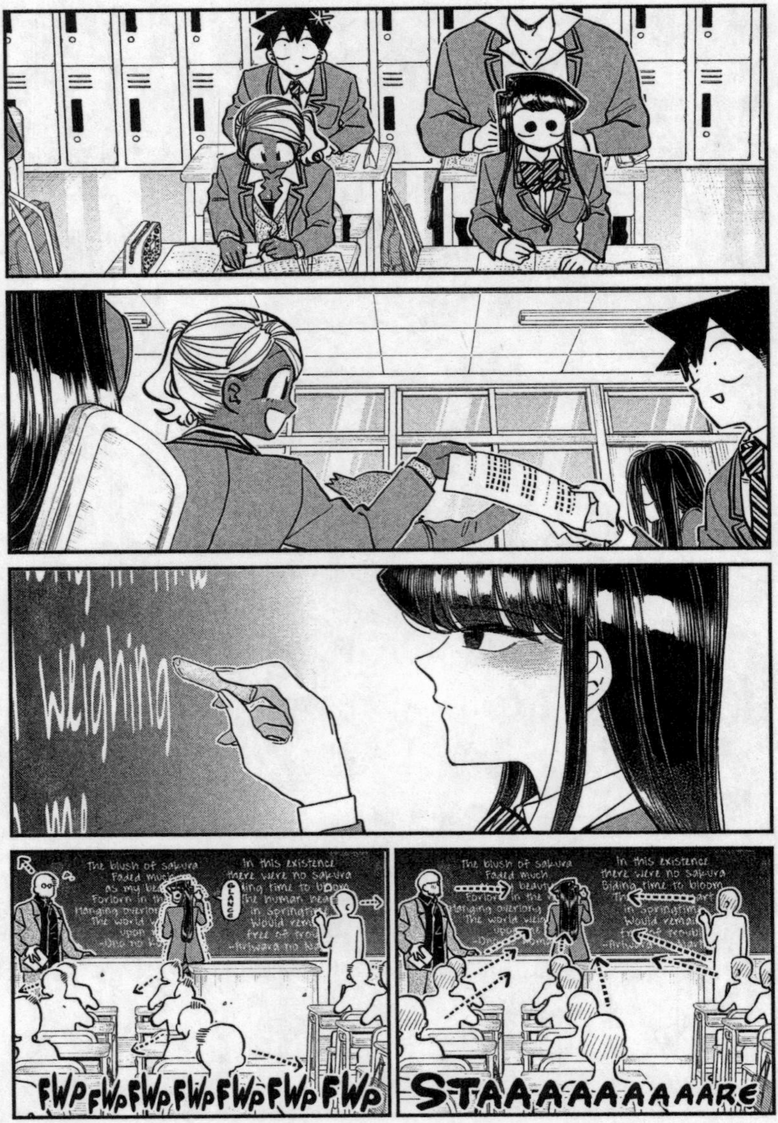

weighing
In this existence
there were no sakura
Biding time to bloom
The blush of sakura
Faded much
STAAAAAAAAARE
In this existence
there were no sakura
The blush of sakura
Faded much
GLANCE
FWP FWP FWP FWP FWP FWP FWP

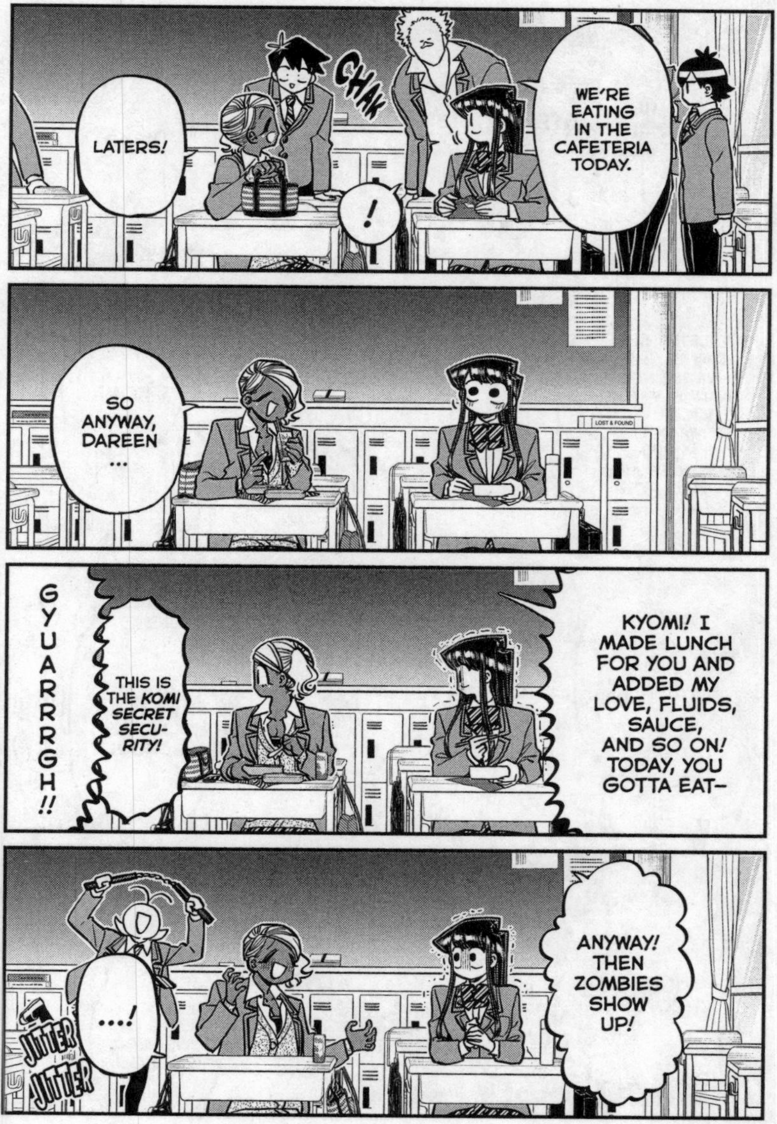
WE'RE EATING IN THE CAFETERIA TODAY.
CHAK
LATERS!
!
SO ANYWAY, DAREEN ...
KYOMI! I MADE LUNCH FOR YOU AND ADDED MY LOVE, FLUIDS, SAUCE, AND SO ON! TODAY, YOU GOTTA EAT–
THIS IS THE KOMI SECRET SECU-RITY!
GYUARRRGH!!
ANYWAY! THEN ZOMBIES SHOW UP!
...!
JITTER JITTER

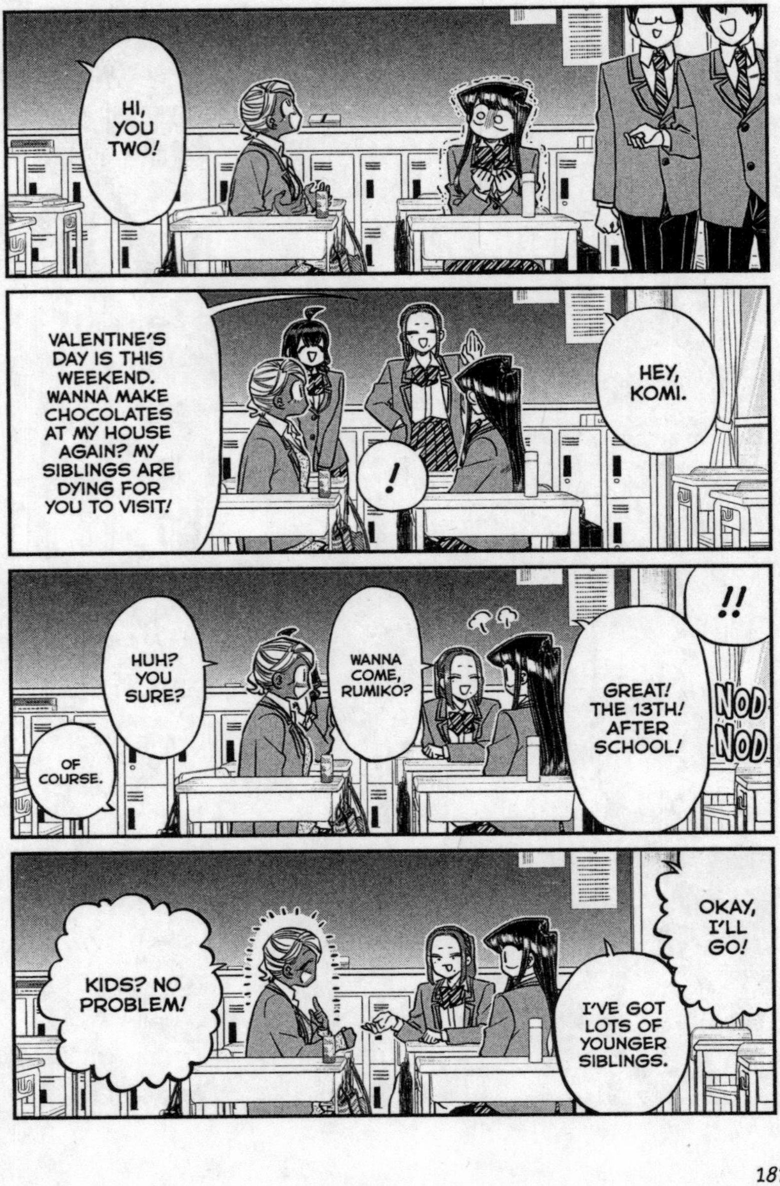
HI, YOU TWO!
HEY, KOMI.
VALENTINE'S DAY IS THIS WEEKEND. WANNA MAKE CHOCOLATES AT MY HOUSE AGAIN? MY SIBLINGS ARE DYING FOR YOU TO VISIT!
!
!!
NOD NOD
GREAT! THE 13TH! AFTER SCHOOL!
WANNA COME, RUMIKO?
HUH? YOU SURE?
OF COURSE.
OKAY, I'LL GO!
I'VE GOT LOTS OF YOUNGER SIBLINGS.
KIDS? NO PROBLEM!

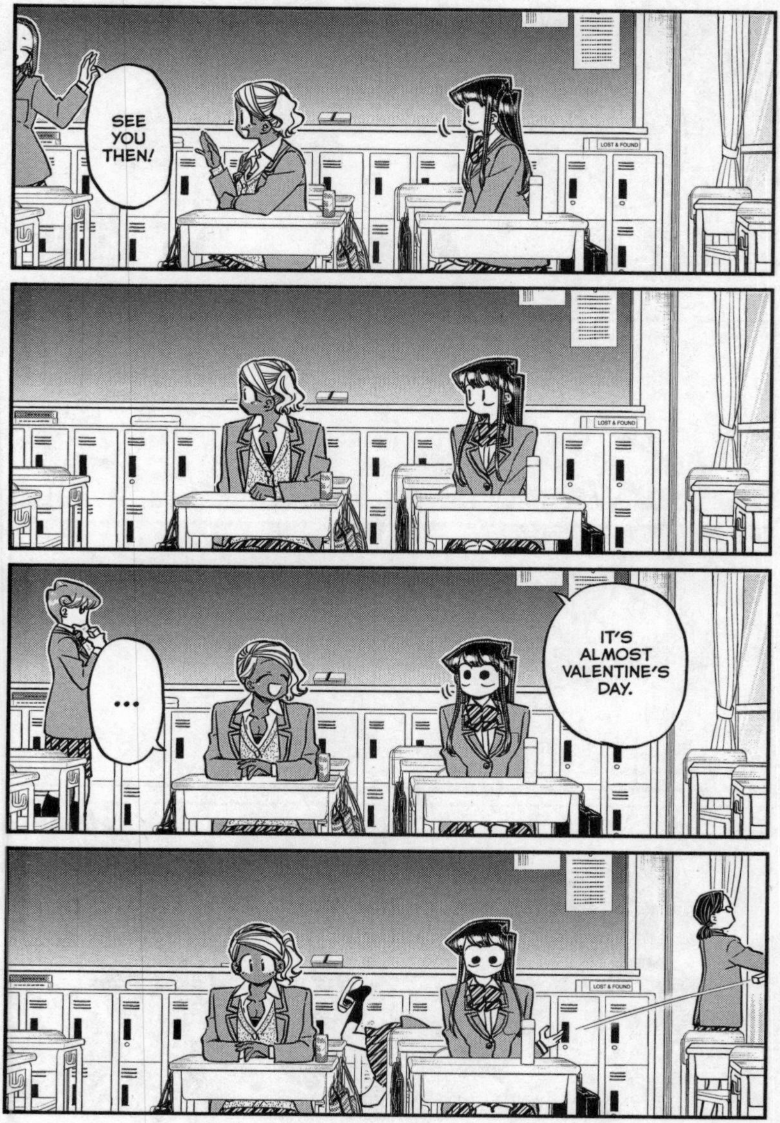
SEE YOU THEN!
IT'S ALMOST VALENTINE'S DAY.
...

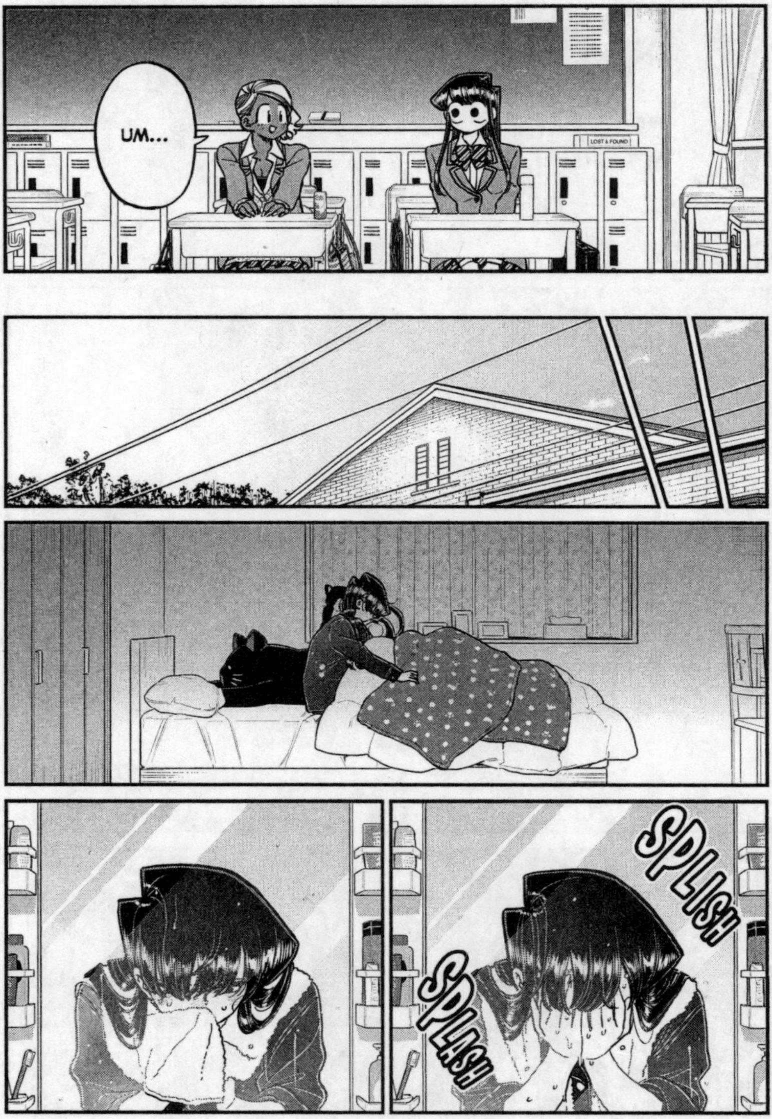
LOST & FOUND
UM...
SPLISH
SPLASH

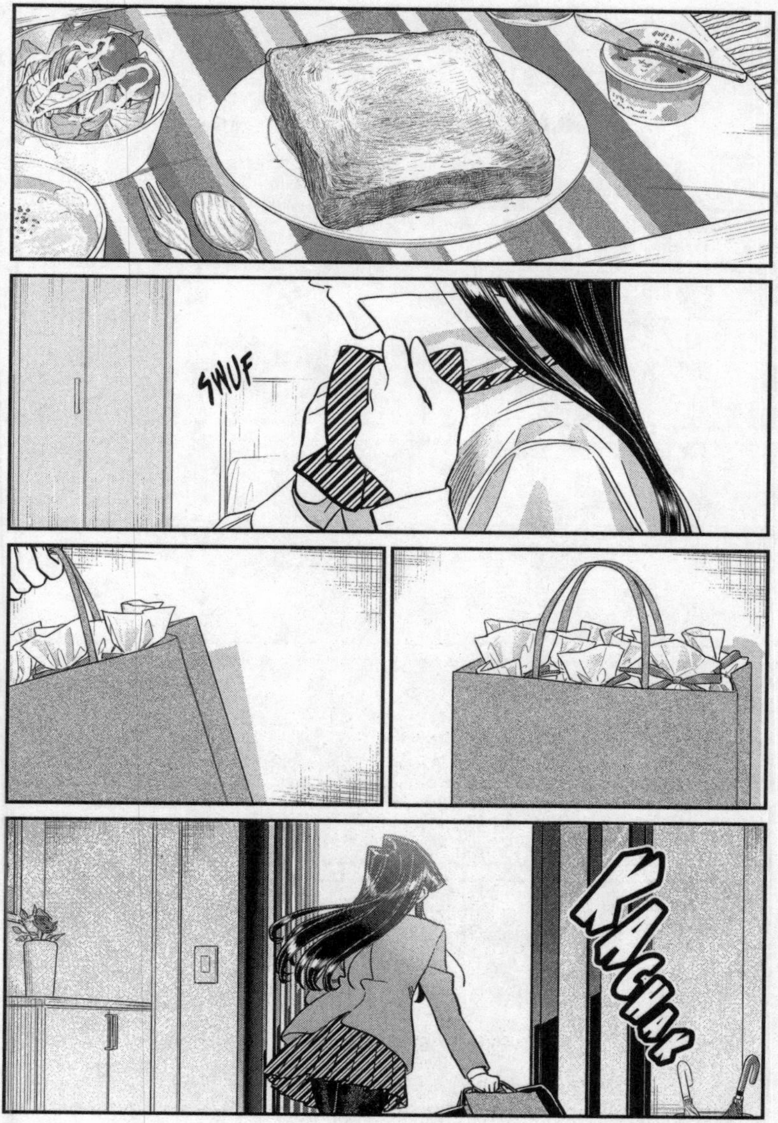
SWUF
KACHAK

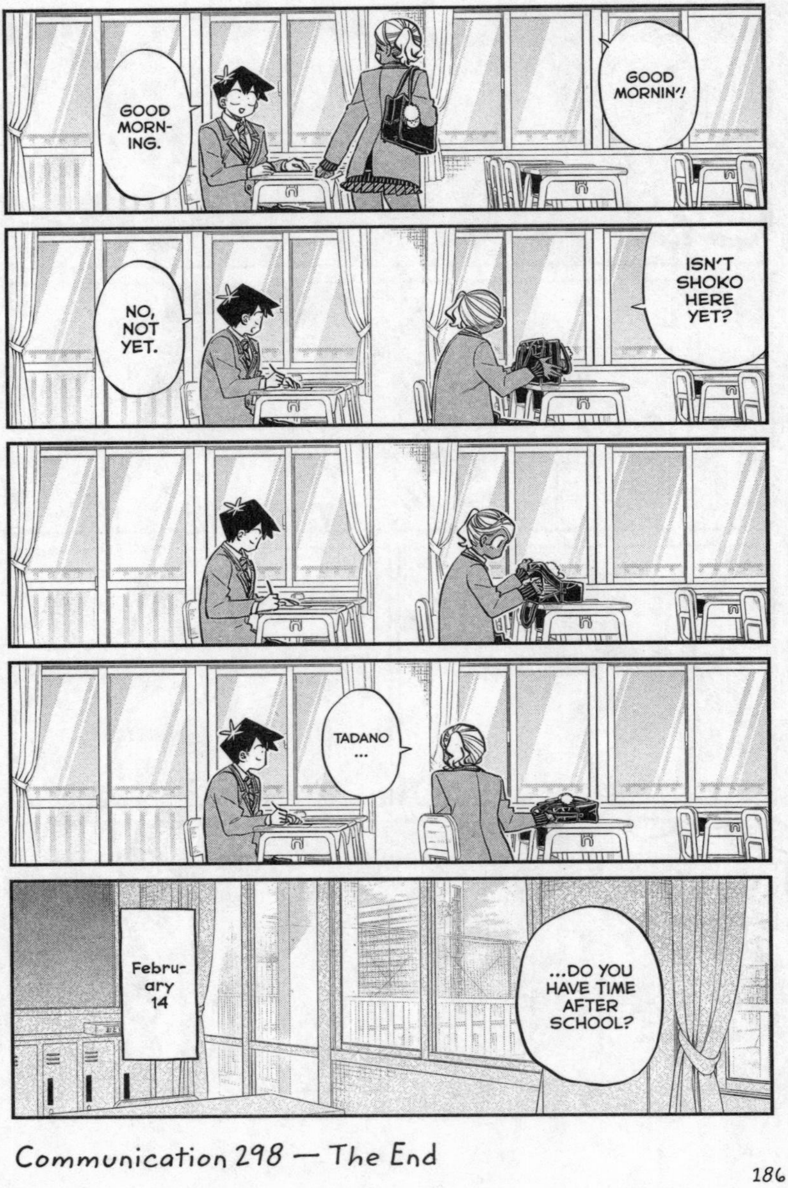
GOOD MORNIN'!
GOOD MORN-ING.
ISN'T SHOKO HERE YET?
NO, NOT YET.
TADANO ...
...DO YOU HAVE TIME AFTER SCHOOL?
Febru-ary 14

Communication 298 — The End

Komi Can't Communicate

Totoi Interrupts a Serious Mood, Part 2

HAVE THEY DEVELOPED AN APP FOR HYPNOSIS YET?

TOTOI INTER-RUPTS A SERIOUS MOOD, PART 2?!

Komi Can't Communicate Bonus

Communication That Would Wake Up Anybody

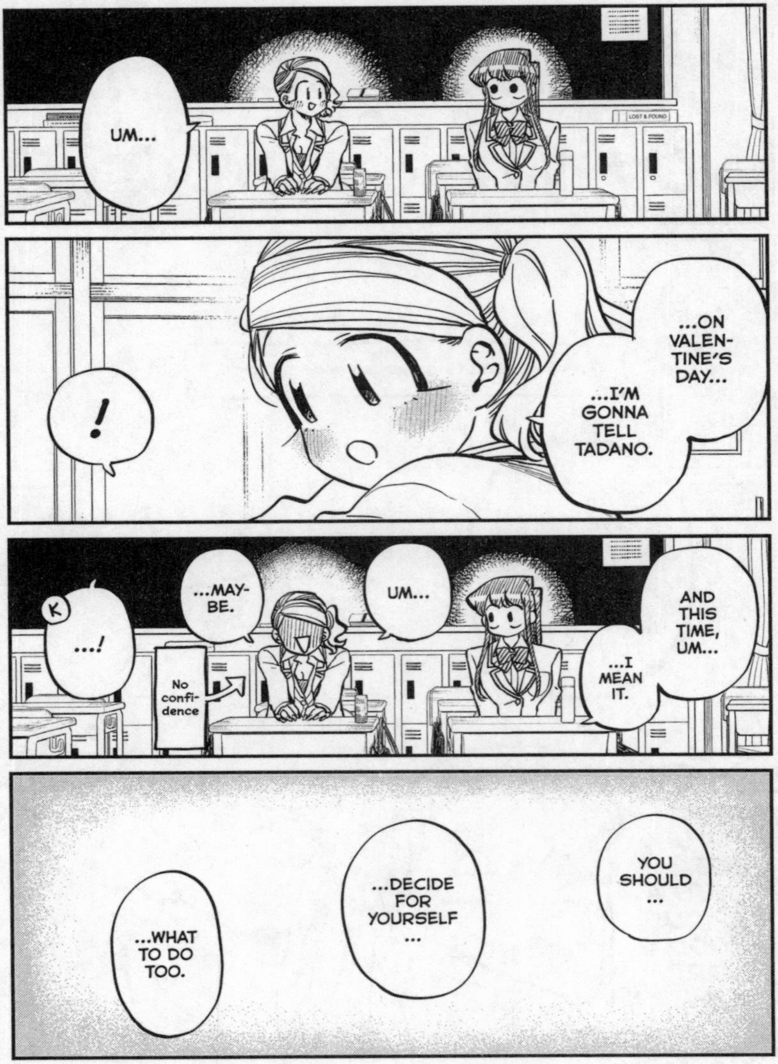
UM...
...ON VALENTINE'S DAY...
...I'M GONNA TELL TADANO.
!
AND THIS TIME, UM...
...I MEAN IT.
UM...
...MAY-BE.
No confi-dence
K
...!
YOU SHOULD ...
...DECIDE FOR YOURSELF ...
...WHAT TO DO TOO.

Komi Can't Communicate Bonus

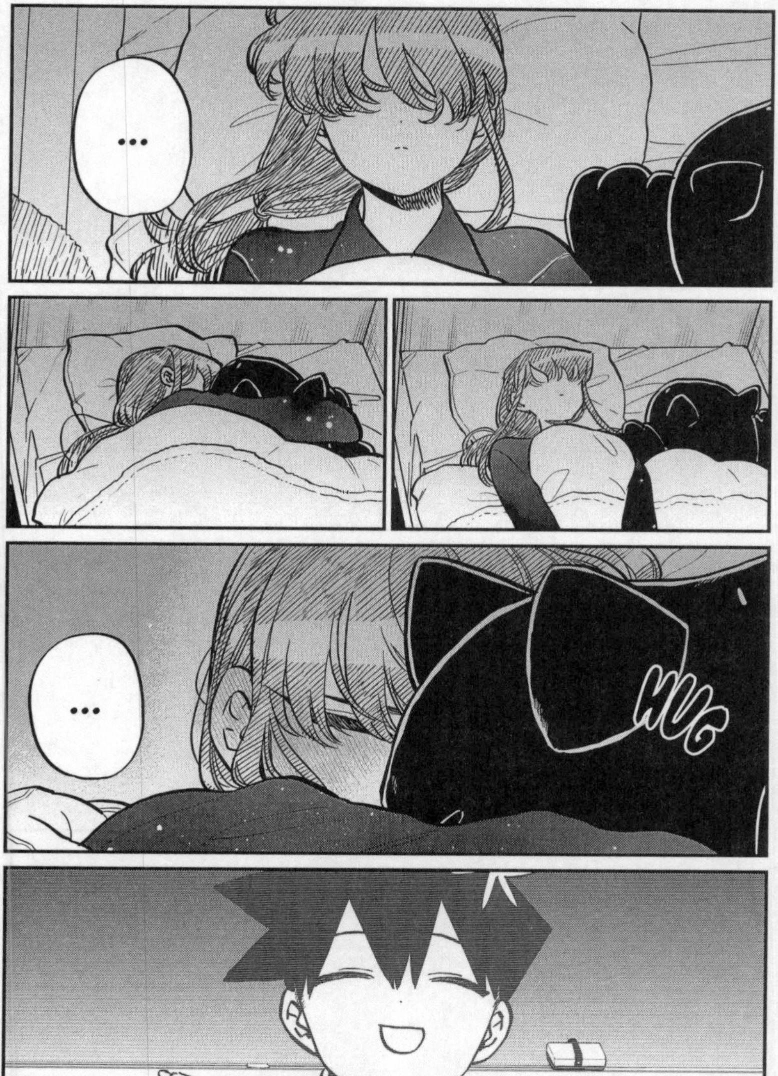
...
HUG
...

Continued in volume 23...

Tomohito Oda won the grand prize for *World Worst One* in the 70th Shogakukan New Comic Artist Awards in 2012. Oda's series *Digicon*, about a tough high school girl who finds herself in control of an alien with plans for world domination, ran from 2014 to 2015. In 2015, *Komi Can't Communicate* debuted as a one-shot in *Weekly Shonen Sunday* and was picked up as a full series by the same magazine in 2016.

Komi Can't Communicate

VOL. 22
Shonen Sunday Edition

Story and Art by Tomohito Oda

English Translation & Adaptation/John Werry
Touch-Up Art & Lettering/Eve Grandt
Design/Julian [JR] Robinson
Editor/Pancha Diaz

COMI-SAN WA, COMYUSHO DESU. Vol. 22
by Tomohito ODA
© 2016 Tomohito ODA
All rights reserved.
Original Japanese edition published by SHOGAKUKAN.
English translation rights in the United States of America, Canada, the United
Kingdom, Ireland, Australia and New Zealand arranged with SHOGAKUKAN.

Original Cover Design/Masato ISHIZAWA + Bay Bridge Studio

Published by VIZ Media, LLC
P.O. Box 77010
San Francisco, CA 94107

10 9 8 7 6 5 4 3 2 1
First printing, December 2022

viz.com

shonensunday.com

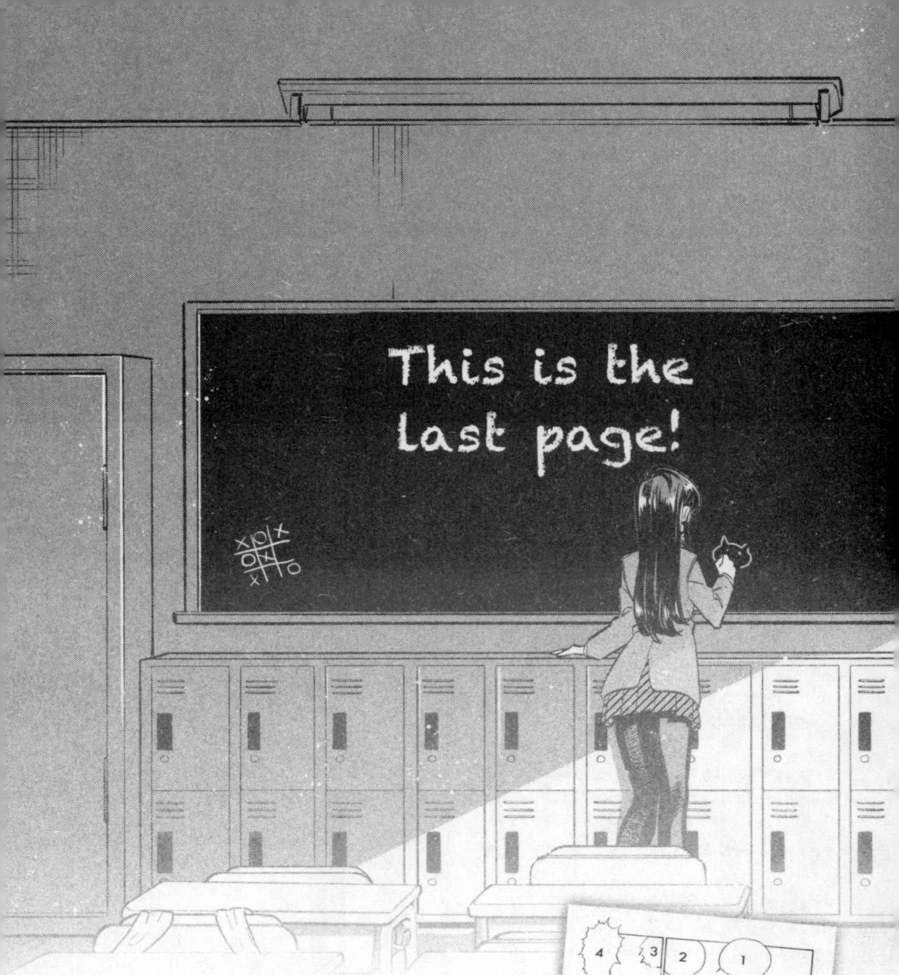
This is the last page!

Komi Can't Communicate has been printed in the original Japanese format to preserve the orientation of the artwork.

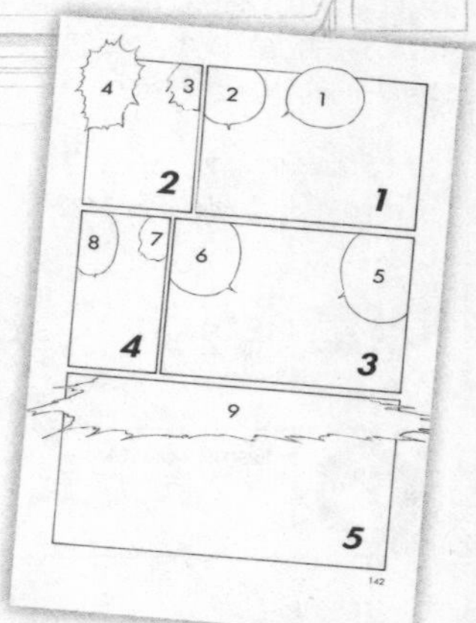
1
2
3
4
5
6
7
8
9
142

Follow the action this way.